MW01641724

THE RESURRECTION OF ARISTOCRACY

THE RESURRECTION OF ARISTOCRACY

Rudolph Carlyle Evans

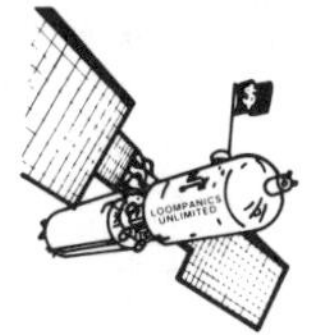

Loompanics Unlimited
Port Townsend, Washington

Dedicated to the noble ones of all races

THE RESURRECTION OF ARISTOCRACY
©1988 by Rudolph Carlyle Evans
All Rights Reserved
Printed in U.S.A.

Published by:
Loompanics Unlimited
PO Box 1197
Port Townsend, WA 98368

ISBN 0-915179-71-7
Library Of Congress Card Catalog Number 87-083445

ABOUT THE AUTHOR

Rudolph Carlyle Evans is 36 years of age. He was born in Kingston, Jamaica, leaving that country at the age of 5 to live in England, where he attended school and college. He is a graduate of Hull University, from which he obtained a Bachelor of Arts degree in Sociology and Social Anthropology. Immediately upon graduating (July '76), he left England to reside permanently in the United States. He has written extensively on heroic vitality, a philosophy which he believes holds the key to the future of western civilization, and feels confident that an aristocratic renaissance will occur before the end of this century. His writings include, *The Resurrection of Aristocracy, Thoughts Out of Season* and *Poets and Prophets.* Evans has recently become an American citizen. He is unmarried and lives in Hempstead, New York.

TABLE OF CONTENTS

INTRODUCTION

by Robert Hertz

It is not just do-gooders, liberals, and wimps who have utopias. The basis of any utopia is a systematic vision of how life could be better. And "better" is a function of desire, not morality. Utopias are fueled by intellectual lusts and obsessions, and not everyone dreams of a gentler and more generous world.

Therefore utopias are not arranged along a straight line of refinement and progress. They can look back to the Middle Ages or even Classical times, as well as to the 21st century. The creator of a utopia simply follows his vision on what society should become, and one man's meat may be another man's poison. Or, as Norman Mailer once noted, "If the essence of God is speed and force, then the Hell's Angels are probably closer to Him than the War on Poverty."

In Rudolph Evans' utopia, the warrior elite will have more style and substance than a motorcycle gang, but will rule without a single apology or hesitation. The very title page of *The Resurrection of Aristocracy* contains a dedication to "to noble ones of all races," and the book's ideas only get more Nietzschean and Darwinistic from there. This is not a reassuring or uplifting book, and if it were popular in the mass market Evans would probably be astounded. He is not bringing good news, but hard news to the majority of readers. He stands for "small is beautiful," all right, but not the way the ecologists imagine it. In Evans' view, the main function of the common people is to beat the lily pads at night to keep the frogs quiet. That, and go to war when their well-rested masters demand it. Evans wants to see a two-tiered social morality: for the leaders — pride and booty and a chance to humiliate their enemies; for the mass of followers — at best, security, and a chance to take orders from those they fear and respect.

What Evans wants is a new feudalism. If the world once moved from castles and serfs into bourgeois cities and capitalism, he sees no reason why it cannot be reversed. Evans has read enough of Karl Marx to appreciate his systematic approach to society, but he totally rejects Marx's determinism and is frankly horrified by his egalitarian philosophy. Evans wants a world where men are men (and sheep are nervous, I presume) — but a harsh and martial world for certain, high on loyalty and internal honor, but lacking in regulation and social improvement. As he states: "The present age is one of equality, the new age will be one of aristocracy; the present age is dominated by urban life, the new age will be dominated by a rural lifestyle; the present age is one of mass production, the new age will be one of homemade goods and craftmanship; the present age has given us the nuclear family, the new age will return us to the extended family; the present age idolizes science and technology, the new age will be hostile or indifferent to these things."

Even though Evans spends far more words and paragraphs, by line count, in attacking air pollution, crime, pornography, etc., what really fuels his anger is the way he is treated. Democracy insults his manhood; one can't put it more simply. A democracy consists of rule by impudents, and mediocrities who cater to impudents. Evans' feudal solution to this species of social decay is that, ultimately, the common people would have no money. They would come to their lords for charity, after they had carried out their duty. As he complains, "This legalistic age of ours with its motto of justice for all, elevating the weak at the expense of the strong, is destroying life not enriching it. The character of western man is being molded in a manner that emasculates him."

Evans does not believe in trickle-down, trickle-up, or any other form of economic redistribution. He feels that scarcity is inevitable, either through ecological limitations or general human wastefulness. Therefore he wants a fiercer scarcity, one which generates a proud nobility that is unashamed about living off others. His solutions for conventional social problems such as divorce, alienation, et. al., are therefore extraordinarily simple — the commoners should go home, stay home, and be glad to be supervised. Instead of learning things, they should forget about intelligence and sophistication. They should get about the business of living by their nature — docile, passive, and brutish. "Life will be hard," he explains, "and the commoners will have very low expectations. They will never question the permanency of their subordinate position....and their joys will be of the most basic kind, such as the birth of a child, the marriage of a son or daughter, and military success of their lord, particularly so when it involves the members of their own community, and of course a good harvest... Communal cooperation will be essential for the common people if they are to survive. No longer will they be able to beg for a living, or live off the charity of some benevolent institution or rely on the government to provide for their needs — put simply, those who do not work really will not eat."

Evans is thus a long way from *National Review*-style conservatism. His two main distinctions from, say, William F. Buckley, are that he does not believe in free enterprise and also that he is anti-Christian. I would place him somewhere to the right of Attila the Hun — and affectionately, too, because Evans has the clarity and courage to organize and articulate what I and other "reactionaries" have been hinting at for years.

Evans understands that ideas have consequences; and if harsh ideas have harsh consequences, then so be it. If bellicose diplomacy results in wars, (and believe me, Evans would have the gunboats and assassins out in force), then good, because small wars are part of the natural Darwinist order. If selfish economics lead to a depression because the masses aren't consuming enough — then fine, let it happen. Depressions knock out inflated social values and pampered lifestyles among the common people, and the nobles by definition will be too ruthless to suffer very much. If the wars or depressions cited above lead to massive shortages of energy, that's no problem either. There's too much travel as it is. And as for commodity prices dropping in a general deflation — that is perhaps the healthiest development of all.

Evans has a special hatred for capitalistic farming; and again, not from a Marxist standpoint of wanting collectives, but from the feudal perspective of land being valuable in itself regardless of what is grown on it. His problem is not that farmers are poor money managers, but that they shouldn't have to manage money at all. The ownership of land should be a noble's prerogative, probably granted in return for military service. It should have nothing to do with the Chicago Board of Trade, and just as little connection to agricultural extension colleges. "All land throughout the nation," Evans declares, "will be held by members of the nobility, and all surpluses will be held by the ruling nobles....Under no circumstances will land be bought and sold in the new age....and there will be corresponding changes in the way we produce and distribute the products of the land. Gone will be complex agricultural implements."

Modern readers are not used to such contempt for economics. Americans generally expect that all parties to political debate will have at least a basic respect for general prosperity, and an underlying desire for the greatest good of the greatest number. Even those who pass for religious fundamentalists in our country — Billy Graham, Black Muslims, etc. — are supportive of more money and more goods and services (if for no greater reason than to line their own pockets). Evans by contrast is like an Ayatollah out of the past, because the one thing he wants — the integrity and power of a new nobility — will not be compromised for any "stomach problems" such as living standards or the gross national product. His nobles will not buy and sell, they will not finance or finagle, and above all they will not explain themselves. (Because any type of self-justification implies a legal or moral standard superior to the will of the ruling group.)

It is worth noting, however, that Evans' nobility will be motivated by something more than a naked lust for power. While hardly an ascetic in his world-view, it would be erroneous to categorize Evans as a pure hedonist. I'm the one who's read *The Story of O* seven times, not him. Evans expects his aristocracy to accomplish something, and not just live off the fat (or the sleek) of the land. He knows if the propertied classes do no more than put their feet up on the porch and watch the darkies haul cotton, sooner or later that upper class will decay — if in fact it is not overthrown. A lazy nobility is not alert enough in today's revolutionary world; it will not be "fit" enough, either mentally or physically, to hold off the serfs in the next rebellion.

Meanwhile Evans dreams of a "class war from above," of new masters who rise up from social cataclysm, returning the masses to rural obscurity and personal servility. Evans does not have a precise road map of "how to get there from here." He does not expect or really want a single race to be classified as masters; he is not a Nazi. Nor does he expect a single nation to do the job; again, he is not a Nazi. The reader comes away from his book without knowing precisely who will step forward — that's the next step, perhaps, something Evans will take up later or in conjunction with other reactionaries. My own estimate of the new nobility is that it would be akin to the men who attend the gatherings of *Soldier of Fortune* magazine — mercenaries, survivalists, martial-arts types, gun-runners, and military philosophers. At least in this group one finds the highest concentration of practical Nietzscheans: arrogant men, dreamers, anti-democratic and pagan to the core, men who could run colonies or at least plantations, men who would have ten wives and forty children if they had the opportunity, and who would eagerly fight wars against upstart serfs and neighboring peasants. I have written to hundreds of such men for several years (I am the founder of a publishing house called The Spengler Group), and believe me, those guys are out there.

And for the most part, "those guys" are no happier with America than Evans is. They are not impressed by computers or the space program or the auto industry or even the defense industry. Technological achievements mean little to them if their society lacks the proper "status" and "dignity." I mean, how much pride can one take in a super-computer, if it is operated by some pinhead who reads Gloria Steinem? It's like spending $100,000 for your wife's birthday party, and at the height of festivities she throws a drink in your face. You have a lot of wealth (or at least credit), but no status, no power. A mechanical servant, even one with 10,000 horsepower, is not as good as a human servant. And America does very poorly in creating human servants, providing them, or teaching you how to take them. Better a drafty castle with real slaves and servants, than a condo on the golf course with *Playboy* and a V.C.R.

Nobility will not come easily, though, nor should it. It comes down to a willingness to shove somebody else into the face of enemy fire. You can call it greed or the survival of the fittest, but either way, it is the unwritten code of an officer caste. It is revealing that Evans cites Joseph de Maistre as one of his inspirations; de Maistre attacked the French Revolution, and wrote brilliantly and cruelly. "Democracy," he stated, "is chiefly distinguished by its unwillingness to sacrifice anyone." Democracy is too calm for Evans, not carnal or tragic or visceral enough. He would sooner have a world where "the aristocracy is fully conscious of the power they will wield over the lives of the common people. They will constantly strive to increase their power, prestige, and influence at the expense of their weaker noble brethren. Unlike commoners, they will not hesistate to relieve their anger with acts of ferocious cruelty against those who have incurred their displeasure....they will read and write as little as possible, leaving most of this type of activity to their trained officials....they will have no interest in the age that went before. Written laws will not be made in the new age, instead, when the need arises, people will be given instruction by word of mouth. Neither will land deeds be drawn up or formal treaties made, for in the new age the sword will once again prove itself to be far mightier than the pen."

Evans expects little from Nature or any God. He feels that the world is inevitably cruel and scarce. The only question is who will get the best of that cruelty and scarcity; and the answer is, those who are mentally prepared for it, unsurprised, undismayed, and even eager to take adavantage of their new opportunities.

In other words, those who read Evans. Those who have realized — even if fleetingly — the thrill and responsibility of total power over others. Those whose personal God is a dark and savage one. Those whose Great Lord is a warlord. Those midnightly men, those upcoming masters of the world. Bear down, hang on. Your day is coming. As Evans describes your future, thusly:

> *"The present age will collapse, and upon this collapse will arise a breed of men with such ambition to dominate their fellow men that in comparison with men of the preceding age they will appear to be superhuman. These men — destined to become lords of the land — will gather around themselves lieutenants and followers. They will push outward across the land until their progress is checked either by natural barriers: forests, rivers, deserts, mountain ranges, or by an equally ambitious individual coming from another direction. The meeting point between two such individuals will be the boundary of their respective domains. The lords will divide much of this conquered land among their most faithful lieutenants. The latter will in turn hold this land as vassals paying homage to their lord and swearing fidelity to him. In this way will feudalism once again be established in the western world."*
>
> *"Those who look forward to this resurrection of aristocracy,"* Evans concludes, *"must ignore the outcry of the weak and insecure...the opinions of those who oppose*

the resurrection will not count because, frankly, people will not be asked to vote on the new age; it is coming whether they like it or not. It will be a great age that truly knows itself like none before it has ever done."

Evans rests, but not in peace. One knows he will be heard from again.

THE CRISIS OF A LOST SOCIETY

Never before has western man been in the predicament in which he now finds himself. So much is wrong with just about every aspect of contemporary life and yet so little of relevance has been written about our state of crisis. At first sight this seems all the more puzzling, since this age more than any other is characterized by man's supposed mastery over nature and his belief in the power of reason. But a deeper analysis leads to the conclusion that the old ways of thinking and the old ideals are now worn out. A new model of reality is needed if we are to understand what is going on at the present time and what the future holds in store for us. Not only must our modern ideals and values be overthrown, but our blind devotion to scientific rationalism must also be carefully reassessed and amended. The man in the street may not be so definite about the problems of modern industrial society, but he is in no doubt that western society is in the doldrums and that there seems to be little that can be done about this. To those who have a feeling for the rich heritage of western civilization, the inability of modern man to make use of this as an aid to understanding his present situation makes it all the more depressing. This is a matter I intend to put right in the subsequent pages of this book.

Explanations of the current malaise to be found in the western world are various. Some consider it to be due to the economic downturn which has left the future uncertain. Others consider it to be primarily due to a feeling of boredom or even disgust with the institutions, beliefs and life style of modern industrial society at its highest stage of development. My own studies indicate that the second opinion is closer to the truth than is the first. More to the point, I believe that we are moving towards a new age, one quite unlike any age that has ever existed, an age that will check our progress towards self-destruction and bring about a closer relationship of man to nature. All signs point to this as the only possible explanation of our present woes. In every direction in which we may turn, we are haunted by the specter of potential breakdown, a situation which is highlighted by Mesarovic and Pestel, who tell us frankly that: "The developed world is experiencing an appreciable decline in the quality and quantity of services in spite of increase in cost; from medical to transportation and postal services one can find an abundance of examples to prove the point."[1] Just as we believe we have one problem straightened out for the time being at least, other problems suddenly turn up to tax our resources and ingenuity. Moreover, some of our current difficulties such as an over-supply of university graduates are totally insoluble within the context of western society as it is presently organized. It is almost as if the advanced industrialized societies were beginning to wilt under the weight of their own complexity. This is not something that could have been clearly foreseen two hundred years ago or even one hundred years ago, but it is something that we moderns must now face up to. The ideal of a peaceful world growing prosperous on the shared benefits of trade and industry is no longer tenable. Instead, time has almost run out for the heirs of the Industrial Revolution. What we now have to decide is not whether or not industrial society as we know it will continue to exist, but rather what will be the form of the society that is destined to replace it. Understandably this is a very sensitive subject, one which no serious writer has yet come to grips with. So far we have had talk of the post-industrial society, but the way in which it has been presented is hardly a convincing description of a future age different from our own. And I stress that *different* is the operative word.

The post-industrial society of Daniel Bell and his disciples is, after all, one that would be little different from the present age, except that there would be more people working in the services sector of the economy. Manufacturing would still be dominated by large corporations and mass production techniques, scientific-technological rationalism would still reign supreme and the social structure would remain more or less unchanged. In other words, the new age of the post-industrial theorists is simply an extrapolation of the old age and, as such, does not offer solutions to those problems and contradictions besetting the old age. Instead, these problems are either expected to disappear or to become amenable to programmatic solutions involving the spending of millions, or if necessary, billions of dollars. This view is hardly acceptable at a time when our political institutions appear to be sinking under the weight of difficulties confronting them, and when public opinion, not without good reason, appears to have lost faith in programmatic solutions. But at least there seems to be general agreement that change is on the way. Unfortunately, lack of imagination and timidity have been the most conspicuous traits so far in the writings of those who have attempted to come to terms with the need for, and certainty of radical change. This seems to be the case regardless of the political beliefs of the authors; it would appear that there is still a lingering hope among writers of all political persuasions that solutions to the world's problems can be found within the confines of contemporary society. None of these writers seem to realize that the continued existence of our high performance industrial societies is creating far more problems than they can possibly solve, a situation which cannot go on indefinitely.

One need only look at the most persistent problems of the developed countries to realize that modern industrial society has serious troubles which it is unlikely to overcome as long as it continues in its present form. The advanced industrial nations, which are also the world's most affluent countries, should therefore have the most contented citizens, but this is far from true, since nearly all these countries are suffering from a veritable galaxy of social ills. Many of their origins, and their rapid growth, sociologists and others are at a loss to explain, but they are with us nonetheless. Our ever-rising crime rate is stretching the police forces beyond their ability to cope. In some western countries, the police station is little more than a registry office as far as the less serious crimes are concerned, the victim having little hope of his or her complaint being made subject of a thorough investigation. Prisons are filled to over capacity, thus stimulating a desperate search for alternatives which, even if successful in keeping the prison population down, will have no effect on containing the rising crime rate. Juvenile delinquency has also continued to steadily increase in most western countries despite the benefits of free schooling and opportunities for recreation which all the advanced industrial nations provide for their younger citizens. Urban terrorism has reached new levels of intensity during the past decade — yet another indication that something is seriously wrong with the present order of things, since the regular employment of mindless violence to achieve vague or unrealizable political objectives is usually a sure sign that change is on the way, change quite unlike that which the terrorist groups have envisaged.

Another symptom of social distress in the advanced industrial nations is family breakdown. The increasing incidence of family breakdown is in its own way just as disturbing as the rising crime rate and the increased levels of politically motivated violence. The divorce rate of the advanced industrial nations achieves a record increase each year. The number of children in the care of local authorities or with foster parents as a result of broken homes continues to grow. The number of children who leave home before the age of sixteen against the wishes of their parents has begun to alarm welfare workers in the cities of Western Europe and North America. Other features of family breakdown which have become very prevalent in recent years include wife beating and baby battering. Both have received a good deal of publicity and a great deal of condemnation, but still they continue unchecked. As a matter of fact, a recent study has confirmed what many had long suspected, namely that there is more violence committed within the confines of the family than in any other situation, except riots and wars. This is a truly horrifying state of affairs. We must also note in passing that family breakdown is not restricted primarily to the lower-income groups, but is affecting upper-income groups as well. This is particularly true of divorce and wife beating, two examples of the crisis of the modern family which are independent of income boundaries. Although child abuse may not be so prevalent among the better off as it is among the not so well off, it too is no stranger to the homes of the upper class. The large number of cases of child abuse and neglect of young children leads one to wonder whether the art of bringing up children is being lost under the pressures of this dehumanizing age. Along with the increasing instability in family ties has gone a rapid increase in the rate of juvenile delinquency among both boys and girls. What is especially giving cause for concern is that juveniles are no longer restricting themselves to relatively harmless acts of youthful excess, such as staying away from school, breaking the occasional window or trespassing and petty theft. Today's juvenile delinquents have graduated to activities which are far more serious infringements of the law, in some cases serious enough to put them in the same category with the hardened criminal. Such activities include extensive vandalism of any building (including their own) on which they can work with little chance of interruption. Other juvenile crimes include mugging, housebreaking, car theft, arson and assault with a deadly weapon. Gang warfare is yet another example of juvenile energy gone astray. Those are just a few instances of the disorientation among the young which is all too common in the advanced industrial societies. The modern family and family life in general is in a state of protracted crisis. As goes the western family, so goes western civilization.

Another scourge of the advanced industrial societies is the increase in alcohol addiction among all age groups, and among women as well as men. The rising incidence of alcoholism among women is particularly alarming, since only two decades ago there were many times more men than women alcoholics. But the fact that it takes a woman only about half as much time as it takes a man to become a fully fledged alcoholic has meant that the number of women alcoholics is rapidly catching up to that of men. Indeed, it is by no means improbable that if one examines a random sample of alcoholics registered at a treatment center, one will find that housewives make up the largest occupational group. But an uncontrollable desire for alcohol is not confined to a particular class or occupational group. Along with factory workers and other manual laborers, doctors, dentists, lawyers, judges, teachers and business executives are examples of the professions which come within the ravages of the bottle. Neither have the under twenty-ones escaped the liquid curse which is more and more becoming the only source of temporary relief for their parents. Statistics on alcoholism among teenagers from nearly all the world's advanced industrial nations indicate that the young are taking to alcohol earlier than they did two or three decades ago and in consequence are becoming addicted in greater numbers than was the case prior to the early fifties. The criminal offenses associated with excessive drinking have also risen dramatically over the past decade. Examples include driving while under the influence of drink and being drunk and disorderly, not to mention such activities as wife beating and child abuse, which are often (though not always) found in families where at least one of the partners is a heavy drinker. The spreading incidence of alcoholism is most unlikely to be halted by setting up more government aided treatment centers, by an increase in the budget of Alcoholics Anonymous or by any other short-term expedience such as an advertising campaign directed against drinking at lunch time. It seems reasonable to conclude that the problem of alcoholism is here to stay — that is, as long as modern industrial society remains in existence.

Another sign of social instability in the advanced industrial societies is the growth of drug addiction. Under this heading must be included cigarettes and certain types of legally prescribed medications (e.g., tranquilizers and sleeping pills), as well as marijuana and the illegal use of narcotics. Over prescription of tranquilizers and sleeping pills may not yet be considered as a long term danger, but the truth is that civilization has become a questionable proposition when one cannot sleep or get through the day without recourse to prescribed medications. The rising level of cigarette smoking is no less a symbol of an empty, decadent culture than is the increasing attachment to heroin and cocaine, not to mention the use of marijuana which has become so common among the younger generation. Smoking has long ceased to be regarded purely from the point of view of a relaxing pleasurable activity. Smokers crave for cigarettes not primarily for enjoyment, as many advertisers would have us believe, but more importantly as a way of giving themselves the psychological support they so desperately need to cope with life in this high-pressure, consumer society of ours. Many people consider marijuana to be relatively harmless — if not quite as acceptable as cigarettes, at least a lot safer than LSD and other hallucinogens which were popular only a few years ago. I do not intend to become involved in the debate as to how safe is marijuana, since the various schools of thought on this matter have failed to become reconciled, although research has been going on for several years now. What can be said with certainty is that the use of marijuana can and often does open the way to the use of harder drugs, particularly heroin, about whose long-term harm there can be no doubt. Once a person becomes addicted to hard drugs, the possibility of successful rehabilitation becomes greatly diminished. Why do a steady supply of young recruits join the ranks of the growing numbers of narcotics users to become the dregs of the city? One answer could be the crushing difficulties of coping with life in societies which give equal opportunity to all even though all are not equally suited to succeed at being model citizens of modern industrial society. For those who fail to live up to expectation, alcohol and narcotics are two readily available alternatives, depending on age and circumstances. Thus, the young user of hard drugs embarks upon a career of crime to support his habit. As for the chronic alcoholic, he usually ends up joining the denizens of skid row, the down and outs who rely on charity for their bed and board.

Another feature of the intense stress of life in all the most advanced industrial societies which I have not mentioned as yet, although it is perhaps causing more concern than many other problems, is mental illness. Mental illness has now become by far the most widespread medical condition to be found in the advanced industrial nations. It is estimated that three out of every five adults will experience the effects of this type of illness at sometime in their lives, though not all will need to be institutionalized. In fact, most people who readily admit to suffering from mental illness can usually be treated as outpatients. But this does not ameliorate the fact that the number of people needing help is enormous and increasing every year. Fortunately for the mental health facilities of the industrialized nations, only a small fraction of those with mental health problems seek professional help; the remainder struggle on as best they can. There seems to very little chance of successfully eradicating mental illness as smallpox, malaria, bubonic plague and rickets have been eradicated. It would appear to be something we will have to live with until far reaching social changes have taken place. In fact some writers (e.g. Baran and Sweezey: *Monopoly Capital*) have speculated that widespread mental illness could itself be one of the primary causes of the collapse of western society. This I doubt for a number of reasons. For instance, a new civilization, be it democratic, aristocratic or other, could hardy be founded by a society a large proportion of whose members are mentally ill. Such a society would have no future. Nevertheless, I do believe that as long as our present high-performance industrial society continues to exist, mental illness will continue to loom large as one of our most distressing and intractable problems. The above are only a few of the better known indications of social distress, which has now reached a pathological condition in several nations. There are many others, such as decreasing levels of fertility among women, and the increasing number of suicides that are reported from all parts of the world, particularly among the young. The list could be continued indefinitely, but it would be futile to do so. For the common message is quite simple — it is now time for a transition to a new age, one more forthright and less complex than our own, an age based on the essentials of human nature which are known to us from history, rather than an idealized version of the good society, something which has been with us for the last hundred years and has almost succeeded in stifling our natural feelings and emotions.

I cannot leave our discussion of the prominent social problems of contemporary western society without mentioning the conditions of the physical background against which this great drama is being played out, namely the modern city. The rapidly decreasing quality of life in our great urban centers has many facets, not all of which we can touch upon here. One of the key problems of the city and of contemporary western society in general is the motor car. The indiscriminate mixing of man and car in close proximity and high concentration is responsible for a large number of injuries and fatalities, especially among the very young and the elderly, which between them compose the two largest categories of vulnerable pedestrians. The highly toxic exhaust gases given off by motor cars and other vehicles have been a very serious worry in recent years, so much so that a lot of time, money and ingenuity has been expended on attempting to lessen the problem. But it is still with us, as is traffic congestion and the problem of big city smog. Traffic congestion seems to be a result of too many cars and too little roadway.

Furthermore, increasing levels of car ownership make the simplistic solution to the congestion problem of building more roads and highways totally impractical. Smog from car exhaust is a serious health hazard in over twenty American cities, several in Japan, and is on the way to becoming a problem in Western Europe and Australia. The motor car has not only appropriated a great deal of space (e.g., a quarter of an average city is roadway) but it is also responsible for producing a great deal of noise which may reach an intolerable level in some localities at certain times. This problem has also increased in recent years with increases in traffic, particularly the fast growth in the number of heavy lorries, so that many townspeople are having their sleep disturbed by the sound of large articulated lorries. Of course, the city has other problems. The streets are not cleaned as often as they should be, with the result that even the more prestigious parts of the city begin to look like a dumping ground. Whether the reason for this situation is that the big cities cannot afford to employ enough road sweepers and garbage collectors, or whether it is because sufficient people are not coming forward to do the job, is really of no great importance. The fact is we are no longer able to keep our cities clean.

A related problem of the large city is the garbage left to decay on municipal tips. Although the problem of what to do with the millions of tons of garbage collected each year has been under intensive study for several years now, nobody seems quite sure what to do about it. Recycling has been attempted on a small scale, but the bulk of the cities' garbage continues to be left exposed to the elements or dumped in the sea for want of better alternatives. Part of the problem is that modern industrial society has produced a great deal of garbage which is not easy to eliminate, while other types which are much easier to eliminate have been produced in such enormous quantities as to tax our abilities to dispose of them. The sewerage facilities of many major cities of the western world are in a terrible mess and deteriorating rapidly because of age. The sewerage facilities of these cities have just not kept up with increases in their population, so the treatment of sewage is rudimentary and much of their effluent is discharged into the sea in a raw state, a fact that is indicative of the excessive demands made by the modern city on the environment. Aesthetically, the modern city is a crushing place in which to live, and has been fittingly called a concrete jungle. The buildings are huge and overpowering, everywhere there is steel and concrete presenting a harsh and austere facade. Simply taking a short walk in a modern city can drain one physically and emotionally. The very concrete on which we walk does violence to our aesthetic sensitivity; the exhaust fumes of motor vehicles accost our nostrils with their pungent, suffocating odor. We cannot nonchalantly stroll wherever we wish without thought of what is happening about us, for we would soon be run over. And the noise, oh! The noise of daytime traffic and construction work is almost too much to bear. Attempts to make cities aesthetically attractive by the planting of trees and the maintenance of parks are not enough. They could never be enough. But they are clear admissions that even the most battle-hardened city dweller is sensitive to signs of his rural origins. Neither do the tree-lined boulevards above ground alter the fact that most city dwellers travel to and from work underground in overcrowded, noisy subways. To get to a park or other open space in the city where there is grass and a relative freedom of movement one usually has to cross several busy roads and even then one is never far away from the sound, sight and smell of the motor car.

The appalling slum districts of the larger western cities are another depressing aspect of city life. As city life becomes more oppressive, those who can afford to, move out, leaving lower-income families concentrated in those districts which are in the process of going downhill. In other cases, large buildings stand empty for years because no one wants to make use of them, so creating a fire hazard, as well as adding to the decline of the inner city. The mobile life style of modern man is having a very destructive impact on the big city, for not only do inhabitants of the city move out to the suburbs and other places, but the corporations and other organizations which make the large city what it is can decide to close down operations and relocate at anytime, and in fact many of them have done so, leading to a shrinkage in the cities' economic base and a cut back in its services. Even when money is spent on slum clearance and large apartment blocks are built to provide cheap housing for lower income families, all is still not right. Vandalism becomes commonplace and has to be met in some instances by the hiring of security guards or tenant patrols. Living conditions are often cramped, and made more so by the lack of a garden, especially for a family with young children. Furthermore, the tenants often complain of a feeling of isolation even though they are living in close proximity to one another. It is not surprising that many inhabitants of the city lose interest in looking after their homes once they see signs of decline, which in the city are easier to see than to disregard. The big city is no longer capable of fostering civic virtue; it has become a cold, impersonal oppressor of all those who have chosen to make it their home. Architecturally, it is an abomination; aesthetically it is a disaster. All in all, it is a thoroughly miserable environment in which to live, work, and raise a family. The decay of our great cities is part of a much broader trend to which we must now address ourselves. For not only is our age one of unparalleled social distress, it is also one of unmatched environmental destruction. It is no exaggeration to say that our chances of having a decent environment to hand onto our descendants are rapidly diminishing. The processes which are taking us to the brink of ecological catastrophe include thoughtless disfiguration of the landscape in our quest to meet the raw material needs of modern industry. This quest has brought us the horrors of strip mining, which are well known to the residents of the Appalachians, and the conversion of high-quality meadowland into coal fields and quarries. Even national parks, those areas especially set aside to be enjoyed for their scenic beauty and as a habitat for endangered species of plants and animals, can fall victim to the onslaught of the great quest. Thus, it is not surprising any longer to find mining activities of one sort or another carried out in the middle of land designated as a national park. The drilling for oil and natural gas, the storage and transportation of these substances has also been an important cause of environmental disfiguration. Drilling for oil on land deprives us of places where we can get away from the oppressiveness of city life and go into the desert far away from the nearest town. But even the desert is fast being appropriated by the producers of oil and natural gas, who do not waste any time in setting up their hydrocarbon processing plants near their drilling operations, i.e., on land which was once tranquil and uninhabited by man. The oil rigs out at sea are supposed to be helping us fend off the energy crisis, but they too are an environmental problem. For one thing, mining operations carried out in the sea represent a superb example of what over-development is doing to us. Not content with plundering the land, man has turned his attention to the sea, which seems to have vast potential for satisfying his insatiable mineral needs, but this has its dangers, and one of them is the possibility of major leakage resulting in large-scale oil pollution, which is always a possibility with oil rigs located in the sea and has happened time and time again, causing the destruction of much sea life and the fouling of beaches.

Then again, parts of a nation's unspoiled countryside that happen to lie along its coastline are being appropriated to provide international petroleum companies with deep water berths for their tankers and facilities for the storage and overland transportation of oil. Neither are the activities of property developers doing much to help conservationists in their losing battle to protect the environment from being despoiled and desecrated. For example, although people are moving away from the cities in favor of smaller communities, well away from city limits, they still require all the conveniences of city life, and property developers have obliged by constructing these small communities as miniature replicas of the big city. Soon they become extensions of the city to form what is now termed a "megalopolis," a great belt of urbanization which may extend for a hundred miles or more. Then there are those large hotels built in places which should have been left undeveloped for their natural beauty to be fully appreciated. But the jet age tourist comes first. He must be pampered and given what he expects, even if in the process the most desirable parts of the nation, owing to climate and scenery, should be ruined both culturally and ecologically by property developers in search of a "quick buck." Road and highway construction is yet another activity whose impact on the environment has been far more destructive than it should have ever have been allowed to be. Too much of our precious wilderness is still being used for the building of highways whose real purpose is to provide an outlet for government revenues and placate powerful interest groups. The above are some examples of western man's calculated assaults on his environment. But this is just the beginning, for we haven't begun as yet to talk in detail about pollution, the most hideous form of environmental destruction, in that it can in the long run destroy man as well as his environment.

The pollution of our lakes, rivers and oceans has become a disgrace to twentieth-century man. When one examines the facts about pollution of our waterways, one sees the great cost at which our technological civilization has been achieved. For instance, there is at least one river in the U.S.A. which has received notoriety on account of the fact that it contained so much inflammable chemical waste as to be classified a fire hazard. The great lakes of North America have become so polluted by the waste materials from local industrial enterprises as to substantially reduce their once great abundance of aquatic life. The state of our great oceans is perhaps the saddest of all: who would have thought that pollution could ever become a serious problem over an area so immense? Yet it has happened. In the oceans we find a lot of flotsam and jetsam, which is quite normal for a large body of water, even though it greatly detracts from the pleasures of sailing upon the high seas. As unsightly as it may be, floating wreckage is not the pollution threat which is most alarming. The real cause for concern is oil, which is doing untold damage to sea life and marine birds. Basically, there are three ways in which oil gets into the sea. The first is through accidents involving an oil rig operation; this we have already spoken about and hence will say no more. Another is through deliberate discharge as when a ship's captain washes out his tanks. The quantities of oil involved are usually not very great, but because this is regularly done by numerous oil tanker captains with little fear of incurring penalty, it has had an enormous impact on our oceans. The third way in which oil enters the ocean is well known to all of us and often involves very large quantities of oil, i.e., the shipwreck of an oil tanker. This has become such a regular occurrence as to drive some people to despair. No solution to the problem has yet been found, but bigger and bigger tankers continue to be built. Surely one does not have to be academically qualified to appreciate that the continuous entry of crude oil into our oceans on the scale of the past decade, by both accident and design, is posing a very serious threat to the ecology of the oceans and to the world's fishing industry, not to mention the damage the oil can do if it is brought ashore, where it may cause irreparable damage to the habitats of sea birds and other creatures as well as ruin large stretches of beach. The size of the problem is well beyond the resources of any country, and even countries acting together, as they are supposed to do through the United Nations Environmental Secretariat, will be unable to halt the pollution of our oceans and rivers. Only a complete change in our lifestyle, with the abolition of modern industry, can possibly reverse present trends, and this provided it does not take place too late.

The pollution situation on land is almost as bad, with innumerable instances of toxic chemicals dumped without the slightest attempt having been made to neutralize them or to ensure that they will not leak into the surrounding land at some future date, and the thoughtless use of pesticides and defoliant agents which do immeasurable damage to the natural ecological balance in the areas where they are applied. Another major source of pollution are those manufacturing plants which use complex and highly poisonous organic compounds in their manufacturing processes. I am especially referring to chemicals used in the manufacture of plastics, in the processing of metals, paper and food and in the production of paints and proprietary products for personal use. Although precautions are taken to prevent lethal chemicals escaping from the plant, this has not prevented large amounts of these deadly substances from leaking into the surrounding environment and causing a great deal of trouble for many thousands of people living in the vicinity. Sometimes small amounts of the offensive substance may be leaked for many years without anyone realizing this until a substantial amount has escaped from the plant and done irreversible damage.

Other times, a large amount of the poisonous substance may suddenly escape from the plant due to an inexplicable malfunctioning. In some cases, the poisonous substance may enter the water supply and pose a grave threat over a very wide area, as did the recent industrial accident in Ohio which led to the discharge of a large quantity of carbon tetrachloride into the Ohio River, threatening the drinking water of people living in Cincinnati and Louisville. Another spectacular case of industrial pollution was the release of dioxin into the atmosphere after the explosion at a plant engaged in the manufacture of supposedly harmless deodorants. This incident took place in Seveso, a small community in northern Italy located a short distance from Milan. It was probably one of the most serious affairs of its kind in regard to the number of people affected and the nature of their affliction, although the amount of chemical released was thought to be very small, perhaps only a few ounces. But nobody knew how the properties of dioxin change when they are heated to the high temperature that they were at the time of the explosion. There are still gaps in the information that has so far been made available about the incident and its aftereffects, but there is no doubt that the small white clouds of dioxin vapor which were unleashed into the atmosphere by the explosion were very injurious to the health of all those within the vicinity. Understandably then, the explosion had a severe impact upon the life of the community. The area where the explosion took place was cordoned off by barbed-wire fencing, the top-soil in the immediate vicinity was declared unsafe to graze animals, and people living near the factory were ordered to evacuate their homes. Some people went down with skin complaints such as rashes and discoloration, as well as dizziness and nausea. Those closest to the explosion were advised to abstain from the conception of children for an indeterminate period of time, while women who were already pregnant were offered abortions by the state. Fortunately, the number of people directly affected was not very great, but this is not the point. What is the point is that the leakage of carbon tetrachloride into drinking water and the explosion of dioxin vapor into the atmosphere are warnings that a future in which these and a whole host of similarly toxic chemicals will continue to be employed is very bleak indeed. No matter how well designed for safety are the industrial plants, no matter how conscientious are those who maintain and supervise them, accidents will happen, and have been happening more regularly over the past few years than ever before.

The atmospheric pollution which is part and parcel of big city life is also becoming a familiar part of rural life and is another situation which has become a serious threat to the health of modern man. Here again, the variety of pollutants is bewildering. They include exhaust gases from motor cars, which was earlier mentioned as a major problem in many large cities, smoke from factory chimneys and other noxious gases discharged into the atmosphere as a by-product of certain manufacturing processes. These noxious gases include carbon monoxide, which can enter the blood stream and prevent corpuscles from efficiently taking up oxygen, sulphur dioxide, sulphur trioxide, hydrogen sulphide and oxides of nitrogen, all of which can become significant impurities in rain water and by this means absorbed into the soil, increasing its acidity and thereby disrupting its pH balance, which leads in the long run to a decrease in fertility. Or the acidic rain water may enter a reservoir, thereby increasing the acidity of drinking water. Neither does breathing air saturated with high concentrations of these gases do much good for our lungs, whose delicate tissue is most sensitive to the minutest concentration of the acids they form when in aqueous solution. The question is not whether pollution is a major menace to the health and vigor of mankind — this has been settled in the affirmative — but rather how much damage will have been done by the time this age has come to an end. The situation is well summed up by Robert Heilbroner, who tells us: "The other side of the coin of affluence has been a steady deterioration in the quality of the environment — a deterioration brought about by enormously enhanced demands for resources, by gigantic scales of physical and chemical transformation of materials and by the need to dispose of gargantuan quantities of end products, including the peculiarly lethal ones of radioactive waste."[2]

Some people still believe that scientific and technological progress, which has served us so well in the past, will again come to our aid in the future. This is the attitude of mind referred to by Mesarovic and Pestel (*Mankind at the Turning Point,* 1975) as the "technological fix" solution. In other words, all problems can be solved given the application of sufficient technical expertise. It is true that on paper many of what appear to be mankind's most stubborn problems could be solved by a selected group of experts, assisted of course by a suitably programmed computer. But as our two authors rightly point out, it is quite another matter to apply these neatly derived solutions to the real world. Furthermore, the technological fix approach can only work within the confines of modern industrial society; it is absolutely no use to us if this society is itself no longer viable, as I believe to be the case. Belief in the powers of science and technology has been with us since the earliest days of the Industrial Revolution and now appears to be the only abiding certainty in an age of confusion. It will only fall with the transcendence of this age. The fact that pure and applied science has served us well in the past cannot be argued with, but whether it would be able to solve those problems which are now with us and which we can reasonably expect to get worse, is quite another matter. We have now reached the point at which scientific progress in a wide range of fields simply adds to the problems facing western society and mankind in general. For instance, a great deal of applied research is dedicated to producing military weapons with enormous destructive potential. The areas covered include nuclear armaments, biological warfare and weather control processes. No one can convince me that the development of nuclear bombs with multiple warheads, or germs capable of causing an epidemic and havoc in an enemy nation, has been of benefit to mankind. Let us leave mass destruction to nature, which can do it just as well as we can, if not better. Going to war should not mean the possibility of the annihilation of millions, as is the case with modern warfare. Let us go back to seeing warfare as part of the natural order of things, rather than as a threat to the very existence of our species as is now the case. Other questionable benefits of scientific progress include supersonic jets, which apart from being noisier and faster than conventional jets, have little to recommend them, and nuclear energy.

Many would argue that the development of nuclear energy for peaceful purposes once again demonstrates the value of science for good as well as evil. I would respectfully disagree with this conclusion; instead, the utilization of nuclear energy for peaceful purposes indicates clearly that as far as scientific progress is concerned western society has reached the point of diminishing returns. For how can our national leaders and many of our most eminent scientists justify the widespread use of nuclear material which will remain lethal for thousands of years, and in nuclear reactors which pose a serious threat to the localities in which they are situated owing to the chance of accident or terrorist attack? Ernest Schumacher, whom no one could accuse of wanting to see the end of modern industrial society, has stated the issues involved in the use of nuclear energy with tremendous force: "No degree of prosperity could justify the accumulations of large amounts of highly toxic substances which nobody knows how to make 'safe' and which remain an incalculable danger to the whole of creation for historical or even geological ages. To do such a thing is a transgression against life itself, a transgression infinitely more serious than any crime ever perpetrated by man. The idea that a civilization could sustain itself, on the basis of such a transgression is an ethical, spiritual, and metaphysical monstrosity. It means conducting the economic affairs of man as if people really did not matter at all."[3] Those who still believe that nuclear power can solve our energy problems should consult Mesarovic and Pestel (1975). They leave the reader in no doubt that nuclear energy is not under any circumstances a feasible solution to our energy problems. The employment of nuclear power is the technological fix idea at its very best and most destructive, a technological fix which, as Mesarovic and Pestel tell us, "might very well become a Faustian bargain — and worse, for we would be selling not merely our soul to satisfy our immediate comfort needs, but the well-being and perhaps the very existence of generations still unborn."[4] For the sake of humanity, we must reject the nuclear alternative, since this age is bound to come to an end well before we have run out of more conventional fuels such as oil and coal. And with the changes in lifestyle which will be brought about by the arrival of the new age we will not need to worry about energy shortages, for there will be plenty of traditional fuel available to support the modest needs of these new societies.

We tend to forget that, despite all his great achievements, man is still very much a part of nature and will forever remain so. Therefore, we can be certain man will never conquer nature, but if he were to proceed along his present path, then nature will one day conquer man with the most dreadful consequences for all mankind. We must take a closer look at our way of life and ask ourselves if we really want it to continue with science and technology coming to dominate all else, with mind and body crippled by the crushing restrictions imposed upon them in order that they should function exactly as the industrial age demands. The balance between man and technological progress is an impossible one to maintain, whereas the balance between man and the land is a most natural one and can be maintained indefinitely, given the right circumstances. The belief that our problems can be solved by the technocrats or by the diligent research work of experts cloistered away in universities or government sponsored research institutions is a species of self-delusion which deserves the title of scientific-technological nihilism. Our foremost problem is the way we live (i.e., our artificial elevation). One does not need to be a Nobel laureate to see that until this is changed — and changed drastically — our major problem will remain very much the same, with a tendency to get worse. New discoveries of wonder drugs or in fiber optics are hardly going to help us to reorient our lifestyle in such a way that we come to terms with nature, in such a way that we are able to maintain a vigorous civilization without the need for large scale industry and advanced technology and all the problems that these bring in their wake.

Over-development has affected our lives in other ways perhaps not so dramatic, but almost as worrying as all that we have been talking about above, especially to those who, through a careful study of history, have become familiar with the values and traditions which are characteristic of a healthy society. Loss of confidence, uncertainty and decline of creative inspiration are usually typical of a civilization which is nearing the end of its existence. Different societies will reflect this loss of vigor in different ways; as a matter of fact, some may hail trends which would be taken for signs of degeneration by more acute minds as a healthy development which should be encouraged. This has been the case at the tail end of our age more than any other. For instance, the cult of the expert has become very pervasive over the last three decades, so much so as to leave those subjects to which expertise has been generally confined and to enter the world of mass consumption. I am not against experts in general, since the average individual of today does need a certain degree of guidance in regard to complex matters whose full implications he or she would not understand without the assistance of recognized experts. There are numerous fields in which this holds true, e.g., international relations, macroeconomics, medical research and other scientific matters. Expert comment on these matters, which is usually found in our daily newspapers and magazines, is understandable. What is not understandable is the mini-industry that has grown up in giving advice on an infinite variety of matters which the average individual should be able to take care of for himself. Our schools and colleges are filled with guidance counsellors. Almost every popular periodical has someone to deal with letters from the weak and insecure. So-called experts on consumer affairs tell us what to buy and when to buy it. Nutrition experts tell us what to eat and what not to eat. Other experts tell us how to pick a marriage partner, how to keep our marriage together, how to bring up children, how to dress and how to relax. Now even people of sound academic standing are cashing in on the cult of the instant expert. Obviously, these self-appointed ministers of the mass psyche must be well received by the general public, but whether or not our society benefits from their activities is quite another matter.

These experts on just about every aspect of our daily lives look at life from the point of view of the average individual and apply their advice as if everybody was cast in the mold of the average man or woman. They do nothing to elevate the mass consciousness and much to depress it. It seems that the complexity of modern industrial society has bred a need for guidance in the simplest aspects of our daily lives. This development has been harmful to an extent that is little appreciated by most people, in that it encourages a superficial attitude to life and stimulates anxieties rather than soothing them. At least religious belief, when it was at its strongest, engendered a philosophical acceptance of life among the masses which took them well above their daily concerns. This is not so for modern man; although many of us still profess to be religious, the vast majority of us have become obsessed with the practical and the rational. Meditation is practiced by only a tiny minority of western citizens; philosophical reflection about man's place in nature, his present discontents and his future is confined to an insignificant group of little-known academics. Much of what they write is unknown to the majority or simply ignored. The literature that appeals to the modern mind are the cheap romance novels, trashy paperbacks spewed out in their millions, or the shallow, trivial autobiography of some highly visible celebrity who might as well be the next door neighbor for all the light his or her life story sheds on the realities of contemporary life. In other words, the depression of good taste, the cult of the instant expert, the flight from challenging literature and serious contemplation are all part of the escapist mentality that has taken over modern man as his affluence has grown greater. The essence of the escapist mentality is that our minds should be anchored to the consideration of the most trivial matters while at the same time believing that, as civilizations go, ours is far superior to any that has ever existed. Quantitatively, this may be true; we certainly have more abundance of just about everything in comparison with any previous age. But qualitatively, this is certainly not true, for there have been ages which have offered a far more spiritually satisfying way of life than modern man has known for the last two hundred years.

The ideal of scientific rationalism has done much to promote this escapist obsession with the practical. The cult of the popular expert is simply an extension of scientific rationalism. After all, does not this so-called expert approach his or her function in a scientific manner? Their advice is based on a great deal of statistical sampling or other research work. But we should remember that science and the scientific spirit is only part of the whole and not all of it, a point made most forcibly by Collingwood in his book *What Is Nature.* In the end, the most important thing is history, and science develops or recedes within the context of history and cannot be separated from it. Therefore, science cannot tell us anything definite either about its own future (i.e, its status in a future age) or about the course that will be taken by contemporary western civilization. Since these things are not possible, the scientific spirit of dedicated research has been harnessed to keep busy those eminent men and women who have more qualifications than can possibly be of use to themselves or to their society, while the principles of modern science have been employed to give respectability to a host of non-scientific pursuits which have popular appeal ranging from astrology to scientology, not forgetting our sex therapists, child guidance counselors, marriage counselors, all of whom would claim their work is scientifically valid.

Our much praised access to education has probably done as much as anything else to make us susceptible to what I can only describe as the enfeeblement of the modern mind. We have been led to believe that the universal availability of education would solve many of the problems of western society and, despite setbacks, people still believe this. They believe it because modern industrial society continues to exist and so to believe anything else would be to turn one's back on the only lifestyle and value system of which the individual, his family and friends are part. And yet, there is a certain amount of unease that runs through the worship of education; it has been most clearly apparent in the past decade during which the application of expert knowledge and careful reasoning (the hallmarks of our educated society) has utterly failed to come to grips with the most pressing problems of western society. The system of trade-offs between different interest groups and different policy objectives, such as high employment and low environmental pollution, is no longer working. Confronted with the truth of this observation, i.e., applied education is failing us in those areas where its success is most vital, the people are bewildered. But they continue to go through the motions and stick to the old beliefs, for they have no other alternatives. In a way, modern industrial society has undercut its own existence by extending the benefits of education to all its citizens, for although an educated individual will function in our society better than an illiterate one, he also has a greater awareness of himself and his relation to others. Thus, he will come to appreciate that education is not nearly as important, in achieving success, as his parents told him it was. He will see educated men in public life, whom at one time he may have considered to be worthy of his respect, change their opinions at the drop of a hat to suit their ambitions or just to keep in tune with public opinion. He will read about the futile wrangles of well-known personalities in various fields as they wage their petty vendettas or scramble for public acclaim. He will watch his highly educated contemporaries struggle with problems they cannot understand and attempt to solve them by applying measures which are bound to fail. All this will breed cynicism and contempt for education and the educated, something which is already happening although it has not yet really begun to shake the establishment.

There is another side to this matter that cannot be passed over without comment. The availability of education for all, regardless of family circumstances and natural capacity, has meant that in theory each person is able to consider himself the equal of any other person, when in truth we all know that this is not so. True, the vast majority of the citizens of western nations can read and write, but very few of them are creators. Their literacy gives them the potential to be prey, not only to the most outlandish ideas, but also to the offerings of the myriads of popular experts who would be most happy to relieve their fellow men of the burden of thinking for themselves. Critical thinking is not a faculty that is found in great abundance among the common people and in the unstructured social order that characterizes the western world, the people are intellectually rootless, for there is no way in which they can properly understand the essentials of world history and their place in its onward march. Unable to be an original and constructive thinker, though literate, the average man and woman have nothing to do but to agree or disagree with the latest trends in fashion, interior decorating, penal reform, medical research, politics and the arts, as set down by the leaders of opinion in these various fields. But many of the leaders of opinion themselves spend much time wondering what thoughts are currently in the mind of the majority and whether or not their own ideas will meet with popular approval. To place matters in their simplest terms we have reached stalemate — stagnation, if you like — in our patterns for living. Those who the people expect to lead them are in turn looking to the people for inspiration. Somehow we must break out of this impasse if we intend to maintain the vigor and vitality of western civilization.

Earlier we talked about the daunting array of social problems to be found in western society. There is one problem about which I said very little, except to mention the declining fertility levels of women — this is the population problem, something which we must now look at in greater detail. Since it first became a matter of international importance, the population problem has always been seen as that of the world having a level of population growth which was far greater than it could possibly sustain. Such terms as the "population explosion," "population countdown" and the "Malthusian nightmare" became commonplace. The Third World countries were encouraged to launch massive birth control programs in the hope that they could head off the coming calamity. There is still a great deal of concern over the rate at which the earth's population is increasing, though mercifully this concern has lessened somewhat compared with the hysterical levels it reached only a few years back. If only our compassionate family planning advocates and the academic busy bodies who support them could realize that their concern is totally misplaced. Population growth in the Third World (and in all other countries for that matter) should be allowed to continue at a vigorous pace and encouraged in those nations where it is slack. For the coming age which is destined to replace the present one will certainly bring about a period of immense turmoil and dislocation owing to major climatic and environmental changes, plus the concomitant changes in social organization which we will be discussing later on. The world's population is bound to undergo an appreciable reduction, at least in the early stages. Of this we can be sure. Why then should man attempt to do the work of nature? The greater the population, the larger will be the number that survive to till the soil and protect the land from foreign invasion. Only by having the largest possible population at the time of the great transformation will a nation have a chance of repopulating its homeland and perpetuating its cultural identity. Also, the larger the population the greater the chance of there being leaders of exceptional ability to guide our now leaderless societies through the difficult times that lie ahead. Two points follow naturally from what I have just said. The first is that the countries of the Third World should not bother themselves to reduce their birth rates but on the contrary should leave matters to nature. The second is that those countries (mainly the developed nations) which are now experiencing a population decline have more to fear in regards to the maintenance of their cultural identity, under the circumstances of the new age, than do the countries of the Third World which have a high birth rate.

There seems to be little that can be done at the present time to reverse the declining birth rates of western nations. The social organization of these countries with its stress on high mobility, loose family ties, equality of man and wife in marriage and the fact that a small family is less of a financial burden than a large family, all militate against a married couple having a large number of children. I deliberately emphasize married couple, for there is a tendency for a couple living together outside the bonds of matrimony to avoid having children and thereby cheat their society of gaining more members and themselves of the joys of parenthood. The women's liberation movement has not helped matters either, encouraging the widespread use of contraception and, when this fails, abortion, as being the most desirable alternative to having children. The attitudes reflected by the wide prevalence of contraception and abortion in the northern nations are a curse upon modern industrial society — a will to national self-destruction, which nobody wants, but which is taking place all the same. Instead of counting children as a blessing and having as many as possible, far more energy is expended in western society on thinking up ways in which having children can be avoided, so as to keep their number down to a minimum. The attitude that sees children as a liability rather than an asset is no doubt largely responsible for the declining birth rate of the developed industrial societies, a trend which must be reversed if these nations are to have a future. Whether or not this trend will be reversed before modern industrial society reaches its end is uncertain, but one thing we can do to improve matters is to stop sanctioning the murder of our unborn children.

The great debate over abortion which has taken place in all major western nations over the past few years and which continues with unabated vigor in most of these countries, is just one aspect of the current confusion in regard to morals and values which now reigns within the mind of western man. The reasons why western man is so confused with regard to his beliefs and values are various. Some would put it down to his loss of anchorage which was provided by the deeply held religious convictions of his forefathers. This is a possibility not to be scoffed at, since religion has undoubtedly played a large part in the maintenance of social tranquility and continues to do so in several countries of the Third World. Others would attribute the insecurity which is gnawing away at the mind of modern man to lack of decisive leadership from politicians and others in a position to lead. Still others consider the problem to be connected with the chronic lack of reasoning power among the ordinary people. Perhaps all of these have something to do with the crisis of values.

But I believe that there are other aspects of the problem which have so far received insufficient attention. One of these is the contradiction between the advancement of science and technology which is felt to be a good for its own sake and the application of the fruits of this advance. Diligent scientific research has given us such enormous barbarities as that which opened the nuclear age in 1945 with the dropping of atomic bombs on Hiroshima and Nagasaki. The need to maintain the balance of terror has ensured that the debate over nuclear weapons is always with us. In exploring the properties of the atom, science has proved to be a greater disservice to man than could possibly be justified by pointing to the knowledge added to man's understanding of the universe. Now we have enough stockpiles of nuclear weaponry to destroy the world several times over. But still we engage in the competitive expansion of our nuclear capability. This insane battle for nuclear supremacy between the superpowers is backed up by their colossal scientific-technological capability, and only by destruction of the latter will we cease to have anything to fear.

The development of nerve gas is yet another blatant example of modern science gone astray. Now our scientific gadflies are working on the biological equivalent of atomic research, i.e., the manipulation of genetic material to produce new forms of life. This is really the limit, for although this research work is not at the present time being carried out with a view to military application, it is an area in which man has no business to be meddling, for such research could ultimately do incalculable damage to the human race. But still the scientists press on in the name of the unfettered pursuit of knowledge, even against the reasoned objections of their more reverent colleagues. Reason is not going to stop these scientific trailblazers, but history will do so one day. How does the ordinary man in the street react when he is confronted with the unquenchable thirst for knowledge — whether in connection with high powered lasers to destroy enemy craft or in connection with the manipulation of genetic material which can lead to the sudden emergence of a highly resistant and virulent type of bacteria? He is of course helpless, for he is a mere spectator. All he can do is to turn his back on the scientific breakthroughs which are occurring with such frequency these days, and concentrate on gratifying his own desires. He can understand the dangers, but is helpless to influence the course of events. Scientific-technological progress is an integral part of his way of life and therefore he has no option but to accept all that it may bring — yet he can see the dangers.

Another source of confusion is the area of morality in international affairs. This problem is of course a legacy of the changes in international affairs since the end of World War Two. The North Atlantic nations made the mistake of setting themselves up as so-called defenders of the free world, a stance which committed them to come to the assistance of all nations which felt in the least bit threatened by communist subversion regardless of geographical locality. One could have understood this posture if the defense of the free world was restricted to western Europe, but what, pray, were the Western powers doing in involving themselves in places such as Egypt, Korea and later Vietnam? These countries and all other members of the Third World, whether communist or anti-communist, should have been left to sort out their own affairs without outside interference. Because the Western powers came to the assistance of several of these nations on the grounds of moral argument, the same argument can be used against this policy when the nations assisted do not live up to the ideals of western democracy. In fact, the moral argument has been used in this way and continues to be used. But instead of drawing the obvious lessons from recent history and maintaining a low profile, the western powers led by the United States have insisted on pressing ahead with their "defense of freedom" in countries of the Third World, freedom now having been expanded to include not only the right to stand up against communist aggression, but also the granting of human rights in those countries which are ruled by anti-communist authoritarian regimes. The quest for consistency in the application of moral values to international affairs is bound to end in a debacle for whichever nation pursues it, regardless of the nation's political or economic strength. For one thing, the ideals of western democracy belong almost exclusively to Western Europe and those few countries which were colonized mainly by people from Western Europe. To expect any other nations to fully live up to the ideals of western nations is the height of folly. All these other nations have their own history and culture. Therefore, a Westminster type parliamentary democracy may not always be able to take root. Criticism of the political situation in authoritarian Third World countries seems all the more suspect when we consider that the political system of an increasing number of western nations is never very far from the brink of chaos and the fact that they have not gone over the edge in recent years is due more to luck than to anything else.

Whatever the political system of these independent countries of the Third World, they should be left alone without moral lectures from statesmen of the Western powers. Military alliances should not be made with them, economic embargos should not be used to get another nation to change its internal policies, and the regime in power should be recognized provided it is in control of the greatest proportion of the country, i.e., regardless of its political complexion, for in the long run no nation can really affect the way in which a second nation treats its citizens, unless it is prepared to go to war with the object of replacing the incumbent government with a new one. If the complaining nation is not prepared to go this far it should hold its peace. Furthermore, each nation has its own destiny different from all others; in the case of the advanced industrialized western democracies and the Third World, the destinies of these two groups will be different. Therefore, the western nations are in effect wasting their time in attempting to foster the growth of western patterns of political morality in most nations of the Third World. A neutralist or isolationist stance will be found to be far more profitable. All thought of morality should be eliminated post haste from the consideration of international affairs. It must be left to each and every nation to find its own salvation. If this could be understood by our present generation of political leaders, then the man in the street would cease to be in a state of confusion over right and wrong in international relations.

Despite the continuous diet of pseudo-enlightenment which they have been brought up on for the last thirty years or so, the common people show an amazing amount of resilience, which leads me to conclude that the purveyors of pseudo-enlightenment will encounter firm resistance to some of their more extreme proposals. The advocates of pseudo-enlightenment would of course be surprised by such a development, for so far they have had things all their own way. But this has been because the advocates of traditional values have had poor leadership and in consequence have been outflanked by their adversaries time after time. Furthermore, the close association between those of conservative outlook (in politics) and corporate capital has not only cast doubt among the people about their sincerity and independence but has also blunted their effectiveness in attacking the ills of western society and fighting for the preservation of those values which are now under attack. Nor would the task be as great as some might imagine, since western society is ready for a well aimed counterattack. For example, the false guides talk about the need to give generous aid to the Third World, the people are not so sure. They speak loudly in favor of the complete abolition of the death penalty; the people are hostile. The cry for abortion on demand meets with the same hostility as does the spread of pornography. The common people have no ambitions to change the world and would laugh loudly at the visions of a classless society held by the most extreme of the "enlightened." They are patriotic, but worried about the future of their society as they watch their leaders struggle with mounting problems. They believe in doing a fair day's work for a fair day's pay and that if someone is exceptionally talented he should be exceptionally rewarded. In this connection they are intolerant of both incompetence and corruption. They believe in the right of self-defense and retaliation rather than stretching out the hand of friendship to their attacker. They believe that an individual's fitness for a job or college place should be based on ability alone and no special concessions should be made to particular groups in giving them preference over others. Despite all the talk regarding equality of the sexes, a large number of men and women remain convinced that women are by nature unable to compete equally with men either on the battlefield or behind a desk. The same people also believe that a woman's most valuable contribution to a well-ordered society is as a faithful wife and mother. These are truths which it would be difficult to deny. But they seem to run counter to the whole tenor of modern industrial society, especially during the last three decades which have been unparalleled in the attempts made to put right injustices real or imagined. All I can say is that modern industrial society will not go on forever, and when it does finally come to an end, we shall find out whether traditional values will be triumphantly reasserted or whether the rooting out of all supposed injustices will finally be consummated in an age of pacifist cave dwellers.

From all that has been said so far we should be able to agree that there is something very depressing about the tenor of our age. Up until now we have discussed those problems which are most familiar and hence most easily understood. But there are other disturbing features about our age, perhaps less well understood, but nevertheless in their own way just as telling. The spirit of adventure, the possibility of great issues being fought out by equally great men, are absent from our age. Creativity in art, literature, poetry and music, which captures the spirit of the age and stirs us deeply, is gone. Contemporary western society is like a lifeless body which is not yet clinically dead. We still have plenty of mental activity, but it barely touches us, for what use is it to an age which has no pulse, no great stirring challenge in which everyone can play his part. Decadence — the disease of a dying age — is eating its way to the core of western society. The artist and the man of letters have no impact on contemporary western society. They are shut out by the realist, the man of business, the technocrat and the bureaucrat. Everything is subordinated to our material well-being; we must produce more and own more this year than we did last year. To ensure that this is so, every aspect of life is precisely regulated to the minutest detail. It seems that even the most vigorous spirits among us have been tied securely to Ixions Wheel, condemned to go through the same motions day after day. Our age is surely the first to be devoid of all challenge, all possibility of finding one's identity in a cause for which one would die without hesitation. This age suffers from a lack of freedom, not the freedom of opinion or of association but the freedom to express one's energy in the undertaking of great deeds involving if necessary great loss of life. Was it not Freud who once said that life becomes impoverished when the highest stake in the game of living, life itself may not be risked? How right he was.

This legalistic age of ours, with its motto of justice for all, elevating the weak at the expense of the strong, is destroying life, not enriching it. The character of western man is being molded in a manner that emasculates him. His traditional vocabulary is no longer good enough, but must be changed to reflect new ideas of equality which are totally erroneous. He is expected to share household chores equally with his wife, he is no longer left in peace when away from home with friends, but is now forced to share what were his former sanctuaries with members of the opposite sex. Laws have been enacted to support these degrading changes. The last thing a society should want is for its women to act and think as its men, competing with men on equal terms. No society has operated that way in the past and no society could long survive if it attempted to operate that way in the future. Contemporary western society is already suffering as a result of the changes in the status and expectations of women, the achievement of total equality would be the final straw. It seems that those who advocate total equality for women cannot accept that men and women are physically and psychologically different, a fact that prevents them from ever being equals. The only reason why the women's movement has done as well as it has, is that for the most part modern industrial society has been set in a "soft age." The food supply has been superabundant, social mobility has been common and the emphasis has been on change rather than conservation. Thus, the cause of women's liberation has been able to gain a high place on the list of "wrongs" to be righted.

In the new age, all this will be changed, those physical and psychological differences which distinguish men from women will once more come into prominence, the penchant of this age for the rights of women and others will be seen as a misunderstanding of the human condition. These days we speak about happiness as if it were the birthright of every man who lives, when in fact it is the birthright of no man be he rich or poor, brilliant or illiterate. The birthright of man is not happiness, but struggle and conflict with nature and with other men. This truism has receded well into the background but will one day return with a vengeance. The superabundance and lax social structure that characterizes western industrial society is, after all, just a brief interlude; it could never be a permanent way of life. The weak, the underprivileged and the indigent who expect happiness to be handed to them on a plate are living in a world of make-believe which is destined to be shattered. Not surprisingly, the strong-willed, independent-minded spirits no longer venture out in public. The one-sided stress of contemporary society on its fatuous attention to the needs of those least able to help themselves has worked hand in hand with our scientific materialism to denude our age of all those qualities which make for greatness. Instead, the popular ideals of contemporary western society embrace the most despicable and ignoble traits of mankind.

Our healthy emotions and freedom of action have been curbed to such an extent that modern man is unable to stand up to a comparison with his pre-industrial forefathers, who would not have allowed silly sentiment to dictate to them what is right and wrong. The devitalizing effect that a fully developed democracy would have in an industrialized nation, was recognized and predicted many years ago by Alexis de Tocqueville in his masterpiece *Democracy In America*. He correctly foresaw that with equality as the leading ideal, mediocrity would come to dominate every aspect of life. As for politics, more time and effort would be spent in pandering to the whims of the majority than on any other activity. Those having an opinion challenging the commonly held beliefs would be ignored or abused. He rightly perceived that such an epoch would be an age without valor or virtue, an age almost devoid of original and penetrating minds, an age in which the people would be occupied by the trivial and the petty. All this is clear from de Tocqueville's description of a new type of despotism for which up to his time there had been no precedent, but which he could sense emerging before his very eyes in democratic America. He concluded that it would be easier than most people realize to establish such an enervating despotism under the guise of sovereignty of the people, and so it has come to pass.

This civilization of ours, of which many are so proud, is characterized by a total lack of heroic quality. What else could one expect of an age in which a leader is judged on his ability to win votes and interpret the will of the people rather than on his ability to take power, hold it against all comers and tell the people what their will should be. A legalistic-bureaucratic age like our own which has so far shown itself to be incapable of producing men of this caliber, will by the same token be an age incapable of inspiring great works of art. Moreover, this is an age in which we have become divorced from the faculty of intense appreciation of art, from the pathos that only great art can produce. This fact more than any other shows us how empty is present-day society, a spiritual and cultural wasteland amidst material plenty. There is much talk in the western world that the arts are under-financed, that their traditional sources of revenue are drying up, that inflation is every year making matters more difficult for the performing arts. These points are true enough, but this way of looking at the arts in crude monetary terms does not allow one to appreciate the fact that modern art has contributed very little to the intellectual formation of modern man. This is the real crisis of culture, it has been found impossible to make a viable and inspiring theme of scientific-technological progress or any of the other varieties of progress on which our age prides itself. The great tragedy of contemporary art is not its lack of financial support, but its inability to accurately reflect the age in which we live in a meaningful way. Art is no longer an irreducible part of the fabric of western civilization; instead it has become another commodity to be priced, packaged and purchased according to the going rate. Present-day society marks the highest development of modern industrial society, and as such is less conducive to artistic creativity than any previous age.

This sick age of ours is as confused about its moral and ethical beliefs as it is about most other aspects of its life style. We have already spoken about the confusion over moral values that exists in international affairs, but the confusion over morality on the domestic front has been of more direct concern to a larger number of people. The breach between public virtue, i.e., the conventional morals of modern industrial society and our private morality, i.e., our inner feelings, inclinations and, not least, actions, has become in many countries a national scandal. On the one hand, public virtue preaches honesty in business dealings, strict adherence to legal form in all matters and the iniquity of using one's position of trust for satisfying one's own cupidity, and of course, the sanctity of family life. But there is enough evidence to show that contemporary western society has been having a very difficult time sticking to its public virtue behind closed doors. Bribery, malfeasance, fraud and nepotism abound in business and politics in the western world, just as much as in the Third World, if recent disclosures are anything to go by. Dishonesty is accepted as a normal part of the game, the honest man is no longer nature's nobleman but a fool! Those who can use their position to enrich themselves or to assist their relatives and friends or in some other way derive benefit have no scruples about doing so, whilst many of those who are unable to derive much benefit from their position envy the good fortune of those who can. Infidelity among those in highly visible public office has become so common as to no longer cause a stir among the lesser mortals for whom they were once supposed to set an example. I hardly need dwell on these matters; the facts are well known to everyone.

The dishonesty of our age is compounded by its lack of candor. Our age seems hesitant, unsure of itself in matters of morality and ethics, almost as if it cannot make up its mind whether to be totally amoral or only selectively immoral. The ethical ideals on which the public virtue of modern industrial society is based have not been specifically rejected, yet we are moving away from these ideals at an alarming rate. We seem to have lost our anchorage; neither attention to duty nor respect for one's own status is sufficient to guarantee consistent standards of competence and integrity. By this I mean that the decisions of a person in an office of trust should be his own, uninfluenced by public opinion or by how much money others are willing to pay him if he will see matters their way. As for sexual morality, we have never been able to straighten this out since the triumph of Christianity and have had particular difficulty over the last five hundred years, either erring on the side of a too strict and puritanical regime, or, like now, on the side of one too liberal and easy going. Either extreme will in the long run be destructive; therefore, both must be avoided. The perplexed state of modern man prevents him from bringing his sexuality under control, therefore, it is breaking out in all sorts of ways which are not to the benefit of his society. The situation would be rather different if there were a warrior class which could set its own standards of sexual morality unbothered by the majority, who would nevertheless live a life of chastity and temperance. Not having such a division within contemporary society, the result is utter confusion and moral discord. A similar situation existed for a brief period of time during the earlier part of the first French Revolution, the people having lost their bearings following the eclipse of the nobility, monarchy and church in rapid succession. But with us the situation is so much worse, for unlike the vast majority of those living in Revolutionary France of the 1790s, we are surrounded by an overabundance of goods and comforts. We do not face the challenge of hard toil in order to eke out a bare subsistence. Neither are we at the mercy of the elements which could wipe out all we have at one blow. Nor can we find redemption on the battlefield, for war between valiant men has become archaic; war between scientists and technicians is now the rule. We live a life that is overindulgent, a life that is too easy, far too easy for our own good. While we are on the matter of ethics, there is another disturbing feature of our age which is closely connected with the decline of standards. This is the invasion of privacy which has taken place in recent years, as all manner of private matters are dragged before the public so that they can gloat and glee. People are given no time to get over personal tragedy before they are set upon by the news media. Details of the serious illness of a well known public figure are soon made public regardless of the patient's own desire. All this is done in the name of freedom of the press or freedom of information. I prefer to see it as nothing better than cheap sensationalist journalism. A review of the last thirty years tends to confirm the belief that this entire epoch has been one long essay in social, political, economic and cultural decadence which is now reaching its peak.

Some people believe that pornographic films, magazines, books and peep shows, together with various lewd forms of live entertainment are the most explicit examples of decadence to be met with in the advanced industrial societies. But although these things are symptomatic of the last stages of decay of modern industrial society, their full significance can only be appreciated by examining them with a view to the future of western society. What should be seen as bad about the commercial exploitation of pornography, from the point of view of the well-adjusted modern man, is that it helps to promote an attitude of mind which is antithetical to the continued existence of modern industrial society. There are two schools of thought in regard to the commercialization of sex which has become part of the contemporary scene. One school believes that it should be suppressed by strict censorship, zoning restrictions and the use of the courts against those who offend against standards of public decency. The venom of this school is quite understandable, but as far as pushing to a successful conclusion, theirs is a lost cause. It is much too late to check the profitable career of commercialized sex by legal means. The other major school of thought on this subject appears to believe that the commercialization of sex should be left to take its own course, and if so, will eventually go out of fashion as the novelty wears off and good sense reasserts itself. This is certainly possible, though in my view unlikely. As far as I can see, the commercial exploitation of sex is here to stay, i.e., for as long as modern industrial society remains in existence. But I also believe that the tension between contemporary man's need for self-discipline and what Daniel Bell aptly refers to as the antinomous value system of contemporary western society is one of the key factors propelling us towards the new age, an age that will place human sexuality within proper perspective. Hence, the successful commercialization of sex is a portent of much greater changes to come. It is an outward reflection of the deep-seated psychic forces which will one day come to the surface and provide the energy for the destruction of present-day society and its replacement by a new society based upon aristocratic values.

THE STAGNATION OF CONTEMPORARY POLITICS

One of the most pathetic aspects of modern industrial society in its last stages of decay is the way in which its magnificent political structure is crumbling into dust. The signs of dissolution are unmistakable and include widespread corruption, disillusionment and cynicism among veteran politicians and an inability to come to grips with the most pressing problems of contemporary life. In other words, the politicians are themselves looking for leadership instead of giving it. The degeneration of political leadership is not restricted to one particular country but is taking place in all countries which have a fully developed industrial civilization, including Japan. This is another example of how the age of modern industry has taken man to a point where he has become helpless and confused.

Now that all the great social issues are behind us, the day-to-day politics of the late twentieth century has little challenge. The practitioner of modern politics is condemned to spend most of his time on monotonous paper work which could just as well be done by any bureaucrat of limited competence. When not involved in meaningless paper work, he is either listening to sterile debate or running for re-election. We often think it a matter of great moment when a country gains a new head of government. This belief in the innovative powers of the modern political leader is most touching, but wholly misguided. How can we expect great initiatives from a person who may remain at the helm for only a few years or less? Even if he is head of state as well as head of government, the politician finds that there is painfully little he can do to affect the course of national affairs. The truth is that this is an age which is too complex for one man to have very much impact no matter how long he may remain in power, unless he is a deranged fanatic intent on establishing his place in history regardless of the cost. Other than this, politics has become a matter of choosing between two or three sets of carefully circumscribed alternatives. It is no wonder that ordinary legislators consider themselves to have very little power; even their President or Prime Minister is powerless in the face of the great Juggernaut which I have called modern industrial society.

An age which requires of its leaders only that they be good bureaucrats is an age that has lost all vitality and spontaneity; it is, in short, an age that is less than human. It is no exaggeration to say that our politicians have become part of the bureaucracy from whose encroachments they were supposed to protect us. Ironically, the reaction to the criticism that has been leveled against our law makers, especially in regard to financial irregularities, has done much to reduce the distinction between legislator and bureaucrat. The state now helps pay for the election expenses of political parties. Independence from the state's largess has become a thing of the past. Members of the nation's parliament are somehow considered to be inadequate parliamentarians if they actively pursue their profession along with their legislative duties. The fact that we now expect our legislators to live off the state rather than on their personal incomes means that we are moving well away from the concept of representative democracy as it has always been understood. To make sure that our legislators have no doubt about their diminished status, codes of conduct have been drawn up for them to follow. Not only are legislators pressurized into devoting a disproportionate amount of their time to parliamentary affairs, in some countries they have to make public their involvement with outside interests while in others they must also give details about the financial affairs of members of their family. This is supposed to produce more conscientious legislators who look to politics as a career. The hope that these measures will do something to revitalize contemporary politics is bound to be disappointed.

To be truthful, the professionalization of politics has so far done very little to improve the low opinion in which politicians are now held. In fact, this move betrays a failure to understand the nature of representative democracy by those who are supposed to be its most seasoned practitioners. The basic idea behind this type of government from its earliest inception was that the elected representatives took time off from their regular occupations to devote themselves to the affairs of state though they still remained active farmers, lawyers, doctors or merchants. The fact that our legislators, like our bureaucrats, are expected to devote themselves full time to affairs of state surely means that representative democracy has almost outlived its usefulness. The job of both the bureaucracy and the legislature of all developed societies is to keep up with the great Juggernaut, rather like a man on a treadmill, unaware that one day the effort will simply become too much for him. The politics of the late twentieth century has become the prelude to a much greater drama — the unfolding of a new age. This thought is all that redeems contemporary politics, for if this were not so we would have nothing to look forward to, except perhaps a nuclear holocaust and an instantaneous return to the primeval tribalism from which we so painfully emerged, or failing this, a slow lingering death from the effects of environmental pollution.

Some people, although aware of the serious troubles of contemporary political institutions, refuse to believe that they have had their day. They seem to think that the root of the problem is that politics no longer attracts men of genius, and since our present day politicians are such a mediocre bunch, not much is to be expected of them. But no matter how brilliant a person may be, once he accepts the institutions of his age as appropriate vehicles through which to bring about change, he becomes subject to the limitations of his age and is likely to find himself reechoing popular sentiment, or struggling vainly to keep an already hopeless situation from going totally out of control. This degradation of the finest intellects cannot be helped in a system such as ours, which demands that our so-called leaders regularly pander to the prejudices and fears of the uninstructed. No wonder why one wit once referred to democracy as the system by which the most unscrupulous are elected to office by the most incompetent.

There are now unmistakable signs that the people are being turned off by contemporary politics. They have had enough of broken promises, enough of meaningless debate, they no longer have any interest in what the politicians say. One indicator of the extent of the present malaise is that voter participation in many western democracies has been steadily declining in recent years and in several has reached an all-time low. The politicians talk about the same old issues, housing, social welfare expenditure and the state of the economy. All these issues, except perhaps the last mentioned, have long ceased to be of much interest to the more thoughtful voter. Probably the most pressing questions in his or her mind are concerned with what lies ahead. Can our present day lifestyle be continued for another hundred years? Is the worldwide recession from which we are so slowly emerging just another in a succession of such events, or is it an indication that great changes are on the horizon? And if contemporary society is nearing its end, what sort of society could we expect to rise out of the ashes of the old one? One can see straight away that these are not the sort of questions to which the average politician would be expected to address himself. Welfare expenditure versus military expenditure is quite alright; this is the type of question he has had to deal with since his earliest days in national politics. But questions on a higher plane than this do not come within his range of competence, and anyway he must deal with reality as it is and not as it could be — a constraint which he shares with all other practical and hard-headed men of the world. Where does this leave those who are concerned with the future of modern industrial society — they have no option but to hold their peace. This they have indeed done, if the cynicism and apathy among both young and old is anything to go by. The futile posturing of our politicians is no longer enough to satisfy a deeply anxious electorate. Further, since the questions I posed above will loom larger as time goes by, politicians will become increasingly irrelevant, for they have no answers to these questions.

Both young and old alike are tired of the petty politics of inter-party bickering, of charge and counter charge, much of which they neither understand and care about even less. What they really want to know is whether or not scientific and technological progress will succeed in laying the world waste and eventually uninhabitable. They want to know whether it is yet too late for man to triumph over machine and regain harmony with nature. In the long run, these matters and the questions broached earlier, will be of far greater importance to the course of western civilization than debate over the size of the budget deficit, the level of taxation or the money spent on defense. The people are no longer expecting their leaders to come up with an economic panacea, for they now realize that such a thing does not exist. But they are searching for a new vision of the future, one that can be understood in terms of their deepest emotions and this is where their political leaders are failing them. If modern industrial society was destined to continue in some modified form, then maybe our political leaders would come up with an inspiring vision of the future. But as it is now, they are incapable of doing so.

Contemporary politicians are certainly not the men who will be leading us into the new age. In recent years (as it has become more professionalized) politics has ceased to be an art and is tending to become a science or as near to one as it can possibly be made. Computers have become essential to modern politics; all the great domestic decisions are based on a most careful analysis of statistical trends. Quantitative criteria are applied as much as possible to almost every issue of major political importance, including these days, foreign affairs. The preoccupation with money matters is turning the chief executive (whether he be President or Prime Minister) into the head accountant. Much of his time is taken up with budgetary matters, whether this be raising sufficient revenue, decreeing spending cuts, making departmental allocations, or bringing forward fiscal proposals whose actual effects he is uncertain of but which he nevertheless believes to be essential for the nation's economic health. With the introduction of zero-base budgeting and the possibility of obtaining large quantities of economic information with little difficulty, we have reached the stage at which the leadership of western society could be turned over to a team of computer programmers chosen for their technical ability rather than their political sophistication.

We should not therefore be surprised to learn that modern politics is not only failing to maintain the support of the old, but it is also failing to gain the allegiance of the young. Those of the young who haven't been entirely overcome by apathy and indifference have joined fringe political groups in greater numbers than ever before. Others have forsaken politics in favor of mysticism or have joined one of the numerous oriental inspired religious cults that have sprung up and flourished in all western countries during the last decade. Very few young people any longer become fully paid up members of one of the nation's established political parties. They seem to have lost faith in the ability of the party system to mirror their highest aspirations, which although confused and rather inchoate are of a different order to those of their parents. Whether or not the majority of today's politicians are aware of the massive disenchantment with contemporary politics among young people, I really cannot say. But even if they openly acknowledged the problem, there would seem to be little they could do about it in the long run. The bureaucratic and technological superiority of contemporary western society over all other ages has reduced our political leaders to impotent babblers, who every election year repeat the same promises together with a string of meaningless cliches and statistics. Our political leaders and opinion makers have proved to be no more incisive than the rest of us in applying the experience of history and teachings of philosophy to mankind's present predicament.

We are living in the tail end of an age which has become devoid of feeling. In our inane desire to stamp out all prejudices, all views which do not conform to the fatuous ideals of late twentieth century liberalism, we are well on the way to draining life of all conflict, all sharp emotion; in fact, we are in the process of destroying the very essence of western civilization. Even the strongest spirits have bended under the pressure towards mediocrity in thought and deed which has come to characterize our age. Our politicians make innocuous statements calculated not to offend this or that minority group. Should a public figure make one slip, one off-the-cuff remark, or voice his true sentiments, instead of oozing the unctuous sentimentality that passes for leadership, he is immediately set upon by insecure weaklings who act as if their very lives have been threatened by one solitary individual who had the courage to voice his true feelings or who just by a moment dropped his guard. The hapless offender is usually quick to apologize to the offended group, but sometimes this may not be enough and he has to resign before his detractors will rest satisfied. When Horkheimer and Adorno tell us that in this day and age "personality scarcely signifies anything more than shining white teeth and freedom from body odor,"[1] it is not difficult to understand what they mean. How can political greatness (or for that matter greatness of any sort) be expected from such an age, with its almost compulsive need to cast everyone in a common mold?

Compromise, toleration, compassion, equality — these are the motifs of our age. Rather than improving western civilization, these ideals pursued to their logical conclusion would destroy it. Nothing of lasting worth has been achieved by compromise and compassion carried to the absurd lengths that they are today. Was Christianity established among the pagan people of Europe, Africa and the Americas by reasoned discussion or by the sword? Did fledging states become great sovereign nations by welcoming their enemies with open arms? Even the great capitalist enterprises of today were built up, not by insecure weaklings, but by men of ruthless determination. Progress means far more than the obliteration of all strongly held convictions which promote vigorous action and their replacement by a sickly humanism which stifles action. Progress means more than the great abundance of material goods and the high development of science and technology. If progress means anything at all, it means mankind using his emotional, sensual and physical faculties to the full to enjoy life in all its natural beauty rather than through the shabby offerings of a decadent, anti-human age.

This over emphasis on compromise, toleration, compassion and self-restraint is tending to emasculate the human personality, but advocates of nihilism will fail. As for the virtues of equality, they simply do not exist. Every great civilization has been based on a structured society, with those of superior virtue at the top. The course taken in recent years by the advanced industrial societies has tended to obscure this truth by its idolization of popular democracy, by its veneration of the market place, and most of all by giving birth to ideals which would rob human life of all its vitality if they ever succeeded in taking hold. No civilization worthy of the name could ever be based on absolute social and economic equality, this would be a prescription for regression and decay. The relatively high degree of social mobility to be found in most advanced industrialized nations has led people to believe that a society which practices equal opportunity is a society to be commended. Nothing could be further from the truth. Such mobility must lead eventually to the establishment of an upper social strata which is hesitant and unsure of itself in times of social stress. It has no standards to protect, no class allegiance to reinforce its vulnerability, since the majority of its members have been co-opted to serve (i.e., on account of their economic success). It has no independent power base, no special status among the people apart from the above average income of its members. It is in truth a non-entity, ready to go along with almost any changes taking place in society at large. This accurately describes the position of the upper class of present day western society relative to their fellow citizens. I wonder how far we can push the trend towards equality for all, how long will it be before we have laws instructing us that children must have a say in all matters affecting them before a final decision can be made by their parents.

The fact that our age does not realize what harm it is inflicting upon itself by its drive to produce the ideal society can only be described as sickening. A society driven by a zeal to regulate every detail of its existence and a desire to give to each man his due is bound to become tedious once most of its members enjoy a standard of living as high as that now enjoyed by the typical family in North America or Western Europe. It is, therefore, not surprising that apathy bulks large among the electors. There are simply no issues which can stir them once the indefinite existence of our super-liberal, super-abundant society is taken for granted. The people know what the politicians or editorial writers are going to say about a particular event or policy issue well before they have said it. How? Because they have been saying almost the same thing over and over again for the last thirty years or more. There is no independent opinion anymore; all opinion which receives the greatest exposure emerges from the mawkish sentimentality which today passes for critical thinking. Those who have an independent point of view are a tiny minority who keep it to themselves. It is this tiny minority which may yet save western civilization from its headlong plunge into nihilism.

The long overdue transformation of modern industrial society will give to the more noble specimens of humanity the opportunity to establish a new society. The dominant ethos of these men of the new age, these noble spirits of enterprise, energy and conviction, will not be the sloppy idealism which characterizes the present age, there will be no room for compromise, compassion, toleration or social justice. These are false values which have been built into a way of life upon the buried bones of all those who would not compromise, of those who would not turn the other cheek to their enemy. For these valiant individuals, freedom from constraint meant more than a guarantee of constitutional freedoms, social justice, or equality before the law; it meant for them the freedom to take any action whatsoever which would contribute towards the accomplishment of their chosen goal. The exercise of this type of freedom has accomplished far more for western civilization than the pursuit of social justice ever will. Energy, courage, determination, conviction, ambition — these will be the traits of the new age. Men who possess these traits in abundance are the ones who will be in the forefront of the reconstruction of western civilization. Their energies will contribute towards the creation of a society which will be socially more stable and economically less complex than the one we have now.

It will be a society in which science and technology will revert to being the servant of man rather than his master as is now the case. For it is no exaggeration to say that compulsive scientific-technological research is a greater danger to mankind's continued existence than would be the total absence of science and technology. Moreover, and perhaps most important of all, such a society would be based on truly human values, rather than on abstract ideals, values which have proved themselves in the past to be the bulwark of all civilizations which have retained their vitality over a long period of time. What I am saying, then, is that the sense of continuity with past greatness has been lost from western civilization as it now stands. And with it has gone the open and unashamed display of those attitudes and qualities which ensured that western civilization right from its earliest days was second to none. It was not so very long ago that imperialism and colonization were considered to be an obligation of western society, an obligation which was cheerfully accepted and which lay the foundations for the emergence of many nations of the Third World which are now independent states. How the West has degenerated since those days. Look at what we have today, an amorphous mass of like-minded individuals all parroting the same slogans and ideals. The very thought that these weaklings, the degenerate descendants of a noble breed, are the standard bearers of western civilization is enough to make one sick. As long as the more noble spirits among us continue to remain unaware of what is happening, the degeneration of western civilization will also continue regardless of what the politicians say or do.

Modern politics is moribund; it is almost devoid of life. This applies just as much to contemporary political theory as it does to the contemporary practice of politics. Instead of the nation being mobilized to overcome great challenges, instead of one particular group holding opinions and principles for which they are prepared to die, we are daily treated to the feeble adversary politics of penny-weight politicians which we may observe in all its splendor from the visitors gallery. Those of us who do not become bored to death may find the spectacle highly entertaining, or simply bewildering. Although responses to seeing our political leaders in action may vary, there is one thing we can be certain of: They will say nothing that is profound, nothing to disturb our smugness, nothing that causes us to lose sleep or to resort to serious contemplation, nothing to show that their insight into the workings of history is superior to that of the average man in the street. In fact, they will re-echo again and again in countless different ways the predominant sentiments to be found in advanced industrial societies of the West. This truism does not only apply to the pseudo-battles fought between the nation's major political parties but also to the propaganda and general ideology of the non-parliamentary socialist groups. Neither the long established political organizations which are part of the mainstream of national politics, nor those groups on the fringe of institutional politics have much to say that is of relevance to the desperate plight of the citizens of the advanced industrial nations.

Even the clear-cut differences which once existed between the major political parties have narrowed down to such an extent as to become almost meaningless. For example, the parties which draw a major part of their support from the working class are supposed to distinguish themselves from their main parliamentary opponents by the fact that they are prepared to spend far more on social welfare in preference to national defence, a commitment to full employment, and a tendency to favor state ownership over private ownership. The conservative parties, on the other hand, have been noted for their fiscal prudence, i.e., reluctance to spend heavily on social welfare programmes, their belief in the need for strong defence capability and their willingness to fight inflation through the adoption of fiscal policies which may lead to high unemployment and, of course, a strong belief in the virtues of free enterprise. These have been the traditional differences between the major parliamentary parties of the western industrial democracies since the turn of the century. But all this is fast changing. The political parties which have always enjoyed large-scale popular support among the working class have been found to cut back on social welfare spending much as the conservatives would have done under the same circumstances; they no longer shy away from fighting inflation through high unemployment. They now believe that there must be a check on government spending even if this would mean that many social welfare goals may not be realized. Finally, the social democrats believe that a large and prosperous private sector is vital to the nation's long-term economic viability. The conservatives in their turn have accepted the need for comprehensive social welfare as well as the need to keep military expenditures in check, if not cut back. In other words, a process of convergence has been going on in regards to the ideological outlook of the major political parties in all western nations. This indicates firstly, that there is a paucity of original ideas, which is not altogether surprising, and secondly, that the alternatives open to our political leaders are so restricted by the social and economic complexity of the typical advanced industrial democracy that no matter which party is in power the policies followed will turn out to be almost the same. The process of convergence has gone further in some countries than in others. For example, in West Germany there is almost no difference in the views and policies of the major political parties. Great Britain is saved by the vigor of the left wing of the Labor party from being a political replica of its far more successful Common Market partner, but is nevertheless fast moving in this direction as economic woes begin to prevail over party ideology, while party politics in the U.S.A. has been in a state of stagnation ever since the New Deal.

It is therefore natural to look at political groups outside the nation's established political institutions for signs of life. But here again the acute observer is liable to be disappointed in his search for new and authentic political ideals. The most vociferous non-institutional political groups are those representing a bewildering variety of "socialisms" ranging from the highly disciplined Communist party (which in many Western European nations does have parliamentary representation) to loosely organized anarchist groups. All the revolutionary socialists appear to be united by the war cry, "Power to the workers!" regardless of all other points of doctrine about which they may disagree. I therefore feel that it is reasonable to lump them together in the discussion that follows. In this discussion I want to impress upon the reader the fact that not only is revolutionary socialism an untenable lifestyle for the new age but also that it draws its inspiration from the very same utilitarian ideals that now dominate the social thinking of our present day consumer society and so must fall at the very same time that this age does.

To begin with, all the major varieties of contemporary radical socialism assume the continued existence of large-scale industrialization. Should circumstances emerge to make the continued existence of modern industry impossible — as I believe they will — radical socialism would automatically become irrelevant, since worker control of the means of production would have no political or economic significance in a society which was overwhelmingly agricultural, with cottage industry catering to the needs of those requiring a large supply of non-agricultural goods. Moreover, let us assume for argument's sake that the radical socialists were to get their own way, worker control of industry becomes the order of the day and the profit motive is abolished. How would this break the hegemony of science and technology which is the greatest danger to mankind in general and western man in particular? How would this reduce the stresses and strains of modern life which are now taking such an enormous toll and have nothing to do with economic inequality, since they afflict the upper and middle-income groups as well as the poor. It seems highly probable that the success of radical socialism would place even more strain on the delicate fabric of the advanced industrial societies by attempting to ensure all goods and services were available in sufficient quantity to give everybody a middle-class lifestyle. This is made clear in one of the most impressive reaffirmations of the socialist millennium to emerge in recent years, namely *Marxian Economics* by the Belgian Marxist theoretician, Ernest Mandel. The last section of Volume Two is particularly revealing from this point of view.

He states that goods in several categories, such as food products, would be allocated free of charge, while the prices of other goods would be steadily reduced as they become more freely available. He feels that eventually money could be done away with after a sufficiently high level of productivity had been reached. Presumably people would then be free to have as much as they liked of anything they took a fancy to. Exactly what such a great abundance of material goods would do to the human soul, I shudder to think. Fortunately, it is most unlikely that we will ever be in a position to find out. The revolutionary socialists have all the programs for harnessing the productive powers of modern industrial society but say little about whether or not the continued existence of this type of society is itself a good thing for the future of mankind. Here they are at one with social democrats, liberals and conservatives. Admittedly, they tend to show a great deal more concern over environmental pollution of all sorts than is permissible within conventional political circles. For instance, Herbert Marcuse proclaims that environmental pollution is becoming a form of mental oppression, as well as a physical danger, and must be overthrown along with the capitalist system: "The pollution of the air and water, the noise, the encroachment of industry and commerce on open natural space have the physical weight of enslavement, imprisonment. The struggle against them is a political struggle."[2] But it is easy to show more concern for the environment than is conventionally allowed when one does not participate in the power structure but is disagreeing with it from the sidelines. Just let our environmentally concerned radical socialists have a small taste of power and we will soon see how quickly they bend to the dictates and constraints of modern industrial society. The dominant politico-economic traits of our age are big industry and big government supported by a highly developed science and technology. No socialist revolution of whatever hue would be capable of changing this reality.

It is against this background that we must look at the values of radical socialism, since, far from representing a challenge to the existence of modern industrial society, it shares many of the utilitarian ideals of the latter and should more correctly be seen as an alternative rationale for the management of an advanced industrial economy. Indeed radical socialism would be the natural outcome of the leveling process which appears to be part and parcel of modern industrial society at its highest point of development. One need only mention the ever-increasing demands for taxes upon the rich (as if this would do anything to solve our deep-seated social and ecological problems), the demand that everybody should be treated as if they are equal, although we all know that this is not so and could never be, the belief that majority opinion is always right when in fact it is often wrong, the belief that we should all conform to one standard of values which by judicious application (i.e. distributive justice) will guarantee the happiness of the greatest number. Thus, in terms of their ideal of the good life, there is little to choose between our modern consumer society and the radical socialist alternative.

Most radical activists and theorists would of course vehemently disagree with this conclusion, citing their insistence on a fair distribution of the national wealth which goes far beyond anything that would be permissible under a liberal democracy, and their belief that a radical socialist society founded in the industrialized West would produce a new type of individual and, therefore, must be judged qualitatively different from present-day society. In regard to a fairer distribution of the national wealth, the gap between democrats and radicals is getting narrower all the time, something which we shall discuss in more detail below. As for the implementation of any program of radical socialism producing a new type of man, one who is both willing to work to the best of his ability and generous enough to forego greater rewards than individuals of lesser talent, this must now be accepted as a pipe dream. Just as the environment of man cannot sustain indefinite industrialization, so is the character of man incapable of infinite perfection. In fact, by his anti-historical acceptance of certain modern values, his character is already being stretched to its limits. Bauman, in his book entitled *Socialism: The Active Utopia,* gives the common sense view of radical socialism and its goal when he states: "The feasibility of the socialist project hinges precisely on the hope that men may, given the right conditions, cease to be as we know them and as we seem always to have known them. To this hope, however, the sobering popular wisdom of endlessly duplicated individual and collective practical lessons is opposed."[3] This statement needs little elaboration.

Because modern industrial society is deeply involved in the production of nonessential goods not directly revelant to the survival of the producers, the latter need some sort of incentive to produce. In some of the less developed countries, so-called moral incentives may be sufficient in the early stages; this appears to be true of China and Cuba. But moral incentives such as exhortations to increase one's output for the sake of one's country and fellow citizens will not work permanently even for an underdeveloped country. As for a country which is already developed, moral incentives would be a hopeless way to increase productivity; only the knowledge that the workers would be materially benefited in a direct way could do this. One is reminded of Stalinist Russia where wage differentials between various occupational groups and between individuals doing the same type of work became very large as an incentive to stimulate high productivity in chosen sectors of the economy, and present day Russia, where incentives in the way of higher wages and living allowances are used to encourage highly skilled workers and professionals to live and work in the more remote parts of the Soviet Union. Contrary to what some writers of socialist persuasion may believe, man does not have a protean personality which awaits the arrival of a socialist utopia. His personality remains essentially what it has always been, though it is covered today with a temporary veneer of obsequious conformity. If natural goodness and brotherly love were the essence of the human personality, man would never have passed beyond his earliest beginnings to create the great civilizations which compose the history of the world.

There was until recently one other feature of the radical socialist credo which set it apart from the ideals and practices of modern industrial society as it now exists. This is the almost fanatical belief in the virtues of economic equality. Whether the objective of this belief is to produce a society of well regimented Pygmies, or whether its proponents sincerely think that it would lead to a healthy and vigorous civilization, I really cannot say. But I do know that, apart from one or two outstanding examples (e.g., the Essenes of Ancient Judea), societies which have made the deliberate choice to live on terms of total equality have not been very successful. I see no possibility of matters being very much different in the new age, which will be synonymous with boundless energy and aggression, hardly traits on which to build an egalitarian society. In fact, a society in which there were no rich and no poor would be a society made up of gods rather than men, to paraphrase the author of *The Social Contract.* Such a society will forever remain a figment of the imagination. Absolute equality is totally alien to the ways of the West or to those of any other culture, for that matter. Wherever one may go, whatever period of history one may choose, there have always been those who lead and those who follow. If life were to be any other way, then mental differences among men would be quite unnecessary. Although inequality is to be found in every nation, the rate of social and economic change has certainly not been the same for all. More to the point, relative differences between the economic performance of the North Atlantic nations and nearly all other countries have been a source of much upheaval and continue to exercise a profound influence over the course of international affairs.

Thus, the theory of scientific socialism, with its emphasis on class conflict, together with the economic interpretation of history and the concept of surplus value, to name several of its better known aspects, could only have developed out of the cauldron of Western European history. But the economic backwardness of first Imperial Russia and later the rest of Eastern Europe proved to be fertile ground for the setting up of a communist state as an alternative to the private enterprise model of industrial development. The essence of the alternative model with regard to politics has been the existence of one legal party only — the Communist party — and the exclusive employment of Marxist ideology. In regard to economics it has meant the introduction of a Centrally Planned Economy which has greatly helped these countries to increase productivity in both industry and agriculture, although their overall performance still lags well behind that of the West. The inability of Eastern European nations to provide a large and industrious bourgeoisie to lead their industrial development is well documented. Instead they had to rely to a large extent on foreign investment and foreign entrepreneurs to give impetus to their industrial growth. This was true of Russia up until the time of the Bolshevik revolution, as it was of the far smaller Eastern European nations up to the time of the Second World War. In many cases, foreign capital was either dominant in a particular sector of the economy or had a substantial, though not majority share in the sector. Another point worth noting in connection with the economic backwardness of Eastern Europe is the fact that the government of these nations played a large part in the management of the economy well before this became fashionable in Western Europe. This, as Chris Harman[4] tells us was especially true of Poland, Czechoslovakia, Rumania and Yugoslavia. For example, credit for economic development was provided by state banks or other state agencies; it was not unusual for the state to own railways, utilities and forests, and in Yugoslavia it was directly involved in the production of goods such as steel, armaments, sugar and cellulose. All this was well before the Soviet Union came to dominate the politics of these nations.

A congenial climate for the expansion of the alternative model of economic development (i.e., communism) is now provided by many countries of Asia and Africa, which stand absolutely no chance of following the Western model of economic development, even if they were inclined to do so, and all available evidence suggests that they are not. Latin America has been slow to adopt the alternative model primarily for two reasons. One is the firm grip on the economy of these nations that the traditional oligarchy of wealthy upper class families have always had since the gaining of independence in the nineteenth century and which has remained firm until quite recent times. The other is that the politics of change in this region have been invariably built around personalities, whether civilian politicians or military leaders, rather than ideologies. All this is of course changing now and Latin America's low level of development compared with the advanced industrial nations also makes many of its member countries suitable candidates for the alternative model.

Since the birth of modern industry it has been those issues connected with distribution, rather than the problems with production, that have dominated the politics of Western society. Formerly Western society was able to consider itself almost immune from the worst excesses of the radical socialist solution — but not anymore. Thanks to the research work of Christopher Jencks and his associates, which has been elegantly set forth in a book entitled *Inequality,* we are now able to see where excessive concern for the underprivileged and downtrodden is leading the most capitalistic of all societies. According to Jencks, neither education, innate intelligence, nor family circumstances account for one's level of material success in an open society, as is the U.S.A. Instead, this is determined by such factors as a combination of luck and on-the-job competence. He therefore concludes that the only way to achieve a socially just society would be to equalize results through various forms of insurance systems working in combination with income sharing, rather than promoting equal opportunity. What this would mean in practice would be that the successful would have little to show for their success, except the fact that the unsuccessful are just as well off as they are. What a ludicrous way to run an industrial society! We all should be indebted to Mr. Jencks and his colleagues for their timely warning of what modern society could have in store for us. For this is the next logical step, once it has become clear to all that the doctrine of equal opportunity has failed to equalize the life chances of all. Only those within whose mind envy has reached the point of a terminal disease could look forward to the coming of such a society with anything but horror.

Let us take a look at what the representatives of our non-political institutions (e.g., private foundations, newspapers and universities) have to say in regard to the diseased state of western society. Have they been able to supply the intellectual leadership of which our society is so badly in need? Have they brought forth creative proposals, bold new concepts? In a word, have they done anything to shake western civilization out of its smug complacency? The simple answer is no. All our intellectual leaders drink from the same well of wisdom, as do our political leaders, and most of the rest of us. Not even the most lionized members of our academic community appear to realize how much conflict has done for the history of ideas. From Machiavelli to Marx, the great political and social theorists have drawn on the lessons of the great conflicts and upheavals that have periodically racked western society. This is true no longer, for it is in the universities more than anywhere else that the stench of intellectual decomposition of western civilization is heaviest. No contemporary academic has struck out on a bold and original train of thought to see where it would take him. The great masters of social and political thought of the nineteenth and early twentieth century still hold sway. Their books are constantly coming out in new editions. Their ideas have been analyzed and reanalyzed. It is all a cozy intellectual game strictly for the initiated.

Most academics are content to remain in their ivory towers, disengaged from the world of affairs, acutely aware of their impotence to influence it one way or the other even if they felt strongly inclined to do so. The contemporary intellectual is helpless before the great material progress of his age, he accepts it as vindication of the weak and overly sentimental ideals of his society. He is wedded to the values of his age to a degree which has totally destroyed his critical faculties. The situation of the typical intellectual of today with regards to the future of western society can be compared with that of the two great Renaissance humanists, namely Thomas More and Erasmus of Rotterdam. Both were highly learned, very pious men, who were eventually unable to come to terms with the harsh realities of human life and history. The first ended his days on the block, with his head displayed on traitors gate as a warning to others not to stand in the way of an imperious king. The second died in obscurity, a man whose writings were ignored by both Protestants and

Catholics alike. Before dying, he suffered several years of anguish because he could see the justice of the Protestants' cause, but could not bring himself to break with the Catholic church although his pleas for reform were ignored by the church hierarchy. Futile stubbornness of the first one, and indecisiveness in the case of the second, were responsible for the miserable endings to the lives of these two great men. So too will almost certainly be the fate of our contemporary academics who are dispassionately devoted to the pursuit of knowledge and are unquestioning humanitarians, but who shy away from the harsh realities of human existence. No attempt has been made to re-interpret to a lost generation the thoughts of those thinkers whose anti-utilitarian ideals have caused the significance of their message to be overlooked. The names of Marquis de Sade, Joseph de Maistre, Bonald, Maurras and von Trietschke come instantly to mind. Although there are others of similar stature who have been ignored and neglected because their message could not be properly understood. On the rare occasions when the writings of these authors are dealt with, instead of an honest attempt being made to creatively analyze the inspired genius of these men, they are usually dismissed as either misguided or as the precursors of twentieth century fascism.

The desire to go beyond the feeble ideals of contemporary mass society is still with us. If it were not, there would be no independent voices of dissent among the academic community. But what do we get from these most learned savants, these independent voices of dissent? Instead of an interjection of newly found ideals which could revitalize western society, we are treated to a critique of contemporary society telling us in effect that it is unjust and its institutions are outdated. A thirteen year old could do better than this. These critics, like Robert Wolff (*The Poverty of Liberalism*), are sure that Pluralism has had its day, but despair of knowing what to put in its place, as our intrepid author frankly admits. Nevertheless, at one point, he comes close to a partial explanation of what is wrong with contemporary society when he tells us how solid citizens with predictable views are always chosen to form commissions of enquiry and promptly proceed to submit a predictable report assuring us that our basic institutions and beliefs are sound. A rather pointless exercise, as Wolff clearly states.[5] Other authors, such as John Schaar in his article entitled *Equality of Opportunity and Beyond*,[6] are highly critical of, not only the politics of contemporary society, but its entire organization and ethos. He characterizes it as "a mass, bureaucratic, technological, privatized, materialistic, bored and thrill-seeking consumption oriented society" and warns us candidly that we are "building a culture that our best men will not honor." But, apart from these cutting observations, and one or two other bright spots, the essay is in general a great disappointment, for he gives us no details of the type of society that our best men would honor. He indicates his belief that the essentials of the Marxist model are still valid, but this hardly seems compatible with his biting, nay blistering critique of contemporary society, which he further describes as "a society of well-fed, congenial, and sybaritic monkeys surrounded by gadgets and pleasure toys." Two more incisive and independently minded critics than Wolff and Schaar would be difficult to find but neither face up to the full implications of the inviability of our age. Schaar comes closest to doing this only to eventually withdraw and take refuge in Marxian dialectics instead of pressing home his attack and calling for the establishment of a new society based on a new system of values.

Neither conventional party politics, radical non-party politics nor independently minded political theorists offer any hope for the future. But we need not despair; smoldering below the surface and waiting to blaze into life is a stronger spirit than the spirit which informs contemporary society, a spirit capable of achieving far greater deeds than the human mind has yet been thought capable of. The political ideals and institutions of our consumer society have become impotent, effete, incapable of inspiring great deeds, but are most conducive to the fostering of cynicism and despair. The energy which will free us from the oppression of bureaucracy and the crushing weight of conformity to the facile values of a dying age will come from within the afflicted societies themselves. There exists even at this late hour a small number of individuals who are superior to the feebleness of their age. It is to these people that the future belongs, not to the meek and the mild. Neither round-the-clock legislation, nor fine speeches praising the virtues of popular democracy, can prevent the arrival of a new age and its dominance by a new breed of man.

When one considers modern politics in this light, one sees it to be a trivial thing hardly worth the attention of the superior type of man. The political leader of today is a marionette rather than an autonomous individual. He has to keep faith with his party, the people who elected him and the special interest groups whose attitude can have a major impact on his chances of re-election. Every decision he makes has to be approved by expert advisers and then by the national parliament before it can become official policy; such are the limitations imposed on leadership by the complex nature of advanced industrial society. Every step of the way the leader of the modern nation state is totally dependent on the judgement of other men; prudence and moderation are the watch words. There is no room for bold initiatives spontaneously conceived and rapidly executed. The political leaders of today do not even write their own speeches, but instead employ a speech writer to do it for them. The modern-day President or Prime Minister has become nothing more than a glorified bureaucrat. He is supposed to be the Commander-in-Chief of the Armed Forces, but knows next to nothing about military strategy. If his office were to be suddenly stripped of its legitimacy owing, say, to a large-scale social and economic breakdown, he would have no hope of rallying the nation around him as an inspirational leader, i.e., independently of the office he formerly held. In short, the leaders of today are men of straw. To place one's faith in them is akin to receiving reassurance from the captain of a sinking ship that all is well.

A bloated bureaucracy is one of the most consistent indications that a society has reached the limits of its development. One need only mention the bureaucracy of Imperial China, which was perfected long before the science of rational administration was known to the West. Still its long tradition of maintaining a very elaborate national bureaucracy did not save Imperial Chinese civilization from decline and eventual destruction. Neither will the rational bureaucracy of contemporary western society save it from inevitable transformation into something far more robust in the new age that is soon to come. It is interesting to note that every major social theorist of the nineteenth century was an inveterate foe of bureaucracy. This includes J.S. Mill, Marx, Spencer and de Tocqueville. The fact that men of such great intellect and diverse opinion as these could agree on the evils of bureaucracy is a most impressive confirmation of the fact that man can never be quite comfortable with the excessive growth of government regardless of his political outlook. Probably the following quotation from J.S. Mill sums up the feelings of most of his contemporaries: "The disease which afflicts bureaucratic governments, and which they usually die of, is routine. They perish by the immutability of their maxims; and, still more, by the universal law that whatever becomes a routine loses its vital principle, and having no longer a mind acting within it, goes on revolving mechanically though the work it is intended to do remains undone. A bureaucracy always tends to become a pedantocracy. When the bureaucracy is the real government, the spirit of the corps bears down the individuality of its more distinguished members."[7]

This accurately describes the contemporary situation, for the mammoth bureaucracies which now characterize the process of government in the advanced industrial societies appear to have become victims of their own growth. The collection of statistical data has become nothing more than an empty exercise of bureaucratic prerogative. It has no real purpose, except to provide a convenient source of details for the countless number of government publicationss which are annually churned out by the state's official printers. Complaints are frequently heard of the long delays even in regard to expediting the simplest matters, of needless duplication, and of the need to answer questions which are clearly irrelevant and demand remembering facts which may have long been forgotten, not to mention the invasion of privacy which is just one more degrading aspect of the inexorable spread of bureaucracy. We should not be surprised that the bureaucrats themselves often have difficulty in coping with the burdensome demands of their job. Several forms are usually required in connection with the smallest matters, and in the case of a matter of great complexity perhaps involving several public agencies, the paper work can mushroom to an enormous quantity which leads one to wonder if it is all worthwhile. Delays often arise from forms duly completed (in triplicate) and returned having been lost. Finally, when a decision is handed down, it is often inexplicable and serves only to underline how harmful is the unwarranted interference of remote bureaucrats. The bureaucracy of the West has become so dominant that it is playing no small part in moulding the nation's political leaders into stumbling nonentities unable to make a move on their own without the helping hand of their trusty bureaucrats. There is no way we can overcome bureaucracy within the context of the present age. We cannot vote it out of existence, since our votes can only serve to speed the growth of bureaucracy on its way. We cannot disestablish it, since it is an integral part of the social and economic organization of modern western society. Neither will we do much to change the situation by setting up commissions to report on and control the bureaucracy, since experience shows that its growth continues regardless.

The phenomenal growth of bureaucracy, especially in the last three decades, has been largely in response to the foolish and misguided belief that all social problems can be solved by increased government involvement backed up by continuously increasing government expenditure. This viewpoint is not only in error, it is also harmful, since it raises false hopes which simply cannot be satisfied. But the futile legislation continues to multiply and give birth to new agencies, new commissions and more bureaucrats, despite the pious promises of successive administrations to cut back or at least hold down the size of the nation's bureaucracy. So now we have laws guaranteeing equal opportunity to various groups (with specific quotas in some cases), and equality among the sexes, while other laws have almost abolished the right of private organizations to decide who can and who cannot become a member. Each of these examples of modern man's wishy washy sentimentalism has spawned more bureaucracy, which has in turn grown and expanded in a manner akin to geometric progression. Where is it all going to end? Laws, whether or not they are formulated by a democratic assembly, will never shackle the human spirit; they will never prevent it from soaring to the greatest heights of which it is capable. How can a facile group of second-rate men legislate to make all their fellow citizens equal regardless of inherited differences, regardless of family connections, regardless of innate differences of intelligence and regardless of historic precedence and traditions? Surely this is nonsense. Our law makers have outdone themselves; they have set themselves up as God. They will one day see how foolish such presumption is. Man's supposed conquest of nature has led him to believe that he has the capacity to create a perfect world composed of millions upon millions of avid consumers patting each other on the back in praise of their mutual moderation. A world free from famine, hunger, war, plague, poverty, illiteracy and, of course, inequality. So concerned are our political leaders and the other guiding lights of our age with being given a pat on the back for their display of goodness and compassion, that they have failed to realize that these examples of adversity and ill luck are the very stuff of life.

They are the spurs which have goaded man onward. Without them life ceases to be a valiant struggle to overcome and achieve. This has been the distinguishing feature of all societies which have created a thriving civilization, and it will continue to distinguish the most vigorous civilizations from those of lesser standing. Advocates of moderation and compassion would have us degenerate into a tame and docile society such as the Arawak Indians, who were the original inhabitants of Jamaica when the Spaniards first discovered the island. Alas! They long ago became extinct, since they were a race ill equipped to survive contact with the expansion of western civilization, just as our decadent consumer society will not be able to survive the impact of the resurgence of that spirit which did so much to establish the superiority of western civilization over nearly all other cultures. So let us not any longer worry about creating a world which would be ideal for everyone to live in. Man must suffer, man must continue to strive, often against impossible odds. Only by doing this will he fully realize his greatness.

I must emphasize that what we have been talking about is not so much the degeneration of popular democracy, since this was degenerate to begin with, but the degeneration of the human spirit, which, under the aegis of our licentious consumer society, has reached an all-time low. This being so, none of the ideas for political reform which have been put forward with increasing frequency during the last ten years could do much to rectify matters. These ideas include the introduction of proportional representation to give smaller parties a better chance of being represented in parliament — a cause dear to the heart of many parliamentary reformers in Great Britain. The idea of a unicameral legislature as a way of improving the efficiency of the legislative process has always had support among those whose politics lean to the left. In the U.S.A., structural reform of the political process has made little headway in thought or deed in comparison with ethical reform and changes connected with the financing of campaigns for national office. The one issue of contention in this area (i.e., structural reform in American politics), namely the abolition or retention of the electoral college, has generated much argument, but very little critical analysis of the failings of modern politics in that country.

The exhaustion of liberal democracy should be no surprise to anyone familiar with the essentials of modern political theory. The devitalizing cynicism which is now found among the academic community was foreshadowed well over fifty years ago by the writings of Vilfredo Pareto, Gaetano Mosca and Robert Michel. The most important ideas of these three authors are discussed by John Plamenatz in his book *Democracy and Illusion* (Longman, 1973). All three concluded that the politicians were more concerned with holding onto power within the party structure than with anything else. Pareto and Mosca talk about this preoccupation in terms of elites and their rise and fall from favor within the party, whereas Michel codified the situation in his famous iron law of oligarchy, by which he meant that the same group of people tended to hold onto power for as long as possible even if this meant turning their back on the party's ideology. Their penetrating critique of the politics of their day left no doubt about the eventual irreversible decline in the vitality of the party system, which has been the chosen instrument of national politics since the earliest days of modern industrial society. So pervasive has the loss of vitality become, that not even the possibility of gaining power over the party can enthuse life into the politics of the late twentieth century.

But by far the greatest prophets of modern industrial society outside the Marxist tradition have been Alexis de Tocqueville and Max Weber. Each said several things of great importance about the social and policital organization of modern industrial society and its future. Alexis de Tocqueville ranks among the intellectual giants of his time and his two-volume *Democracy in America* was a masterpiece of social analysis and remains today one of the great works of western political thought. Some commentators have criticized de Tocqueville for not giving enough attention to the impact that the industrial revolution would have on the politics and lifestyle of western society and tending to concentrate almost exclusively on the ways in which a democratic society will differ from an aristocratic one in its values. This is simply not true, for more than anything else de Tocqueville attempted to explore what sort of society would be produced by the full development of unrestricted democracy, in conjunction with equal opportunity for all to succeed regardless of family background, and increasing material abundance, which he saw as an inevitable outcome of the industrial revolution. He rightly discerned that such a society would be highly bureaucratic and technocratic, with its citizens having very little say in the way it was run and little to do but fill their stomachs and participate in the numerous diversions that would be available to them. "I see an innumerable multitude of men, alike and equal, constantly circling around in pursuit of the petty and banal pleasures with which they glut their souls. Each one of them, withdrawn into himself, is almost unaware of the fate of the rest. Over this kind of men stands an immense, protective power, which is alone responsible for ensuring their enjoyment and watching over their fate. Having thus taken each citizen in turn in its powerful grasp and shaped him to its will, government then extends its embrace to include the whole of society. It covers the whole of social life with a network of petty, complicated rules that are both minute and uniform, through which even men of the greatest originality and the most vigorous temperament cannot force their heads above the crowd. It does not break men's will, but softens, bends, and guides it; it seldom enjoins but often inhibits action; it does not destroy anything, but prevents much being born; it is not at all tyrannical, but it hinders, restrains, enervates, and stifles and stultifies so much that in the end each nation is no more than a flock of timid and hardworking animals with the government as its shepherd."[8] Thus de Tocqueville intuitively perceived that the full development of modern industrial society would smother the potential of differences in wealth to be a source of revolutionary strife, and so it has turned out. He also predicted that this very same process would seriously undermine the vigour of western civilization in just about every area, and again events have proved him right.

Like many of his great nineteenth-century predecessors, Max Weber also warned of the debilitating effects of excessive bureaucracy. In this respect, he was one of the first people to see capitalism and communism as essentially alternative models for the management of an advanced industrialized society, for he sincerely believed that, whatever the nature of the political system, bureaucracy was destined to play a dominant part, to the detriment of innovation and individual initiative. If he were alive today, he would see that his greatest fears have been realized in both the "capitalist" West and the communist East. But as far as his contribution to political theory is concerned, Weber is best remembered for his typology outlining the three basic forms of political authority, a typology whose full significance to the future of mankind has not been realized by the host of political and social theorists who have analyzed it or used it for the purpose of analysis. According to Weber there are three types of authority. These are Traditional, Legio-rational and Charismatic. Now the point to note is that these three types of authority are the only viable types to have arisen in the past and, furthermore, it would be reasonable to assume that no other type of authority will arise in a future society.

At the present time, the western world is ruled by legio-rational authority and has been for much of the last two hundred years. The distinguishing characteristic of this type of authority is one we have all become familiar with, i.e., a highly developed and well ordered bureaucracy whose motif is the process of rational decision making. Furthermore, the way in which authority should be exercised is precisely laid down by laws, rules and regulations, the exercise of authority can only be challenged by legal means. One of the most important points to remember about legio-rational authority is that it has no aristocratic component. In theory at least, positions in government are open to all, provided one has acquired the necessary degree of competence to carry out effectively the job to which one aspires, a fact which is usually ascertained by competitive examination or similar means. With the transcendence of modern industrial society, legio-rational authority will also disappear. Thus, the new age will be dominated by Traditional and Charismatic authority. But we can go further than this in attempting to get some idea of the course of events in the new age. Charismatic authority can best be understood as being the catalyst for a sudden explosion of pent-up energy which sweeps away the existing structure of authority. The appearance of Charismatic authority usually indicates a serious loss of confidence in the established institutions, leadership and customs, by the ordinary people, and deep divisions or visible insecurity among the society's upper strata. Thus, the chaos that would be triggered by the total disintegration of modern industrial society would produce ideal conditions for the emergence of this type of authority. Because of the enormous human energy which it sets loose, Charismatic authority can often do great things, especially if, as in most cases, the Charismatic leader is an individual of exceptional personal magnetism. But as Weber himself pointed out, Charismatic authority never lasts for very long. It is either institutionalized or the Charismatic leader fades from the scene and the old status quo reasserts itself, perhaps with one or two defensive changes.

In the new age, there will be absolutely no possibility of the old status quo reasserting itself; it will be gone for good. Therefore Charismatic authority (leadership) must become institutionalized and transformed into a mode of Traditional authority. This is the type of authority which best reflects the highest state of civilized man, for there is no artificial attempt to lump all men together. The distinguishing feature of traditional authority is that it is inherited and can typically be acquired in no other way. An elaborate bureaucracy and highly developed judicial system is superfluous to this type of authority, although certainly not incompatible with it, as was demonstrated by the history of ancient Rome. An important feature of a society in which this type of authority is dominant is the importance attributed to one's rank, i.e., whether one is a noble or commoner, and the status one enjoys within the nobility if one is of noble birth. In those traditional societies in which central authority is relatively weak, or non-existent, those of noble birth exercise power at will, acting in accordance with the dictates of their conscience. Under these circumstances, traditional authority is concerned almost exclusively with power; the material welfare of the people is their own affair. If central authority is fairly well developed, the sovereign (if an individual) rules by fiat rather than by detailed laws or ordinances. Those who participate in the process of government at the highest levels are usually of noble birth. The legitimacy of this type of authority is unquestioned by the common people. Public opinion in this type of society is the opinion held by members of the nobility; all other opinions are of no consequence. These characteristics will become the main features of authority in the new age once stability has returned. Thus will order and good sense also be returned to human affairs.

THE BANKRUPTCY OF MODERN ECONOMICS

The state of contemporary economics is just as dismal as the state of contemporary politics, which is perhaps hardly surprising, since they are merely different sides of the same coin. In fact, what we are faced with today is nothing less than the total bankruptcy of modern economic theory and practice. The problems include persistent inflation, high unemployment and all-round disenchantment. One of the most consistent indications that the old order is dying and a new one is on the horizon, is the failure of old remedies to solve new problems. This is exactly the case at the present time, a fact that has long been recognized and accepted by some of the more acute politicians and intellectuals of the western world.

There was a time when economic theory and practice were closely linked at all levels. Thus, William Pitt the Younger, when Prime Minister of England, was a keen supporter of the theories of Adam Smith and tried to do all he could to put theory into practice. This, of course, meant strict observance of the rule that counselled the non-interference, by government, with market forces. So familiar was Pitt with the ideas expounded in *The Wealth of Nations* that after he had met its author and discussed its content with him, Adam Smith was heard to exclaim that "He (Pitt) understands my ideas better than I do myself!" A rare compliment for a politician to receive from a celebrated academic, a compliment that would be quite inconceivable today. For the present-day politician can barely understand the latest advances in economics, let alone discuss them fluently with their author. The close ties between the political establishment and laissez-faire economics continued in the earlier part of the nineteenth century as England, the world's first industrial nation, forged ahead. lt was during this period that Lord Liverpool, the Prime Minister of England, had to remind the working class that it was not the government's job to improve working conditions and pay rates. Unions were vigorously suppressed as an obstacle to free bargaining between employer and employee, for this was also the period of the Tulpuddle martyrs. The high point of classical economic theory (i.e., the period during which it reigned supreme) also marks the era of the closest tie up between theory and practice in production and distribution of the national wealth. Companies in financial trouble did not get a loan from the government or any other sort of assistance but either improved their situation or went bankrupt. When demand was slack for an article, the price went down until demand picked up or the manufacturer went out of business. The early classical economists fitted exactly what was happening in the real world into a fairly straightforward body of theory for understanding the essentials of economic affairs. Classical economics was in this sense an empirical discipline (hence the early name political economy) rather than a body of theoretical knowledge painstakingly worked out to the smallest detail.

But the advent of Marginal Utility changed all this. Thus over the last hundred years a great deal of effort has been put into the "scientific" development of economic theory, with the theory of marginal utility replacing the classical economics of early industrial society. But I am not so sure that our understanding of economic affairs has progressed as much as one would be led to believe by the huge amount of literature on economics published in recent years. Many contemporary economists would agree with this statement in private, if not in public. The attempt to turn economics into a science has been a complete failure and has left the more sincere practitioners of the discipline frustrated and bewildered. We can best sum up the situation by saying that "The theory of economics, magnificent to behold, is considerably less impressive to use: welfare theory has not yet resulted in a single substantive proposal that has added significantly to the welfare of mankind. Price theory fails to explain the pricing operations of the great corporations. International trade theory does not adequately account for the most important single fact about international trade — to wit, the failure of an international division of labor to shed its benefits on poor countries and rich countries alike. The theory of economic development does not tell under-developed countries how to grow."[1] These are not my words, but those of a distinguished American economist, Robert Heilbroner (*Between Capitalism and Socialism*). Advanced industrial society has been able to become independent of economic theory in a way that early industrial society was never able to do.

One need only recall that during the heyday of laissez-faire, economic theory and social arrangements were closely linked. Each of the three factors of production, land, labor and capital was represented by a clearly defined and homogenous sector of society, i.e., land by the hereditary and capitalist landowners, capital by thc industrial entrepreneurs and financiers, labor by the propertyless working class. All classical economic theory was intimately tied up with what appeared to be a clearcut and permanent social reality. Perfect competition between industrial enterprises was taken for granted. Freedom of contract between employer and employee was a basic article of faith. Under these circumstances, the classical theorists not only wrote books, but took an active part in the economic affairs of their time, as did David Ricardo, who became a successful investor on the London Stock Exchange, or Nassau Senior, who represented Manchester industrialists against those calling for reform of working conditions in the textile industry. The rise of the monopoly joint stock corporation, the greater involvement of government in the economy, and the increasing size of the clerical labor force and the service sector in general, all contributed to make classical economic theory untenable. Advanced industrial society has never really needed economic theory to legitimate its existence. In the last hundred years, only one economist has enjoyed public acclaim approaching that which was given to the classical theorist — J. M. Keynes. And all he did was to put into words what had been made obvious by the enormous growth in productive capability over the previous sixty years, namely, fiscal conservatism was no longer feasible. With the apparently permanent expansion of industrial productivity had to go a permanent expansion of the money supply. All previous impediments to this expansion such as the belief in a balanced budget or insufficient gold and foreign currency reserves were no longer to be given a second thought. This is what the logic of advanced industrial society demanded, and this is what it got, i.e., an unlimited expansion of the money supply, with the government in the forefront as printer and the biggest spender.

Once deficit budgeting had received the stamp of approval from the most distinguished of those progressive economists with a social conscience, economics may be said to have fulfilled its historic mission as far as modern industrial society was concerned. Contemporary society can get along quite happily without the slightest reference to modern economic theory. This is just as well, for as the earlier quote from Heilbroner reminds us, modern society has become far too complex for modern economic theory to accurately interpret its needs and guide its destiny. Under these circumstances, our modern economists have withdrawn from the world of practical affairs where they are no longer wanted and expend their creative efforts on the construction of mathematical models depicting the workings of model economies which have very little relevance to the real world, and whose theoretical significance can only be fully understood by the most gifted of their colleagues. It is no wonder that Heilbroner asks the rhetorical question, "Why is it that modern economic theory presents the spectacle of superb intellectual achievement without much social relevance?"[2] Perhaps the answer lies in the fact that modern economic theory is one thing and modern economic organization is quite another.

The limitations of mathematical economics have always been apparent to the adherents of this school, and as we learned earlier, go beyond the inability of marginal utility to account for differences between nations in their economic growth rates. Indeed, it is probably true that, like many theories in the higher realms of the physical sciences, the greatest appeal of "marginal utility" lay in its mathematical elegance. That is, the fact that it most readily lends itself to the mathematical manipulation and interpretation of economic data. It is certainly true that modern economic theory has not remained static, but has developed over the years. The names of Hicks, Hayek, Samuelson and Friedman are among a few of those that spring to mind. But this is the least we should expect from a discipline which can be made so easily amenable to complex mathematical techniques of analysis. The important point is that, despite these advances in the development of more sophisticated theories and more precise analytical tools, the day-to-day functioning of modern industrial society continues entirely unaffected. The trade cycle remains as untameable as ever, bringing in its wake those characteristic booms and slumps which set at nought the most intricate calculations of politicians, businessmen and the expert economists who are supposed to advise them.

Neither have our mathematical economists been very successful in dealing with the problem of "stagflation," a problem which has far deeper roots in our social and economic structure than anyone would care to admit. Some have advocated the same old tired formulas such as a return to market conditions, i.e., no subsidies or other assistance to producers and no regulation of prices or wages, combined with strict monetary management by the central government. The latter would include such things as an attempt to move away from deficit budgeting and return to a balanced budget, a drastic reduction in social welfare spending and perhaps in other areas, and finally, restrictions on the growth of the money supply. This is what is commonly known as the monetarist solution to our economic woes. If applied wholeheartedly, it could have some very interesting results. It would undoubtedly tame inflation in no time at all, but the cost would probably be a level of unemployment not seen since the thirties. Whether any democratically elected government could again survive such an event is highly debatable. As for the economic stagnation that is now gripping the West, the monetarist solution is more likely to further depress production than to stimulate it. But at least one can understand the monetarist's viewpoint. Others have come up with wild theories (e.g., the Cambridge School 1975) which are so complex as to be totally incomprehensible to the average mind, and even if they could be deciphered and put into operation, would probably make matters worse instead of better.

The more honest of them are prepared to admit quite frankly that they do not know the answers as far as the long term attainment of economic stability is concerned. This is indeed a pathetic record. It would seem that our economists are like everyone else, keeping their fingers crossed that we will emerge from our present economic doldrums without the foundations of the system having been shaken beyond repair. The truth of the matter is, the theoretical advances which have been made in economics over the past few decades have not given us new ways of interpreting reality or altering the economic facts of life. Furthermore, even those principles of modern economics which have proved to be useful in helping to construct plausible models of the economic functioning of contemporary society have no more claim to everlasting validity than did the categories and principles of the classical economists. Not that modern economists should worry too much about their inability to produce ideas transcending the confines of present-day reality, since their decline is only part of the general decline in cultural creativity of modern industrial society. It is a process, I may add, which seems to have accelerated within the last thirty years.

One thing underpins all aspects of the economic disintegration of our age; this is contemporary man's obsession with economic growth, something which was quite alien to our preindustrial forebears. They neither understood the dynamics of economic growth nor fretted over the fact that articles in daily use could not be produced by mass production. All contemporary evidence indicates that continuous economic growth is no longer sustainable and hence by any criteria of judgement must be considered as irrational. No one puts this better than Schumacher, who tells us that: "An attitude to life which seeks fulfillment in the single minded pursuit of wealth — in short materialism — does not fit into this world because it contains within itself no limiting principle, while the environment in which it is placed is strictly limited."[3] The accuracy of this statement is undeniable. The energy crisis has so far been its most dramatic demonstration. We have to face the unpleasant fact that the natural gas and petroleum which we use to fuel our cars, provide heat for our homes and industries and electricity for distribution throughout the nation, may all be gone within forty or fifty years at the most. We also know that the belief in the need for continuous economic growth is a product of modern industrial society and will not be relinquished until modern industrial society has itself been transcended.

Nevertheless, it would not be too far-fetched to say that all the economic problems which the advanced industrial societies are now experiencing are indications that the socio-economic structure and hence the consciousness of this age is beginning to give way — a condition which is a prerequisite for transition to the new age. Thus, Schumacher is not the only person to have come out strongly against further economic growth. Robert Heilbroner has also expressed his opinion on this matter in no uncertain terms, He tells us that: "The worship in the West of a growing Gross National Product must be recognized as not only a deceptive but a very dangerous avatar."[4] He concludes his discussion with a powerful warning to the rest of us: "There is... the possibility that the ecological crisis will simply result in the decline, or even destruction, of Western civilization, and of the hegemony of the scientific-technological view that has achieved so much and cost us so dearly."[5] These are the words of one who is aware of the dangers facing mankind from the continued existence of modern industrial society. The politicians and their allies (the conforming economists) can talk all they want about the need for continued economic growth — they are wasting their breath. The days of non-stop economic growth are almost behind us. They have been characteristic of an age which more than any other has been anxious to push the boundaries of human knowledge and productivity to their upper limits. The societies of the new age will have no such desire. In these societies, life on the soil will take precedence over life at the work bench, and they will have no inclination to retrace the footsteps of their "modern" predecessors.

The consciousness which demands an annual increase in the standard of living will no longer exist. The abolition of modern industrial society, and with it the emphasis on economic growth, will be no great loss. The vast majority of the articles manufactured by modern industrial society are not essential to our well-being and those that are, will, for the most part, be made at home by those who need them, though members of the ruling elite will employ artisans when necessary to minister to their needs. The age in which we now live compels us to pollute our environment, develop previously unspoiled open spaces, destroy our mental peace and break up our families. The keynote of the new age will be the emergence of a new and distinct aristocratic elite and the free and unhampered exercise of their will, unrestricted by utilitarian considerations of what would be in the best interests of the greatest number. Their main concern will be how they can extend their power and influence or in some other way gratify their most pressing desires. Economic growth will be the last thing on their mind. Such a way of life is hardly compatible with the self- discipline required for the operation of a highly industrialized society. True, not even the new elite will be able to undo the past; we will have to live with the damage that has already been done to our environment. But at least the process of environmental destruction will be permanently halted with the arrival of the new age. Without the leadership of an elite class, the ordinary people will have neither the inclination nor the capacity to embark upon the economic growth trail once more.

A sign of the times is the persistence of inflation and unemployment in the economies of the world's most advanced industrialized nations. Despite all the talk, the legislation, the price and income freezes, and the opinions of experts, these two problems remain with us and stubbornly refuse to go away. One is reminded of the Great Depression, which showed that even under the conditions of a highly developed industrial economy, man's control over his long term economic performance is tenuous at best. At the time of writing, control and understanding have again become almost nonexistent. The advanced industrial nations are rapidly becoming driverless juggernauts. None of the old remedies appear to work any longer. The money supply is held constant, the bank lending rate is increased, bank loans are cut back, government spending is reduced, and wage demands are moderated, but still prices mount and the costs of production increase inexorably. All western nations are officially committed to an economic policy which guarantees full employment, i.e., an unemployment level of no more than 4 per cent at the very most. But in many of them unemployment is above 7 per cent and is either still rising, as it is in several countries of Western Europe, or stubbornly refuses to go down, as is the case in the U.S.A. Some have attributed this persistently high level of unemployment to structural changes in the economy by which less people are required to maintain the high levels of production that we have become accustomed to. The more conventional view is that while certain structural changes may have taken place in the last decade or so these have not been great enough to account for the high levels of unemployment. Instead, we are told that we are going through a period of economic recession and full employment will automatically return once it has come to an end.

Even if inflation can be brought under control (for a while) and economic activity picks up, there is no guarantee that the level of unemployment will go down. In fact there is every indication that it will stay the same. No doubt a new conventional wisdom will emerge to cover this situation; there are already signs that this is happening. We will soon be told that an unemployment rate of 7 to 8 per cent is now normal for an advanced industrialized country and is nothing to worry about. The real situation will be that the new figure for full employment will be just another omen that modern industrial society is nearing its end. Thus, it is my contention that neither tax cuts, increased government spending, job creation, decreases in the interest rate charged by lending banks, nor increased levels of investment by industry, will make any difference to the long term trend in the unemployment rate. As for inflation, it can only be permanently defeated by the transcendence of modern industrial society. The fact that persistent inflation is something that the advanced industrial societies have only had to cope with for the last three decades is itself rather revealing. We now seem to have reached the point at which the complex economic structure that characterizes a highly developed industrial society has simply become too much to handle. Perhaps this discovery should not really surprise us, for we have ample evidence to indicate that no economist (and very few noneconomists for that matter) of the last two hundred years has fully understood the logic of modern industrial society, that is, it could be beneficial and destructive at the same time, and its destructive effects would eventually far outweigh its beneficial effects. Few realized that wage restraints, freezes and squeezes or a touch on the tiller would be insufficient to control the economic affairs of modern industrial society, once it had achieved its highest level of development, a truth which Great Britain more than any other western country has had to live with. Again, it was once believed that one of the great benefits of industrial production was that it not only increased the availability of goods but was also able to reduce costs of production as the volume of production increased. Alas, this has not happened; quite the reverse has taken place. Costs of production have continued to go up regardless of volume produced. We cannot concern ourselves here with the reasons for this as they are complex and highly contentious, but two observations are in order. One is that the rate of increase in costs of production has tended to take place at a much faster rate since World War Two than previous to World War Two. Neither slow down in demand, high unemployment and improved technology, nor increased productivity has done much to affect this trend. The obvious question that begs to be answered, then, is this: Assuming the above trend to be irreversible, will it continue indefinitely? Rapid price increases followed by equally rapid wage increases would seem to be part of the dynamism of modern industrial society albeit a very recent phenomenon. Thus, theory would seem to indicate that this trend must continue indefinitely, whereas common sense indicates that it cannot.

The second of our two observations would seem to confirm that there are intrinsic limitations to the indefinite development of modern industrial society. Not only is modern industrial society based on continuous growth in productivity in its most competitive form (i.e., capitalism), it also demands continuous changes in the techniques of production, and new investment opportunities, which means new markets and new products. This fact was first brought forcefully to public attention by Karl Marx in his *Communist Manifesto.* It was one of the most remarkable pieces of writing ever to come from the pen of Marx, for in the same article he both praises the achievements of the capitalist mode of production while condemning the class responsible for them and also the way in which they were achieved. He tells us that, "The need for a constantly expanding market for its products chases the bourgeoisie over the whole surface of the globe. It must nestle everywhere, settle everywhere, establish connexions everywhere."[6] Other later writers have felt the same way about the logic of the capitalist system of production. Joseph Schumpeter, in *Capitalism, Socialism and Democracy,* places the situation in a more modern context, but says very much the same thing: "Capitalism . . . is by nature a form or method of economic change and not only never is but never can be stationary. . . . The fundamental impulse that sets and keeps the capitalist engine in motion comes from the new consumer goods, the new methods of production or transportation, the new markets, the new forms of industrial organization that capitalist enterprise creates."[7]

But for just how long could we expect this situation to continue before exhaustion of both resources and ideas begins to set in? There are now unmistakable signs indicating that we are slowing down with respect to ideas and will soon be having trouble meeting our raw material needs without making still greater sacrifices in regards to pollution control, environmental destruction, land use and nuclear power. Furthermore, with regard to the exhaustion of ideas, David Riesman states, "The basic stockpile on which our society's dynamism has rested — the stockpile of new and exhilarating wants — seems to me badly depleted."[8] Baran and Sweezy in their book *Monopoly Capital* reach a similar conclusion, although arguing their case from an entirely different viewpoint. They draw our attention to the increasing surplus that is accumulated by the American capitalist system and to the fact that there is no way in which this surplus can be fully reabsorbed into the system. It is a situation which they believe gives rise to the possibility of a serious economic crisis at some future date. They also note that, even when the American economy is working at full production, there still remains a very large reservoir of unemployment, and conclude from this that the world's most advanced economy must be in real trouble if it cannot provide full employment for all those who want to work, even in times of an economic boom. I am sure few would argue with this assessment.

We need only mention in passing that America is not alone in this predicament, for it is increasingly affecting other western nations which find themselves with an improving economy together with a large number of unemployed. Schumpeter felt that the stagnation of modern capitalism, and the social tensions generated thereby, would be one of the key factors leading to the triumph of socialism and "rational" planning of the nation's economic affairs. As much as I respect his analytical powers, I must strongly disagree with this contention and remind the reader of the alternative model thesis which sees communism primarily as an alternative form of socio-economic organization (albeit a far less efficient one) to a free-market economy. By this reckoning, we may say that as capitalism goes, so must communism. Therefore, when capitalism is superseded, it would under no circumstances be replaced by socialism, since this too will be superseded at the very same time. What we can say is that a so-called capitalist society is able to give us a much better understanding of the problems of modern industrial society and hence a guide to its future, than a far more restricted communist society, every aspect of which is managed by a government agency with its own commissar.

In connection with the economic decline of the West, it is also interesting to note that the last two or three decades have also been ones in which quantity has greatly increased while quality has greatly declined. This applies to just about all fields, whether university graduates, industrial patents, new consumer goods or scientific research (with a large number of published papers, but very little achieved in the way of useful advance). We have more opportunity to do more things than we have ever had before, and yet we are more discontented and more confused than we have ever been before. We seem unable to accomplish anything of lasting worth; everything about our era seems ephemeral. . . notoriety, success, popularity; we are quick to set up tin gods only to knock them down again as our taste changes. Often those in whom we placed our confidence turn out to be broken reeds hardly worthy of the great faith that had been placed in them. Everything about our era is cheap, tawdry and second-rate; little if any of it seems worth preserving. The only thing that matters is that the people should get all that keeps them happy, whether this be more sensational entertainment or novel consumer goods. So this is the way our age is coming to an end, with a great deal of frantic activity, (but very little to show for it), and much of which is either harmful and disruptive or simply depressing to anyone who hankers after the straightforward simplicity of ages gone by when reason devoid of passion had not yet come to dominate mankind's entire lifestyle as it does now.

For we have now reached the point at which the only sure test of right reason is whether or not the action in question would have the approval of the majority. Such beliefs dilute all standards into an insipid concoction. They tear away all passions and strong emotion, reducing man to a soulless automaton. Their long-term tendency is to produce a perfectly pliable nature with no biases, no pride, and no prejudices, in fact, no strong feelings of any sort, except the desire to be a good liberal, whatever that may mean. This outrageous abnegation of man's birthright ties in nicely with the economic practices of our age which bid us that whether we are corporate presidents or workers on the factory floor, we maximize our self-interest by producing more and demanding more. This self-seeking, short-sighted behavior is perfectly acceptable, whereas any behavior or opinions which deviate from the norm of what is expected of a good liberal is not. I should add that one may hold the most conservative economic philosophy but can still be a "good liberal" provided he accepts the touchstones of modern liberalism, e.g., equality of opportunity, equality of the sexes, to name two of the more important. Since most conservatives now also believe in these things, this usually presents few problems. Modern industrial society at its highest state of development has all but abolished both classes and class conflict, reducing almost everyone to docile consumers. But in so doing, it has robbed western civilization of much of its vigour and energy, leaving a vacuum which will remain unfilled for as long as modern industrial society continues in existence. We have been reduced to watching horror movies and reading cheap romance novels in order to break out of the dreary, castrated existence to which we have been confined by the dictates of modern industrial society.

Many so-called experts, especially those who are called upon to give advice to our political leaders, believe that the disintegration of modern industrial society can be reduced to a simple bookkeeping problem, say, more or less government spending, more or less discipline in school and at home, harsher sentences for criminals or softer sentences, and so on. These people obviously underestimate the magnitude of the problem. Not only has our age reached a point at which it is beyond saving either by charitable or repressive reforms, but also the new elite which will arise after the demise of the present age will be entirely out of sympathy with the values of this age. In other words, the entire way in which we moderns of the present age look at problems and attempt to solve them is misguided and inadequate when considered from the perspective of the real nature and needs of mankind, and is something which will only be revealed once the new age makes its appearance.

Modern industrial society has tended to concentrate on the satisfaction of man's material needs to the exclusion of all else. The sensual side of man's personality has been stifled in order to accommodate the self-discipline and routine which is one of the hallmarks of the consumer lifestyle. The rhythms of contemporary man are not those of nature. His day-to-day activity is not determined by the seasons of the year, but by the demands of modern industrial society, which remain the same all year round, a life ruled by the incessant ticking of a clock. He wakes up with his alarm. Before he realizes it, he is on his way to work. He clocks in on arrival. He clocks out to go to lunch and in again upon his return before finally clocking out to go home. When he gets home he is not by any means "off the clock," for he may have to eat hurriedly and change quickly to get to his appointment with a friend on time. In short, we have become a civilization of clock watchers. Such has become the fate of the culture which has consistently shown more energy and has had more accomplishments to its credit than almost any other.

As if to make up for our loss of vitality we have allowed our lives to be dominated by the "big is best" philosophy, believing that great size alone is a sign of national greatness and cultural superiority. Only modern man could be so crass, so unbelievably insensitive. We are now paying the price of our foolishness for belief in the virtue of large size, which has been for so long taken for granted and has left us with many big problems — which include big government, big but useless military establishments, big monopoly corporations, big impersonal manufacturing plants, big energy problems, big decaying cities and many others. These are the debilitating symptoms of our age. The converse idea, small is beautiful, has come too late to have much effect upon our predilection to think big.

Big government and big industry have done more than any other factors to impart to our age this peculiar penchant for bigness. The modern government has tried to do all it can to protect us from ourselves, from external enemies real or imagined, from being underfed, underpaid, underclothed, overworked, overexposed, from inferior merchandise, inferior education, inferior health care and from numerous other possibilities, too numerous to remember and too tedious to list. It seems that with each year that passes there is more for us to be protected from. And our ever-conscientious legislators are only too happy to busy themselves drawing up laws which are meant to protect us from the evils of modern industrial society. Thus, we have laws compelling us to have seat belts in our cars, to wear a crash-helmet when riding a motor bike, while other laws instruct radio and television stations to allow equal time for different opinions and automobile manufacturers to place engines of a particular specification in their cars. On top of all this we have dozens of watch-dog commissions and regulatory agencies. None of this prolific extension of government is able to do anything substantial to improve the quality of life as experienced by the average urban dweller of the advanced industrial sites. Although big government is able to do very little to substantially improve the quality of life, it has done a great deal to help make life at times an almost intolerable burden for many of those who have had occasion to deal with the monster.

One can end up being drowned by an avalanche of paper work, answering questions which are either irrelevant, impertinent or just plain silly. Each department, agency and commission has its own petty rules and regulations which can mean further long delays, more forms and more correspondence. It's enough to drive one to the depths of exasperation. Local government is not making matters any easier for the sorely harassed law-abiding citizen. In fact, the combination of central and local government is proving to be most effective in regard to frustrating the citizen who seeks redress of a legitimate complaint. In several western countries, central and local government employment can be claimed as the only growth sectors in an otherwise stagnant economy. Even as employment in the manufacturing sector continues to shrink in all the highly industrialized societies, employment in the public sector continues to expand. We are told that the decentralization of government helps to reinforce a sense of community as well as giving to people a chance to participate in the affairs of their community. But as most of us should know, this is a lot of phoney baloney. Since when did the payment of local taxes ever help to reinforce a sense of community? This is something which has ceased to exist in all but the most remote part of the underdeveloped countries and perhaps in a few developed countries — but only a few. In the typical community of an industrialized nation, our rubbish is removed by the municipal garbage collectors, rather than burnt and buried, water is supplied to us from some distant reservoir through the medium of the local water works, rather than taken directly from a communal well or fresh water stream. Children in need of care and accommodation are usually taken in hand by a municipally run foster home, instead of by other members of the community, as is the case in many of the less developed parts of the world. For every community need, from the maintenance of local cemeteries and highways to the care of the indigent and incapacitated, there is a particular department of local government concerned with it.

But if there is not sufficient money available then the need in question is just not met. Hence, the dreadful state of the nonresidential parts of many suburbs, areas for which no one feels any responsibility. One would hardly call this the highest expression of civic virtue, to allow some parts of the community, such as wasteland and unpaved sidewalks, to be clogged with litter while the paved sidewalks in front of suburban homes are kept clean to match the neatly trimmed hedges and lawns of these houses. A community certainly does not need the manipulative powers of the cash nexus to qualify as a bona fide community. In fact, the development of a true community sentiment and solidarity probably proceeds far better without the operation of the cash nexus, i.e., we have no other choice but to do things for ourselves. As for the virtues and advantages of big government — whatever these may be — we have lived without them in the past and survived, and can do so again in the future. To be honest, we will be much better off without the protection proffered by big government. Since the fact that we no longer need such protection will mean that we have gone beyond the age of modern industrial society and so are no longer threatened by ecological disaster, and the other innumerable dangers of modern living which now beset us.

Big industry has stamped its character upon our age so indelibly that many would believe that it would be impossible for us to live without it. But nothing could be further from the truth, as we will one day find out. When I speak of big industry, I am referring to both the large size of the individual production units which make up these monopoly corporations and to the corporations themselves. Whether or not we have really benefited from vertical integration, horizontal integration, and economies of scale, is not for me to say. Still, I am certain of one thing, that growth of big industry has given a tremendous boost to the cult of bigness in most other walks of life. After all, this would seem to be what the people demand. They have no interest in aesthetics, but are only concerned with practical considerations, and these can best be met by huge housing projects, enormous hospitals and stupendous office blocks. Big industry has also meant that the industrial capacity of a typical developed nation greatly exceeds that which would be commensurate with the size of the domestic economy. Therefore, its industries must sell large quantities of their goods abroad (in competition with industries of nations in a similar position) in order to maintain economic viability. This, by the way, is one of the most powerful arguments for the continued existence of the European Economic Community, in that it greatly expands the home market of manufacturers (and agricultural producers) in its member countries while protecting them from excessive competition with foreign imports. Thus, politically the EEC has been a total failure as was only to be expected, but in economic terms membership has paid off handsomely — for some of its members at least.

So far we have talked about the situation of modern industry, but what of the other sector of the modern economy, i.e., agriculture? The general reader hears little about the problems of this sector and particularly their long-term implication. The only thing we are told is that the number of those working on the land continues to decline. But this is not the only fact that we ought to know about the present state of farming in a modern industrial economy. All literature written in the last decade or so in connection with modern agriculture either states explicitly or implicitly the opinion that modern farming has ceased to be a special way of life and has become in fact a business like any other. No doubt this is perfectly true — one could hardly expect otherwise given the economic circumstances under which most farmers must now operate. But such a trend carries inherent dangers which we overlook at our own cost, since farming can never be simply a business like any other. All those who participate in it are in a very special position vis-a-vis all those for whom they produce, which cannot be said of the average non-farming enterprise. Since not only will a very large proportion of the nation's best land be devoted to farming (which is as it should be) but food — the basic product of farm labor — has no substitute.

This should naturally lead us to concern regarding the performance pressures under which the modern farmer operates. I do not only have in mind the iniquities of factory farming, or the raising of livestock for slaughter on vitamins, high protein steroids and hormones, which has led to the development of high incidence of cancerous tumors and other disturbing physiological abnormalities in these animals, or the spraying of crops with highly toxic pesticides which endanger the health of farm workers as well as having adverse long-term effects on the ecological balance of the area, or the excessive use of fertilizer which can also have a serious long term ecological effect (see *Mankind At The Turning Point*, p. 172). I am also talking about the pressures which could force farming in non-communist advanced industrialized countries to go the same way as industry did from the late nineteenth century onwards. This would mean the divorce of management from ownership (which is already taking place on a small scale), the integration of many farming units into the operations of large food companies and the rise of monopoly production through the emergence of agricultural finance holding corporations owing to the increasing capital needs of modern farming. These dangers are not the products of a fervid imagination, but are real and quite possible. Already we are told that by the year 2005 A.D. the most important qualification for farm management will not be a knowledge of land, livestock and related matters, but a thorough acquaintance with mathematics, evidently needed for the purpose of model building and making computer projections. Then again, finance capital is stealthily making its way into family farming through the back door as the corporate Moguls look around for opportunities to invest surplus funds. The question is not if corporatism will eventually take over farming in its entirety, but when, assuming the cash nexus is allowed to continue along its course.

With material affluence has come spiritual degradation. Mass production has now been taken so far as to become a blight on the lives of a large section of the population in all the advanced industrial nations. It denies to the worker either a sense of pride in his work or a sense of fulfillment in its end result. One would be mistaken to believe that such things do not matter to the average worker. Although he may not have had the experience of being a craftsman in the generally accepted sense of the word, he is well aware of the fact that his creative potential is not being fully utilized by his repetitive daily labors on the assembly line. Thomas Carlyle, who was a contemporary of Marx and Engels, was one of the few people who fully perceived the disruptive potential of large-scale industrialization. Unlike the "scientific" socialists and middle-class Victorian optimists, he did not romanticize what was going on, but attacked it unsparingly. He bitterly regretted that the thirst for profit was rapidly destroying the last vestiges of the traditional rural organization that had persisted down from the middle ages. Carlyle was the first person to coin the term "cash-nexus" which was later taken over by Marx and Engels. He knew that spiritual strength was not compatible with the enormous material affluence that would eventually be brought about by large-scale industrialization. Engels at one time seriously hoped that Carlyle would come over to the Socialist camp — needless to say Engels was disappointed when this never happened. The reason why Carlyle did not become a socialist is not difficult to understand. He never had sympathy for the plight of the masses as such; he was an elitist, a believer in the existence of a natural hierarchy among men.

What he lamented was the disappearance of this hierarchy as commercial relations came more and more to supplant custom and obligation in the countryside, the place where the existence of a natural hierarchy among men received its most simple and forceful expression. He saw that capitalism would only foster base and ignoble traits, for it gave to all men the opportunity to acquire a great fortune in a short time, provided they were prepared to efface themselves, lie, cheat, grovel, beg and beseech. In fact, no behavior would be too low, provided success was ultimately assured. The sole purpose behind this facile personality was to acquire wealth, nothing else. Yes, Carlyle saw better than anyone else the debasing vulgarity of capitalism at its most competitive. He wanted no part of it, not the capitalist mentality or the capitalist industry of which his age was so proud. Not so Marx and Engels, who were quite prepared to contemplate the passing away of the capitalist mentality, but considered the existence of capitalist industry to be essential for obtaining the better life. Thus, the two patrons of scientific socialism were quite happy to see industrialization continue its course, even though they had on occasion been critical of its destructiveness. How then could Engels dare to expect the support of a man such as Thomas Carlyle, who once stated that society is built on hero worship, a man who had always been a consistent critic of the rapid industrialization that was taking place throughout this period. Thomas Carlyle was not the only major literary figure of the nineteenth century to forcibly express his resentment of industrialization. Another enemy of large-scale industrialization was John Ruskin, an Oxford professor and notable art critic. Like Carlyle, Ruskin foresaw that the success of the Industrial Revolution would produce a society lacking in cultural vitality as far as nontechnological matters were concerned. Ruskin praised craftsmanship and the dignified simplicity of rural life. It was Ruskin who pointed out that great art can only arise from a nation of warriors — warriors, that is, who did not look upon military service as a regrettable waste of time, but who welcomed the opportunity to display their courage and valor under the leadership of their natural superiors. But at the time Ruskin was speaking, England had already become the workshop of the world.

Despite the great material success of industrialization it has tended to rob life of the wholeness it once had. Modern man considers his work to be quite separate and distinct from all other activities. The very thought of one's job often elicits feelings of disgust, a fact most eloquently stated by Marx in his early writings, especially the 1844 *Philosophical Manuscripts* and *The German Ideology*. A typical example of Marx's early tirades against industrial society is the following well known quote: "The worker...feels himself at home only during his leisure time, whereas at work he feels homeless. His work is not voluntary but imposed, forced labor. It is not the satisfaction of a need, but only a means for satisfying other needs. Its alien character is clearly shown by the fact that as soon as there is no physical or other compulsion it is avoided like the plague."[9] Numerous other examples can be found of Marx's early distaste for the lifestyle and values of industrial society, but from about the age of twenty-nine onward his views took a somewhat different turn. He virtually ignored his earlier references to alienation and took the view that workers would never enjoy doing industrial work, but as it came within the realm of necessity, it had to be done. Furthermore, improvements in technology and the rational organization of labor after the proletariat had taken over the means of production, would increase productivity to such an extent that the worker would not have to spend too much time in the factory.

By this means, Marx could rest comfortably with the view that the full development of industrial society would bring about the salvation of mankind. In recent years there has been much discussion among sociologists regarding the difference between the young Marx and the old Marx. As we have seen, the early writings of Marx are filled with indiscriminate attacks upon industrial society. These early critiques were most often sensual and unsystematic. But Marx, unlike say, Rousseau, was not going to advocate that men turn their backs on industrialization. For this would be to break faith with the forces that were shaping the destiny of his age, and this he could never do. So enter the older Marx, author of, among other books, the *Communist Manifesto, Critique of Political Economy* and *Capital*, for Marx intended above all to be a scientifically accurate theorist of the development of industrial society. Thus, logic compelled him to take a more systematic, less sensual view of his subject, i.e., the future of industrial society. Though, apart from a few sentences in his *Critique of the Gotha Programme*, he never had very much to say about how a modern industrial society would be organized once the great Socialist Revolution had come. This perhaps is because there was not very much he could say in this respect without tending to cast serious doubts as to whether a socialist society could be qualitatively very much different from a capitalist democracy.

To be honest then, it is not really difficult to reconcile the discrepancies between the Young and the Old Marx. Shlomo Avineri does an admirable job of it in his book, *The Social and Political Thoughts of Karl Marx.* But even Avineri is unable to overcome the aura of Marx, and allows the richness of Marxian theory to get the better of him. He ends his book by telling us that everyone has so far failed to accurately interpret and apply the Marxian message: ' '. . . a popularizing emasculation of his theory went hand in hand with an idolatrous attitude towards a mythical image of the person of Marx. Kautsky and Bebel were guilty of this no less than Lenin and Stalin."[10] Somehow I think Avineri has got it all wrong, for the message was in the myth. If only our modern Marxist theoreticians would lift their heads from the completed works of Marx and Engels and take a look at what's happening around them, they may yet be able to write something of value for the edification of contemporary man. There are some encouraging signs that this is happening; for instance, the reaction against the strong belief held by Marx and Engels in the long-term benefits of industrial progress has already begun. Thus, many contemporary Marxists are taking an active part in the movement against environmental pollution and have become advocates of a no-growth economy.

The mature Marx was totally out of sympathy with any attempts to restrain the growth of industry. In the *Communist Manifesto*, he refers to all those who opposed the progress of large-scale industry as reactionaries and had far less respect for them than he did for the bourgeoisie. By the very nature of his social theory, Marx could only see industrialization in terms of its tangible advantages (i.e., its enormous productive power). He was quite incapable of appreciating the potential menace it would be to the future of mankind. The limitations of the viewpoint held by Marx regarding the future of industrial society was eloquently pointed out many years ago by the brilliant but erratic Georges Sorel. According to Sorel, "The Marxian theory of revolution supposed that capitalism, while it is still in full swing, will be struck to the heart, when — having attained complete industrial efficiency — it has finally achieved its historical mission and whilst the economic system is still a progressive one. Marx does not seem to have asked himself what would happen if the economic system were on the down grade; he never dreamt of the possibility of a revolution which would take a return to the past, or social conservation, as its ideal."[11] Now that it has become abundantly clear that capitalism is not going to collapse in the way that Marx thought it would, perhaps all contemporary Marxists will take their cue from Sorel and make an honest assessment of the relevance of Marxism to modern man.

Although modern industrial society has been in existence for some two hundred years, man has never become fully adapted to it. It is a fact that many might find strange, but which is nevertheless true. Moreover, man's maladaptation to his industrial environment is becoming more apparent with the passage of time rather than less so. One need only look at such figures as the levels of industrial accidents which have continued to rise despite improved standards of safety and a great deal of experience with industrialization; or the level of absenteeism, which remains high for several industries in which the average wage places their workers among the highest paid wage earners in the land. The large number of unofficial (wildcat) strikes in industry and the tendency of young office and factories workers to change jobs at frequent intervals are further signs that adaptation to our high performance industrial culture is deteriorating rather than improving. They are all strong indications that the worker of today is failing to take pride in his work. The late C. Wright Mills has expressed well the languid disenchantment with the work ethic that now seems to pervade all types of work. He informs us that, "For the white-collar masses, as for wage earners generally, work seems to serve neither God nor whatever they experience as divine in themselves. In them there is no taut will do work, and few positive gratifications from their daily round."[12] With this thought in mind, an obvious question begs to be answered: How long can we continue to demand the effort and self-discipline needed to maintain a highly evolved industrial culture when the attitude of those on whose performance this culture depends is so negative towards its continued existence? Several prominent sociologists have recognized the serious implications of this question, including Martin Riesman, in *Abundance For What and Other Essays* and Daniel Bell in *The Coming of the Post Industrial Society*. In speaking about the tensions in the industrialized societies of the future, which could cause problems, Bell puts the situation this way: "The deepest tensions are those between the culture whose axial direction is anti-institutional and antinomian, and the social structure which is ruled by an economizing and technocratic mode. It is this tension which is ultimately the most fundamental problem of the post-industrial society."[13]

With the domestic economies of the world's leading industrial nations in such disarray, we need hardly find it surprising that international economic relations are tottering on the brink of collapse. Two problems have been fundamental to the present state of international economic affairs. One is trade and monetary relations among the developed countries, and the other is the utter confusion which surrounds economic relations between the advanced industrial nations and the Third World. These two problems are of course closely connected, and are further examples of how it is impossible for man to disentangle himself from the intricate web he has been spinning since the beginning of the age of modern industry. It now turns out that policies which we thought at the time were both sensible and expedient have committed us to proceed on a path which must lead to breakdown and dissolution. The present state of international financial affairs is a very good example of what I mean. It seems that no currency can keep its value for too long before it has to be devalued or revalued against all the other major currencies. A few years ago, it was the dollar which was falling drastically. Recently, it has been the pound and the lire, whereas the Dutch guilder, the German mark and Swiss franc, along with Japan's yen, are perennial candidates for revaluation. Millions are spent by these countries in order either to shore up the value of their ailing currency or to keep its value from going so high, as to threaten export performance, but all to no avail. Long term currency stability has become a thing of the past. Several countries have given up the attempt to maintain a fixed exchange rate and instead have allowed their currency to float on the international money market, i.e., find its own level according to the exigencies of the moment. Only a short time ago, this would have been looked upon as a species of economic heresy, but not anymore. It is an admission that governments no longer have the ability to control the exchange rate of their currency, so they have left the field to foreign currency speculators, who include not only multinational corporations but also many Third World nations with substantial holdings of western currency. Then again, there is the possibility of the complete breakdown of the international financial system as a result of default by one or two large debtors, either from among the developed countries or from among the less developed countries. Debt rescheduling has become a regular part of international monetary affairs, but this only means that the day of reckoning is put off to a more distant time.

The root cause of this situation is the reckless expansion of the money supply in all developed countries which has taken place since the gold standard was abandoned. The lack of the monetary discipline which was formerly imposed by adherence to the gold standard has played havoc with international trade and finance. Neither the pound nor the dollar has been an effective substitute for gold. In fact the use of these as reserve currencies has undoubtedly fueled the tendency towards international monetary instability. The pound's value suffers from the permanent weakness of Britain's economy, whilst the enormous quantity of dollars outside the U.S.A. (including the so called Eurodollars held in Western Europe) makes the currency highly susceptible to the machinations of currency speculators. But many countries, especially some members of the Third World, are not content even with present arrangements which are already straining international economic relations to breaking point. They are calling for a further boost in their purchasing power through an expansion of Special Drawing Rights (SDRs) — the brain child of the International Monetary Fund. The effects of such an expansion of international liquidity would be catastrophic, to say the least, and especially so in an age of liberal fiscal policies such as our own. What with the Eurodollar market and the enormous incomes of the Arab oil producers, international liquidity is already far too great for the good of the international monetary system. The woes of the international economic order continue to multiply without break. There are now too many nations involved in the economic growth stakes. All of them want to maximize their income from international trade, or failing this, to borrow as much as they can from the various sources of international credit available to them.

But ultimately, if some countries are doing well from international trade, then there will be other countries which are not doing so well. Some of the countries which are suffering serious economic dislocation brought about in part at least by an adverse balance of trade are highly developed nations such as England, Denmark and Italy, but most of them are members of the Third World. Frustrated by their inability to cope with this situation, many countries of the Third World are not only demanding more loans and financial aid from the wealthier countries, but also a moratorium on the repayment of previous loans. Because of their stronger position in the world of trade and finance, the developed countries which are in economic trouble do not need to ask for interest free loans and a moratorium on previous loans; all they need to do is make a request for aid from the International Monetary Fund which will be granted regardless of the amount they have previously borrowed. To be quite honest, whether it is assisting nations of the First World or the Third, the IMF has simply become an instrument for throwing good money after bad — all to no effect. Look how many billions of dollars have been received by Britain and still it is struggling with what are to all intents and purposes insurmountable economic problems. Neither have the many billions lent to countries of the Third World (at very low rates of interest) done much to cure their poverty and low level of industrial development. But it must also be admitted that the IMF and related organizations have played an important part in providing advanced industrial nations in deep trouble with a way out of their problem. The point is, how long can the weaker industrial nations continue to borrow themselves out of trouble?

Thus, without the direct intervention of governments in their efforts to stimulate the nation's economy, the assistance of friendly central banks and the IMF, the present world-wide recession would have long ago turned into another Great Depression. The rules of classical economics would once again apply to the exchange of goods and services, thus automatically readjusting the relationship between supply and demand. The lack of demand during this period led not only to a dramatic slow down in economic activity, producing very high levels of unemployment, but also to a decrease in price levels and a commensurate reduction in wages and salaries. There is no possibility that this would happen again to the same extent, mainly because our large corporations (publicly and privately owned) are far more dominant than they were in the Thirties, and utilitarian sentiment is far stronger than it was then, among all groups, regardless of ideological outlook. The truth of the matter is that we have been caught in a dilemma from which there is no way out other than a total transformation of present day realities.

On the one hand, there is the desire of late twentieth century man for maximum economic performance year after year; all his thinking, his economic arrangements, institutions and beliefs are geared to this end. On the other hand, we have the lessons of history accumulated over the last two hundred years, which tell us that a period of economic boom can only take place for a relatively short time, after which comes a period of economic downturn and retrenchment. But since a lifestyle based on continuous economic growth "has within it no limiting principle" (Schumacher, 1973), it would seem that the wisdom gained from history and the desire of late twentieth century man for permanent economic security within an advanced industrial culture are on a collision course. We will no doubt continue to print money and watch the inexorable increase in prices and incomes until the arrival of the new age. Only then will the economic woes of modern industrial society be put right — permanently.

As for the less developed nations of the Third World, loans from the IMF, the World Bank and friendly governments are simply piling on more debt than they can ever possibly repay. No amount of economic assistance will improve the conditions existing in the Third World much beyond what they are at present. In discussing the economic relationship between the Third World and the First World, we must first of all make the point that the developed countries are in no way responsible for the poor economic performance of the less developed countries — despite charges of colonial plunder, imperialism, neo-colonialism and unequal exchange. History has denied to the Third World countries the opportunity to develop economically to the same extent as the advanced industrialized nations. This is a fact of life which no amount of material and technical aid will change. Unfortunately, as long as indefinite economic growth remains as the most important thing to the developed nations, so will the nations of the Third World seek to obtain from these advanced societies all that they wrongly believe is owing to them. Literature on the gap in living standards between the rich and poor nations of the world, and between the minority of well-to-do and the vast majority of the impoverished within the poorer nations, has flourished in recent years. Many radical academics have turned their attention to analyzing the causes and the long-term social, political and economic implications of these differences.

This activity has provided our boisterous radical authors with an outlet for their aggrieved consciences, but has done little to put the situation into proper perspective. Those writers who have been critical of the economic involvement of western corporations in the Third World, such as Andre Gunar Frank and Antonio Galeano, have been suffering from gross delusions by which fact and fantasy are hopelessly confused, since foreign investment has done more for the economy of Third World nations than the remitted dividends have done for the economy of the advanced industrial nations. Nevertheless, these authors have not been entirely ignored, in that many leaders of opinion in both the developed nations and the Third World have become convinced of the need for a New Economic Order regarding finance and trade relations between developed and less developed nations. But not surprisingly, no one seems to know exactly what this would mean, or how it could be brought about. Even if a new economic order could be successfully worked out on paper, there are a number of reasons why the implementation of such a plan would be doomed to failure. Not only would there be numerous technical problems to be overcome, but also political rivalry and opportunism would be bound to wreck any agreement founded upon idealism, as a new economic order would be. I strongly believe that even with the best will in the world, there is no way in which countries of the Third World can be helped by the advanced industrial countries to make substantial economic progress.

Thus, increased access to the markets of the developed countries is not going to help the less developed countries; neither will commodity stabilization schemes which guarantee price levels for raw materials; nor will low interest loans or free gifts. In the first place, it is unlikely that by stabilizing the export earnings of most Third World countries, this would automatically mean that they would be able to achieve large economic gains over a reasonable period of time. We may note in this connection that most developed countries already do allow unprocessed commodities from Third World countries to enter without being subject to a tariff charge. This indicates that many Third World countries have been doing as well as could be expected from international trade, but such factors as their high birth rate and general backwardness combined with a desire for manufactured goods from the West have left them struggling to make ends meet. Even if a less developed nation could increase its earnings from a particular commodity as a result of the new economic order, there always remains the possibility that income might fall substantially with a decrease in demand due to the use of a substitute product or changes in taste. There is little the developed countries could do for less developed countries facing either of these possibilities, except perhaps to extend further aid in the form of low interest loans, to help pay the interest on earlier loans contracted in the days of prosperity. It is a situation which would be all too familiar to those who specialize in the financial aspects of international affairs.

Thus, stabilization of income from commodities could easily prove to be of little benefit to all the less developed countries, except those whose income is derived from oil and natural gas or which have a relatively small population situated over extensive reserves of a valuable mineral. Neither would those less developed countries who managed to export manufactured goods in large quantities be in a much better position than those who relied primarily on the export of raw materials or semi-processed goods. They would always remain dependent on the whim of the trade cycle, and in periods of recession such as we are now passing through, they would almost certainly have to contend with the re-erection of tariff barriers or some other form of import control. The less developed country which embarked upon a highly successful manufacturing career may not even have to wait for a period of recession in world trade to experience a check to their penetration of the market of the more advanced countries, as is instanced by the reception given to manufactured goods from India (e.g., sewing machines) and Brazil (shoes) in Western Europe. There is no reason to believe that these same western governments would allow themselves to be bound by paper conventions, if they could allay industrial unrest by capitulating to protective sentiment which was aimed at manufactured goods from less developed nations.

As for technical aid and other special forms of assistance such as free food, this only helps to increase the dependency of Third World countries receiving such aid. This is especially true of free food, which can create a false sense of security and a high level of expectations which the receiving country will never be able to satisfy. For what happens when the donating country is itself low in food stocks and unable to send any abroad to those nations which cannot pay? It is far better for the less developed nations to buy what they can on the open market while trying to do the best they can to feed themselves from their own resources. A number of agricultural economists are coming to realize that this is far better than the artificial brotherhood that dictates the more agriculturally productive nations of the West make up for the inability of the nations of the Third World to feed themselves. With regards to the long-term goal of western style industrial development for the nations of the Third World, I can do no better than to quote the words of the editor of *The Ecologist* magazine: "Affluence for everybody is an impossible dream: the world simply does not contain sufficient resources, nor could it absorb the heat and other waste generated by the if not the only goal our industrial society gives us."[14] Instead of chasing an impossible dream, the future of Third World countries lies in the reaffirmation of the importance of agriculture and the traditional patterns of social cohesion.

It should be clear now that the economic success of western man has turned against him. A process of disintegration has begun which will be consummated in the arrival of a new age, an age which will be the negation of all that has led mankind to its present precarious state of existence. Most people who are deeply troubled by the present course of western society believe that reforms, controls and restrictions can save us from suffering the consequences of overdevelopment. These people are not yet fully attuned to the seriousness of our situation. While carefully thought out legislative proposals may help in the short term to alleviate certain problems of modern society, we must await more fundamental changes to turn around modern industrial society from its onward march to psychological and ecological dissolution. Listen to this summary of the desperate plight of mankind put forward by one of the few contemporary academics who is capable of looking above the mundane, day-to-day affairs of his society: "The ills of our time — the drab sprawling cities, the scum-choked lakes and rivers, the derelict and waste-strewn land, the incessant noise and poisoned atmosphere, the clogged motorways, the reeking dump heaps — are all interconnected with the life-force and life span of our spaceship Earth. They reveal a deep-seated flaw in modern society which is a threat to ourselves and the biosphere — the thin layer of earth, air and water on which man and his related eco-systems depend for survival. They are products of our so-called virtues — technology, mastery over nature, productivity, progress, prosperity and of the tyranny of the profit margin and the Gross National product."[15] These are the truths which modern man must face up to, and not until he has faced these truths will he begin to understand his future.

THE COMING AGE OF REACTION

Up until the present time, the conventional wisdom of our age has held that history shows no conceivable pattern that could be of use to us in helping to predict the future of mankind. In this chapter, I intend to challenge that view with certain views of my own. I believe, far from being simply a succession of random events or a chronicle of the follies and stupidities of the overly ambitious, history — especially that of the West — does have a clearly discernable pattern which links the past with the future.

Although the grand historic design is no longer in favor, this was not always the case. For example, Oswald Spengler's book *The Decline of the West* received critical acclaim when first published, on account of the breathtaking ideas brought forward by its author. Nowadays, Spengler's boldness is roundly criticized and he is accused of all manner of sins, including that he successfully capitalized on the mood of despair which afflicted the society of his time. Stewart Hughes, for instance, in his book, *Consciousness and Society,* is one of those who is most unfavorable to one of the great prophets of the decline of Western Civilization. Other writers have harped upon the inaccuracy of his predictions, especially in regards to the occurrence of future wars (e.g., Kahn and Wiener, 1967). What these writers fail to understand is that although Spengler's book might have been indefensible from an academic standpoint, it nevertheless represents something of far greater importance than the trivial outpourings of contemporary academics, namely, man's attempt to understand his past and future in a way to which he can easily relate. Besides Spengler's *The Decline of the West*, there have been other valiant attempts to impose some sort of order on the events that have been the most significant in shaping the destiny of mankind. Thus, Ibn Khaldun, the great Arab historian of the thirteen century, was the first person to attempt an economic interpretation of history in his *Prolegomena of World History*, part of which has been translated into English by the distinguished American oriental scholar Charles Issawi. Although Khaldun's book could hardly have been expected to have had the impact on his society as those of Marx, it is all the same rightly hailed as a remarkable achievement, considering the time at which it was written. Another writer who viewed history on a higher plane than merely as a casual sequence of events was Gambatistta Vico, who put forward a cyclic theory of history by which he conceived history in terms of, say, the rise and fall of civilizations or ruling ideals. Vico's cyclic theory of history was not particularly original, for the ancient Greeks had held similar ideas about history and nature in general. But the great importance of Vico in regard to the history of ideas is that he reintroduced the wisdom of the ancients in an updated form, thereby breaking with the linear view of history which saw it as a continuous unbroken progress towards moral and material excellence. But for the most part Vico was ignored by his contemporaries and the unilinear view of history as uninterrupted progress continued to become more influential as time wore on. Not until later did people come to reassess the inevitability of progress and Spengler's *Decline of the West* was a major part of this reassessment, accurately capturing the mood of the period in which it was published.

The above examples have of course not been the only attempts to produce a convincing philosophy of history. Every great modern historian has tried his hand at the task with varying degrees of success. One thinks of such men as Tarde, Mommsen,

Toynbee, Taine and Niebuhr and numerous others. But in considering philosophies of history two giants rank head and shoulders above all others. These are the theories of Hegel and Marx, to which we must now turn our attention. Both writers can be said to have raised the study of the philosophy of history to new heights. Therefore, anyone who attempts to put forward a theory of the historical development of western civilization must be familiar with the pioneering work of these two theorists. Both writers were products of the modern industrial age and the writings of both were goal oriented. That is to say, they both postulated a specific outcome of the historical tendencies present within their age. For Hegel, this goal was the full realization of human potential through the highest development of the state. For Marx, this goal was the displacement of capitalism by socialism and the demise of the all-powerful state.

Hegel's philosophy of history has never been popular, partly because he committed the mistake of depicting the Prussia of his day as the highest development of the state and even more so because it was superseded by the genius of Marx. But disregarding Hegel's praise of his native Prussia, his belief that history would be fulfilled through the highest development of the nation-state has to a large extent come to pass. In the eloquent and prophetic words of Alexis de Tocqueville, the state has become an "immense, protective power which is alone responsible for ensuring the enjoyment of its citizens and watching over their fate."[1] Because there were so many uncertainties regarding Hegel's philosophy of history, it has been the inspiration for the ideals of many writers of sharply differing viewpoint. Those who were the leading students of Hegel's philosophy in Germany shortly before he died were eventually to split into two groups, the right wing Hegelians and the left wing Hegelians. Because Karl Marx was among the latter group, they are of vastly greater importance than the former group, who tended to go along with the belief that authoritarian Prussia epitomized the nation-state at its highest level of development. Marx, on the other hand, was much more imaginative, and to use his own words, turned Hegel's idealism on its head to come up with the economic interpretation of history. Then again, T.H. Green and other late nineteenth century English Hegelians, such as Bosanquet, were moved to redefine classical liberalism in a way which was rather more sympathetic to the aspirations of the working class but left the basic structure of their society untouched. To be more specific, they took the position that it was the government's job to introduce social reforms in favor of the working class. Green in particular, with his ideal of positive freedoms, was a most consistent campaigner for the new liberalism.

Although Marxism has lost much of the force it once had, it is still by far the most widely accepted philosophy of history and is of course a conflict social theory par excellence. But the impossibility of bridging the gap between classical Marxist theory and present day reality is apparent to all, except perhaps a few lost souls who will not come to terms with the real world, insisting upon seeing it in terms of the original conflict model propounded by Marx. As I have indicated in the earlier chapters, Marxism was not the only view of the long-term development of modern industrial society to make its appearance in the nineteenth century, and neither was it the most accurate. This is one point on which I am in complete agreement with Professor Raymond Aron (see his discussion of Alexis de Tocqueville in *Main Currents in Sociological Thought*, Vol. I, p. 192). But the Marxian interpretation of history does provide us with a starting point from which to begin our reevaluation of the past and future of western civilization. In speaking about the coming of the new age, we must disregard the natural tendency to project trends of this age one hundred years hence — a favorite pastime of Herman Kahn and his associates. How these technological optimists can be so confident of a future based on highly advanced technology, when all signs point to an imminent breakdown, is quite beyond me. Even in the area which is supposedly under our control, i.e., technological progress, serious doubts have been voiced as to whether we would be able to cope with further advances in our technological capabilities.

For instance, Kahn and Wiener, in their book, *The Year 2000,* supply us with this striking piece of information: "In the final decades of this century, we shall have the technological and economic power to change the world radically, but probably not get very much ability to restrain our striving, let alone understand or control the results of the changes we will be making."[2] It would seem that even the most committed technological optimists are capable of voicing serious doubts regarding the direction presently being taken by western civilization. In his outstanding collection of essays published under the title of *Between Capitalism and Socialism*, Robert Heilbroner pinpoints the reason why our futurologists have so far only been able to draw up a sterile inhuman future for their fellow men. According to Heilbroner, "We have come more and more to define the future by those social changes whose causes we can identify and whose course we can, with some degree of certainty, project forward. The rise of population, the steady advance and diffusion of technical knowledge, the ubiquitous national commitment to economic growth and, to some degree, national planning, all give rise to tremendous hydraulic pressures that push society into the future in more or less foreseeable ways."[3] But we have already seen that this is not at all a very reassuring process for all indications are that modern industrial society is nearing its end. Thus, the visions of the techological determinists are hardly worth bothering about. They offer us nothing that gives us hope that man will one day be again able to live a life of human dimensions as his pre-industrial forebears once did, a life which does not oppress his senses and disfigure him into a caricature of his real self.

What we do have to look forward to is the transcendence of our age and the emergence of an age which will reconcile man with his environment and with the truths of human existence. We cannot expect our political leaders or our leading academics and opinion makers to understand all this, for their limited mental horizon does not allow them to see how such an event would give new opportunities to mankind's creative energy, as well as check our headlong rush to self-destruction. As I do not believe in nihilism, I cannot accept that our present age will not indeed be swept away to make room for a new civilization. An important clue to the social organization of the new age is given by Marx's philosophy of history, assuming it is carefully interpreted in the light of developments since the death of Marx. Now according to Marxist doctrine, the world's history could be divided into a very long period of Primitive Accumulation followed by three major periods, plus a fifth which was still to come: i.e., the Asiatic Mode of Production, Antiquity, Feudalism, Capitalism and Socialism. The first was never of great significance to Marxian philosophy. It was supposed to denote the special nature of oriental despotism, in which most of the society's wealth was concentrated in the hands of an all-powerful ruler who represented the state, instead of being diffused throughout the ruling class as a whole. According to Marx, this arrangement was desirable because of the special nature of the land which constantly required the undertaking of mammoth irrigation projects needing tens of thousands of laborers. Such projects could only be successfully undertaken by a centralized state. Ancient China would be a good example of the type of society Marx had in mind when using this designation. The fifth period is a theoretical construction destined never to be realized, rather than representing a bona fide age or civilization. This leaves us with Antiquity, Feudalism and Capitalism as the three major types of civilization known to western history. Both ancient and feudal societies were class societies in the truest sense of the word. Power was held by a wealthy nobility, rather than an all-powerful monarch or popularly elected assembly, and economic processes were carried out with the aim of reproducing the traditional lifestyle, rather than with the aim of raising the society's standard of living.

All this was to change with the advent of capitalism, which appears in recognizable form from the late fifteenth century onward to mark a distinct break with the past. The physical assets which a man possessed, whether land, tools, buildings, livestock or commodities become his capital and are given a specific monetary value to facilitate rational accounting. Thus the emphasis of the economic process is transferred from simply reproducing the traditional lifestyle to increasing one's original stock of capital (i.e., both money and physical assets). And so began the process of capital accumulation which was later to give rise to modern industry. Similarly, the hallmark of modern industry is that all of the processes involved in its operation are carried out with the objective of gaining more wealth for the producer (i.e., the owner of capital), and greater choice and abundance for the consumer. We may go further and say that the reproduction of capital is a fact of life in modern industrial society regardless of whether the nation's economy is centrally planned or is an unplanned market economy, only that in the latter case, it is enshrined in the profit motive, whereas in the former, the government determines production priorities rather than leaving this to market forces. It is this dedication to capital accumulation (i.e., the increasing of one's original stock of wealth) rather than antagonism between worker and employer or proletariat and bourgeoisie, which is central to the age of capitalism, for it has existed from the earliest days of capitalism (i.e., with the beginning of rational accounting) right up to the present time. On the other hand, conflict between proletariat and bourgeoisie did not exist until it was invented by Marx, and has now all but ceased to exist in both the real world and in the writings of modern Marxists. They now either ignore it or give it a very low priority, behind economic disequilibrium, environmental pollution, the decay of our cities and other problems of modern industrial society. Although Marx may have been wrong about the essence of capitalism and, hence, the coming of socialism, I believe that his three-age topology is valid. I also believe that the age which is destined to replace the present one will show characteristics of previous ages in the history of western civilization, that is, Antiquity and Feudalism but not Capitalism, for an age which depends on the continuous reproduction of capital (i.e., an indefinite increase in one's original stock of wealth) cannot also foster an ecologically stable society, and such a society will be one of the hallmarks of the new age. So we can expect the new age to show characteristics of only Antiquity and Feudalism. Thus, control of the land would once again revert to a special class — the nobility — and with it control of the affairs of society in general. We would naturally expect the exact nature of a society's social organization and productive techniques to differ according to such factors as its geographical situation, which affects soil and climate among other things, and its historic traditions. According to Marx, the leading economic principle of Antiquity was chattel slavery while that of Feudalism was serfdom. Both types of organization will be found in the new age. We may also note that the economic feature common to both Antiquity and Feudalism was that agriculture ranked far above both industry and commerce in regard to the wealth derived from it and the number of people engaged in it. This will be the same for the new age, but even more so. Therefore, the most important economic resource of the nation will not be its industry, its coal, oil, or natural gas or other buried minerals, but the fertility of its soil and the willingness of the people to work hard in order to provide for all their most essential needs. As was the case in the pre-capitalist ages, communal cooperation will be essential for the common people if they are to survive. No longer will they be able to beg for a living, or live off the charity of some benevolent institution or rely on the government to provide for their needs — put simply, those who did not work really would not eat.

Obviously, there could be no straightforward linear relationship (i.e., a smooth, steady development) between our present age and the future age whose characteristics I have just described. This is what makes the new age so special and the transition to it so different from the other major transitions of which we have historic records. For as far as we know, every previous age of pre-history as well as of written history has merged with very little difficulty with the age succeeding it (e.g., Stone Age to Iron Age; Antiquity to Feudalism), so much so that the dividing line between adjacent ages has not always been clear-cut. The later age gave full expression to several trends which could be detected near the end of the preceding age, perhaps with the benefit of hindsight in some cases. The new age to come, on the other hand, will not be a development of trends in the age that preceded it (i.e., our age). On the contrary, its arrival will bring about an almost instantaneous reversal of just about every significant trend associated with modern industrial society in its last stage of decline. Thus, the present age is one of equality, the new age will be one of aristocracy; the present age is dominated by urban life, the new age will be dominated by a rural lifestyle; the present age is one of mass production, the new age will be one of home-made goods and craftsmanship; the present age has given us the nuclear family, the new age will return to us the extended family; the present age idolizes science and technology, the new age will be either hostile or indifferent to these things. So the list could be continued almost endlessly. We may summarize this situation by saying that the new age will not be a continuation of the material and moral "progress" which has come to characterize this weak age of ours. Instead, its appearance will mark an abrupt break with the beliefs and lifestyle which were dominant in this age. It is for this reason that the coming age of reaction could just as well be termed an age in opposition, since unlike all previous ages it will be on all fronts diametrically opposed to the age which preceded it. The enormous significance of this point should not be lost to the more penetrating thinkers.

Such a spectacular turn of events requires an equally mighty mechanism to bring it about, and it is the nature of this mechanism that we must now proceed to discuss. There is only one mechanism that could bring about such large-scale changes in consciousness and the environment, right across the globe. This mechanism is cataclysmic evolution. One should not be alarmed by this prospect for it is the very process that has been responsible for the emergence of man from prehistoric darkness to civilization, while at the same time giving to him an environment in which he could make the fullest possible use of his abilities. We have of course been familiar with the idea of biological evolution for well over a hundred years. But our understanding of this phenomenon has been superficial and incomplete. Much of the early evidence for biological evolution brought forth by Darwin and his supporters came from paleontology, which often has to be studied in conjunction with geology to gain a clear idea of the evolutionary implication of fossil remains found in rocks. In fact, the study of fossils embedded in rocks was one of the important sources on which the early evolutionists, Darwin among them, drew for support. But this also meant that right from the start Darwin and others introduced certain misconceptions into the theory of evolution which have stayed with us ever since and are only now being questioned.

The most important of these misconceptions is the doctrine of uniformity which is associated with the name of Charles Lyell. According to this hypothesis, change in the earth's features occurs in a slow, gradual and continuous fashion over a long period of time. But as Webre and Liss explain in their book, *The Age of Cataclysm*, this view is no longer tenable, neither in regard to the earth sciences nor biological evolution. The difficulties connected with the uniformity principle as regard to biological evolution are particularly acute. It was Darwin's belief that species evolved through competition that results from the struggle for survival, and those organisms favored by advantageous characteristics would survive and breed at the expense of those members less so favored. By Darwin's reckoning, this process was gradual and took a very long time to produce a new species. Eventually, perhaps over several million years, a new species would move so far away in structure from the species from which it originated as to enter another class or even phylum. The regular manner in which the modified fossil remains of hard bodied animals were distributed throughout rock of several geological epochs appeared to substantiate the gradualist position. But all this shows is that appearance can be deceptive, for the gradualist approach to the process of evolution was soon found to be unsatisfactory in a number of ways.

For one thing, it did not explain how advantageous traits could be passed on from one generation to the next to produce a new species. Neither did it shed much light on the problems concerned with explaining the appearance or disappearance of certain species. Then again, there was the fact that the evolution process sometimes produced features which appeared to be a disadvantage to adaptation (such as the enormous size of the antlers of some extinct species of elks), but the animals nevertheless flourished for a long period of time without, it would seem, suffering ill effect. Nor did the arrival of Neo-Darwinism do much to improve the shaky logic of Darwin's views. The Neo-Darwinists felt they had discovered the key to evolution in the fact that the physical and physiological characteristics of an organism were transmitted to new generations by its genes, and these sometimes underwent mutations to produce deviations from normal which could be inherited, and so explain biological evolution. Unfortunately, the Neo-Darwinists ran into trouble on several fronts. In the first place, they were at a loss to find an agency which could bring about mutations leading to the appearance of new features in the offspring while leaving the parents relatively undamaged. Radiation, mustard gas and several other substances were found to be powerful mutation-inducing agents. But the concentration in which they appeared under natural conditions were hardly sufficient to induce significant inheritable variations, let alone cause a large segment of an interbreeding group to mutate into an altogether new species. Another disconcerting point in regards to Neo-Darwinism is that it was found that most mutations, whether experimentally induced or occurring naturally, were harmful to the offspring, rather than stimulating the emergence of favorable characteristics. But despite its numerous shortcomings, modern biological evolution theorists have more or less stuck with the belief that evolution is brought about as a result of the struggle for existence through the transmission of inheritable variations from one generation to the next.

Of course, the phrase "struggle for existence" is no longer in use. Instead, we have natural selection, implying that nature painlessly selects those most suited to survive. Thus, when the habitat of a species undergoes a change those members showing superior adaptation to the new environment will survive to reproduce at the expense of those showing a lower degree of adaptation. The modern evolution theorists have had some (rather limited) success with this approach, in that they have been able to explain changes in the coloration of certain insects (e.g., butterflies) due to the pressure of natural selection. But this is a long way from explaining how organisms which were formerly members of one species come to evolve, not only into a new species, but into an entirely different class. Surely this could not have come about through the inheritance of such minor variations as we have just described, and if the variations were larger (as they would have to be), what could have produced them without producing irreversible damage to most of the fauna and flora as well? Then again, the gap between members of one phylum and those of another in the animal kingdom is in no case bridged by intermediate organisms, something which would be expected if biological evolution had taken place as a gradual, orderly process. When challenged along these lines, the advocates of classical evolution theory have either claimed that all intermediate organisms ever produced were fragile and transitory and, therefore, no trace remains of them, or have dismissed the criticism as the ravings of fundamentalists and theological dogmatists who are incapable of persuasion by reasoned argument.

In an effort to further improve the standing of a theory of evolution based on the steady accumulation of inheritable variations, modern evolution theorists have introduced the concept of genetic drift. It postulates that genetical change is always taking place within an interbreeding group as a result of internal and external causes, not all of which are fully understood. But the result is to produce adaptable variations over many generations, corresponding with changes in the environment. But this is still not sufficient to explain how a supposedly random process of evolution could have led from the simplest unicellular organism to the most complex mammals without producing an infinite number of intermediate types which defy clear-cut classification. Nor does it help to explain the perplexing problems connected with man's evolution, especially the problem of how he came to develop his remarkable capacities which set him apart from all other animals. Furthermore, mankind's changes in lifestyle and ideals from one age to the next cannot be attributed to genetic mutations, though they clearly represent an evolutionary process. Neither can modern theories of evolution throw much light on the apparently inexplicable phenomenon of sudden extinction which has haunted biologists since the days of Darwin. For instance, how does one account for the disappearance of mammoths or the great reptiles of the Jurassic age? Other puzzling occurrences which do not tie in with a gradualist theory of evolution are the extraordinary finds of frozen animals and tropical flora in the Arctic and the presence of extinct mammals encased in ice in a state of almost perfect preservation in the upper reaches of the Northern hemisphere (e.g., Siberia and Alaska). Such finds are more compatible with sudden and abrupt environmental changes than a gradual and uniform process of change.

Thus, we have ample evidence to demonstrate that enormous changes in climate and topography have occurred in the past and are likely to occur again. It is surely not too far-fetched to postulate the possibility of the occurrence of equally sudden and far-reaching changes taking place in plant and animal life at about the same time. Such changes would bring about the elimination of some long established types and the appearance of entirely new forms of life through substantial modification of the genetic material of existing forms. The "how" and "why" of these occurrences are really no concern of ours, for in the final analysis we are dealing with matters outside the realm of causation, i.e., a straightforward cause and effect relationship simply does not apply. The existence of this class of events has long been known to and studied by mathematicians and astrophysicists, whilst the possibility of their existence can be said to have been anticipated over two hundred years ago by the Scottish philosopher David Hume, who stressed, among other things, that just because two events may always appear together in the same order, this is not proof that the first causes the second, but only a consistent observation which may be elevated to a principle for the sake of convenience. In fact, "proof," outside the realms of certain branches of mathematics, is impossible, for there is absolutely no guarantee that a phenomenon will always occur in the future as it has done in the past. Thus, causation is simply a convenient link between two or more events which regularly occur together, but it is not an infallible doctrine.

It is, therefore, not beyond the bounds of possibility for certain major events to take place in the future which today would not be given credence by any rational man. Indeed, it is almost a sure thing that such major events took place before man became "rational." Moreover, during the last 2000 years, civilized man's penchant for rationality has again and again been turned upside down by a whole gamut of inexplicable religious experiences. Many of these have profoundly affected the lives of individuals and in some cases entire societies. Nothing sums up the situation better than Hegel's famous dictum, "what is real is rational, what is rational is real." The importance to human affairs of sudden changes which cannot always be easily rationalized has been acknowledged by the emergence of a new discipline known as catastrophe mathematics. This is, in fact, a way of representing events which do not take place in a gradual, predictable and regular manner, but in leaps and bounds, by the use of four-dimensional graphs. The most important benefit of this approach is that one can gain some idea of the complexities of a particular process much better than by using regular three-dimensional methods of graphical analysis. We can therefore say in all truthfulness that irrational cataclysmic events are as much an integral part of our universe as are "rational" non-cataclysmic events.

For man, who has existed in his present physical form for at least half a million years, these great cataclysmic changes have meant corresponding changes in his way of life and mode of thought. Such changes must have taken place 11,000 years ago with the recession of the last ice age. This meant that land previously uninhabitable could now be inhabited, allowing many of the peoples of the Northern Hemisphere to disengage from their nomadic wanderings and live a more settled life. We can expect the great environmental changes which will come in the future to be associated with similarly profound change in the lifestyle and consciousness of man. One of the features of the new age which will result from the cataclysmic changes will be the highest possible adaption of man to his environment. The most complete expression of this high level of adaption — higher than in any previous age — will be displayed by the aristocratic elite which will provide leadership in the new age. Furthermore, because of its unique nature, the new age will have certain special qualities which could not have been found in any other age. Hence, the coming age of cataclysm does not mean the end of western civilization but the beginning of an entirely new chapter in its development. Mankind will be given a new lease on life, an opportunity to face new dangers and new hardships, and to recapture the glorious triumphs of his forefathers.

The concept of evolution had of course been applied to the study of society well before Charles Darwin published his *Origin of Species.* One of the first social theorists to do this was Adam Ferguson, a product of the Scottish Enlightenment. Ferguson's most important claim to fame was the distinction he made between rude and polished societies. Since polished societies represented a higher level of civilization than rude societies, it follows that all polished societies must have existed in a rude state at some time in their life history. He also pointed out that polished societies showed a greater degree of division of labor than did rude societies, and stressed how important this factor would be in regard to the long-term future social organization of industrial society. Later these themes were taken up with relish by the writers of the French Enlightenment, including Turgot, Holbach, Diderot, Helvetius and others. But none was more committed to progress through enlightenment than Condorcet who constructed a most elaborate theory of progress beginning with primitive man and ending with a fanciful sketch of fully enlightened man, who would be free of all irrational prejudice and have all his reasonable needs satisfied with a minimum of effort. Condorcet's unbounded optimism is all the more to be admired, for at the time he wrote his eulogy to progress he was a fugitive hiding in the attic of a friend's house and hunted by Danton's secret police. A simplistic linear interpretation of the relevance of the concept of evolution to the study of society continued to inspire social theory in the nineteenth century.

For instance, most of those who have studied sociology will be familiar with Comte's law of three stages. According to this viewpoint, human society evolved through three stages, namely the Theological, Metaphysical, and the Positive. The first stage is denoted by the fact that explanations of naturally occurring phenomena are given in terms of supernatural causes. At the second stage, phenomena are explained in terms of vital forces or inner essences, but not by divine intervention or in terms of the mood of the spirits. Finally we reach the Positive stage, at which time explanations are based on careful observations and calculations. Understandably, the simplistic application of evolution to the development of society came to dominate the thinking of nearly all nineteenth-century social anthropologists

(Sir Henry Maine was a significant exception). The writings of these social anthropologists were in turn to do much to reinforce the smug complacency of the shallow-minded Victorian middle class. But undoubtedly the most thorough and systematic sociologist to employ the idea of evolution as the central part of his theory was Herbert Spencer.

He was also one of the most able and dedicated supporters of *laissez faire* in the latter part of the nineteenth century. Spencer felt that the principle of survival of the fittest was not only the essence of biological evolution, but was also the key to the material and intellectual progress of human societies, a cause to which he devoted the greatest part of his life. No social theorist before or since has ever drawn such a close parallel between biological structures and processes, and human societies. In his search for a complete science of man, Spencer became a master of casuistry. But perhaps Spencer's greatest mistake was to believe that his society was in a process of steady evolution towards a higher type of social organization, when in fact it was in a process of cultural and spiritual decline. This fact was obscured then (and continues to be so now) by modern society's enormous gains in material productivity and technological efficiency. All major critics of Spencer's system have sighted the demise of *laissez faire* as the most important factor which has made his writings irrelevant to the affairs of contemporary western man. This criticism is true as far as it goes, but as I have indicated above, there are deeper reasons why Spencer's ideas have become an historical anachronism rather than a body of vital social theory — something which started to happen even before he died.

For one thing, Spencer was, unlike say Marx or Rousseau, very much a child of his time, believing that the only possible future for western man was a projection of the profit-seeking mentality of Victorian England, with freedom of opportunity for all to make use of their talent in the most remunerative manner — a situation not very different from the present state of affairs in the U.S.A. But as the post-industrial society theorists of today are destined to find out, simple projection rarely, if ever, makes good qualitative social theory. Yet when presented in a quantitative manner, they may be useful for other purposes, such as aiding predictions for the planning needs of business and government. Another indication of Spencer's inability to go beyond the optimism of his age was his belief that although conflict and military conquest were important in shaping a society in its early stages, war had outlived its usefulness in this respect. Instead, the conflict inherent in the economic system of the day would be sufficient to provide the necessary driving force for the future development of western society — how wrong he turned out to be. For there can be no substitute for war, no other way to rebuild and discipline a shattered society; sublimation of the warrior impulse is futile.

When one uses the concept of evolution as the central part of a comprehensive social theory one must use it in a way which (to quote Max Weber) is "value free." This is something which Spencer and all his predecessors and contemporaries failed to do. By this I mean that the social theorist should take his cue from nature, i.e., nature as understood by the Marquis de Sade rather than by Rousseau or the Romantic Movement. Nature knows nothing about moral progress, nor does it guarantee indefinite material progress. Growth and decay, supremacy of the strong over the weak, a period of calm followed by one of calamity, these are the invariables of nature, and these must be given their due weight in any body of ideas which attempts to apply the concept of evolution to the development of human society, in a manner which is anything other than banal. Thus, one must avoid looking at one's own age as if it is some kind of high water mark in the ascent of man. Instead, he who takes the truly evolutionist approach to the study of society must look beyond his own age, as Marx attempted to do (with rather mixed results), and recognize the importance of cataclysmic change. If he is not capable of doing this — as was the case with Spencer, Comte and many others — then his ideas will become commonplace not long after they first see the light of day.

Contrary to what most social theorists in the past appeared to have believed, social progress and social evolution are two entirely different things. The first is value oriented, the second is value free. For western man, the idea of social progress has meant such things as greater sensitivity to the needs of the underprivileged, equal justice under the law, advance in science and technology, greater productivity and democratic political institutions. Social evolution on the other hand may give rise to these things, as it has done in the past, or may sweep them all away and replace them with a new set of values, as it will do in the future. In other words, social evolution is the law of the universe, whereas social progress is the law of modern industrial society. One is permanent, the other is ephemeral. It seems that neither Spencer (the supreme evolutionist), nor his followers realized that evolution takes place as a series of gigantic convulsions, rather than in small incremental steps. Nor did they understand that no society simply changes into another type of society by the deliberate application of reason, but explodes into another society as a result of a sudden growth in consciousness, often accompanied by environmental changes. Further, no society spends its time evolving into another type of society. This is not necessary. But in most cases, we would expect the new society to be better adapted to its environment in comparison with the adaption displayed by the society from which it emerged. Those societies from the old age which could not adjust to the new conditions brought about by the cataclysmic changes would simply become extinct.

It seems reasonable to assume, therefore, that a newly emergent society will reach a high point in its adaption (within a particular environmental era) at which it may remain for some considerable period of time, spreading out geographically and occupying a wide range of terrains. But eventually a society will enter a period of declining adaption corresponding with environmental changes which may be apparent or which may not yet have made an appearance. Man is unique among the animals, in that his own activity greatly contributes to decreasing his adaption. Significant signs of a society's declining adaption will probably not appear until it is very close to the end of its existence. Persistent population imbalance appears to be a universal sign that a society is no longer enjoying the high level of adaption it once did and is nearing its end. We may note in this connection the generally low or declining birth rates that prevail in nearly all nations of the northern hemisphere (also in Australia and New Zealand) even though these nations could quite easily support larger populations than they now have. True, this is not so for the countries of the Third World, most of which are still experiencing rapid population growth. But this is understandable, bearing in mind that these countries are going to bear the brunt of the difficult agricultural conditions which will characterize the new age. Therefore these countries understandably have very high birthrates and several of them can be said to be overpopulated in regard to the amount of fertile land available for farming. The arrival of the new age will tend once more to bring population into balance with the availability of fertile land in both the northern and the southern nations of the globe.

I cannot stress too strongly that man is an integral part of nature, just as are all other living organisms. Thus, one would expect as a matter of course that man would also experience certain changes in his perceptions of reality to help him cope effectively with the conditions of the new age which will be so very different from what he had been used to. Nature does not guarantee mankind a carefree existence. It provides the resources and circumstances and man must do the rest to guarantee, not merely survival, but a flourishing civilization — a task which has been accomplished under the most adverse conditions. One need only remember that the pontine marshes on the outskirts of ancient Rome were a breeding place for malaria-carrying mosquitos, but still nothing could stop this irrepressible city-state from going on to gain mastery of the ancient world. Life will be hard in the new age, but it will only be "primitive" in those areas in which a clearly defined aristocratic class does not arise.

In the past, great cataclysms, i.e., of continental proportions, have led eventually to the emergence of a new era of stability and ecological balance. If this were not so, highly complex and vulnerable animals, as are all of the higher vertebrates, could not have survived and increased in number as they have done over the last million years or so. During this period, ice ages have come and gone, climates have changed and flora and fauna have become extinct or developed into higher types. The period subsequent to the last great cataclysm also provided the conditions for a great abundance of plant and animal life within the context of a balanced environmental *milieu.* Unfortunately, the increasing impact of man's activity on his environment has increasingly contributed to the serious signs of ecological imbalance which we can see all around us. One of the effects of the coming period of cataclysm will be to reestablish ecological equilibrium, which has been so seriously disrupted by the cumulative activities of modern industrial society.

To understand how the coming period of cataclysmic change will improve man's adaption to his environment, one must understand what it means for a society to be well adapted. Throughout the course of recorded history, mankind has shown various levels of adaption, enough that is, to give us a fair idea of the features that we would expect to find in a well adapted society, which exists in a state of ecological equilibrium with its surroundings. One of the first things to note is that a well adapted society must give the impression of timelessness, almost as if it could exist forever, barring an act of God. The people go about their affairs in an unhurried manner; the ruling class does not entertain grandiose visions of ruling the world. Neither is there a strong desire to excel in any intellectual pursuit, except the art of war, which occupies the highest place in its scheme of things. A well adapted society is, in fact, almost devoid of all ambition except the ambition to maintain its territorial integrity and traditions. Even the smallest changes in such a society take place over many generations and larger changes may never take place until it has reached its end.

Thus, although ancient Greece and Rome were ecologically balanced societies, they were also societies of destiny. The destiny of ancient Greece (as represented primarily by Athens) was to take man almost to his limits of theoretical speculation and artistic creativity. The citizens of Athens always aimed for excellence in everything they did whether it was politics, rhetoric, military affairs, prose or poetry, drama or philosophy. They were not afraid to innovate, and as a result peace was often disturbed by conflicting opinions. This is a situation which extended also to the practice of religion, with various cults in conflict with one another. Apart from the perfection of a rational system of jurisprudence which was later to be very influential in the formation of the legal system of several Western European countries, ancient Rome had another special destiny. This was to expand its military power to encompass a great empire. In the process, it brought territorial boundaries to regions where they had been lacking and unified previously warring tribes into one nationality. As we indicated above, a society with a special destiny cannot at the same time be a well adapted society in comparison with a society which does not have a special destiny. The former will undergo change at a far more rapid rate than the latter and effort to improve upon previous accomplishments is always required of its members. Furthermore, such a society is highly vulnerable to internal turmoil and breakdown.

This is why, of the ancient societies, the early oriental ones can be said to have shown better adaption to their environment than the later societies of the West such as Greece and Rome. True, for the most part these oriental societies were almost culturally static, but this is the essence of adaption and as such should not be frowned upon. Some of these oriental societies, such as Babylonia and Assyria, were eventually to disappear without a trace, whereas others such as Egypt and Persia, have survived to see most of their original culture make way to accommodate the culture of successive waves of conquerors. Some remained almost culturally unchanged right down to the modern era, e.g., India and China. It was under Feudalism that the western world was to experience its highest level of adaption so far. This was a type of society just as confident of its position in the universe and almost as timeless as the oriental societies of the ancient world. For most of its existence, the people of the feudal world had no particular goal, except to live in the manner of their forebears. Neither did they show much interest in the advancement of art, science or literature. But it was a society of greater internal flexibility than the oriental societies of ancient times. The king was always considered as first among equals and not as a god among men, as was the custom in oriental civilizations. The result was a vigorous society which was both submissive and yet aggressive, a society very far from the slave societies of, say, ancient Egypt or Persia.

Having completed our short survey of what constitutes a well adapted civilization, we can return to our discussion of those features we will expect to find in the well adapted societies of the new age. To begin with, man is best adapted to his environment when he does not need to rely on the state to provide for his material welfare in any way whatsoever except in times of an extreme national emergency such as drought, famine or threat of external aggression. Other than this, the common people and all other members of the society should be able to fend for themselves, i.e., assuming normal conditions. Few have put this point better than Tom Paine in his *Rights of Man*, where he tells us: "The more perfect civilization is the less occasion has it for Government." I am not saying that Paine actually understood the essentials of civilization, for in common with all other egalitarian thinkers, it would have been impossible for him to do so. But this fact does not invalidate the accuracy of the statement I have just quoted. In this connection, we may note once more that the term civilization implies a highly developed culture; in other words, the existence of a specific group or groups which are free to pursue activities other than providing for their own sustenance and that of their family. This point was charmingly illustrated for early industrial society by Bernard de Mandeville in his "Fable of the Bees." As for the process of adaption within human societies, it is also greatly aided if no more is demanded of the understanding of the common people than is compatible with the limitations of their mental horizons. Finally, equilibrium between town and country is also essential for a well adapted civilization. This means that many more people must live in the countryside than live in towns, and further, that for any sovereign territory there should not be many large towns (none at all if the territory is small), since large towns and cities encourage decadence and are breeding grounds for crime, poverty, disease, dilapidation and shiftlessness.

Now compare the above requirements for a highly adapted civilized society with conditions which prevail today and one will see how ill adapted is modern industrial society to the needs of an ecologically well balanced civilization. The state has grown to such enormous proportions that no contemporary western nation could function for more than a day, without the onset of paralysis and eventually total breakdown, if the government was suddenly to stop functioning. Many people can barely cook their own food, let alone grow it, and the art of making their own clothes is unknown to the vast majority of men and women in our culture. No matter whether we stayed at home instead of working or worked a forty hour week, most of our wants are automatically satisfied by the system and we hardly need to lift a finger. This is life in a fool's paradise, and yet many people have the nerve to talk about the need for more social reforms to produce a truly "just society" — the idea is ludicrous. Then again we tax the mental powers of the ordinary people by obliging them to participate in affairs which they barely understand and can do little to influence one way or the other. This situation can only lead in the end to confusion and cynicism among both the people and their leaders. If this were not enough, we also live in an age in which the imbalance between town and countryside has become chronic. Only some three to four percent of the peoples in Western Europe and North America earn their living from the soil, the rest live in a combination of small towns and large cities. The result is that the quality of life in all these cities and many of the towns has deteriorated well beyond the point of no return, i.e., they simply cannot be reorganized to provide a healthy living environment.

Paul and Anne Ehrlich paint a vivid picture of this situation when they tell us that: "The deterioration of the environment, both physically and aesthetically, is most apparent in our cities." They proceed to explain that "The dehumanizing effects of life in the slums and ghettoes particularly where there is little hope for improving conditions, have often been cited as contributing causes of urban rioting and disturbances. Crime rates usually reach their zenith in these neighborhoods. Such symptoms of general psychological maladjustment suggest that modern cities provide a less than ideal environment for human beings. There seems to be abundant evidence that traditional cultural patterns break down in cities, and also that the high number of contacts with individuals not part of one's circle of regular social acquaintances may lead to mental disturbances." Our intrepid authors conclude with an ominous warning: "The possibility that our cities could eventually deteriorate to the point of causing complete social breakdown is something to consider."[4] I have quoted these two authors at length because this is the clearest and most forceful statement known to me of the fact that late twentieth-century man is becoming progressively unadapted to modern city life, and we may add, to modern industrial society in general, despite his enormous technological and scientific progress. There is no doubt in my mind that this process of increasing maladaption will end in the social breakdown of modern industrial society at the same time as the beginning of the cataclysmic changes in the environment which will be experienced throughout the entire globe. From the subsequent period of chaos will emerge a restructured environment and better adapted societies. Man will interact with his new environment with greater feeling than is now possible. He will have a real love for the soil and rural life just as his ancestors once did. The hustle and bustle of modern industrial society will no longer be for him. He will not even be aware of the absence of modern conveniences, electrical appliances and all other things which we moderns in our ignorance consider to be the very essence of civilized life.

The only time when a succeeding age has distanced itself from a preceding age with anything approaching the force of the coming transcendence, was the displacement of feudalism by the spirit of the Renaissance. The Renaissance brought forth a number of men of extraordinary genius, which alone makes it a period of almost unmatched creativity in just about every major field of human endeavor. But what we are mainly concerned with here is the way in which the mental horizons of Renaissance men were altered by the momentous events of this period. For the purpose of comparison with the coming age of reaction, we can divide the mental impact of the Renaissance into three aspects, the spiritual, material and spatial — the same three categories that could be used to distinguish the coming age from the present age. The spiritual realignment that took place during the Renaissance era led directly to the Reformation and the breakdown of the ecumenical nature of religious authority, a blow from which it has never recovered. Protestantism, to which the reformation gave birth, was a most subversive movement, in that it tended to belittle the importance of religious guidance while also further subordinating the world of the sacerdotal to that of the secular. It was also a central belief of protestant doctrine that a true believer did not need an intermediary to interpret the bible to him. The result of all these innovations is to be seen today in the nations of Western Europe and North America. Commercialism and freedom of choice have triumphed totally over the teachings of the Christian church, including those parts of it which it is essential for a well constituted society to observe. Thus we now have abortion on demand, divorce on demand, legalization of homosexual acts, and commercial activity seven days a week. The new age will not be Christian in an institutional sense, but it will have a definite spiritual quality. This is to say that all those life preserving and life furthering ideals of pristine Christianity which sophisticated modern man in his foolishness has turned his back on, will become an integral part of the way of life of men of the new age.

A brief review of the more important of these values will give one some idea of the "spiritual" context of the new age. Most of these values were part of the teachings of the Roman Catholic Church at its height of influence, power and prestige. They include a belief in the necessity of hierarchy as essential to a well ordered society. This belief was reflected not only in the structure of the Catholic Church but also in the political theory of the period, most of which was written by the Church fathers and a number of able but lesser clerics. Closely associated with this belief in the need for hierarchy was the belief that the common man should accept his fate with good grace whatever it may be. In other words, he who is born a peasant should not aspire to be a lord, an attitude of mind which will likewise be displayed by the common people in the new age. Another important aspect of medieval Christendom which deserves comment is the almost paternalistic attitude towards authority. Thus everyone knows that the word "Pope" is derived from the Latin word for father, and the Pope in Rome was indeed looked upon as the spiritual father of all Christian peoples. Also a monarch, be he emperor, king or lesser prince, was always looked upon as the secular father of his people chosen by God to reign over them. Hand in hand with this paternalist view of sacerdotal and secular authority went naturally enough the belief that parents should exercise strict control over their children. It is therefore ironic that today in this age of lukewarm faith and religious skepticism, we are seeing the results of the breakdown of parental control, i.e., child prostitution, vandalism and other serious examples of juvenile delinquency.

Belief in the sanctity of the family and strong opposition to divorce were also worthy ideals of the Catholic Church which will have renewed vigor in the new age. Thus, at least one Holy Roman emperor (a direct descendant of Charlemagne) was forced to change his mind about divorcing his wife after the move was opposed by the reigning Pope. Neither could the French king Philip Augustus obtain a divorce from his Danish born wife, while Henry VIII had to make himself head of the English church before he could obtain his much desired divorce from Catherine of Aragon. Together with belief in the sanctity of marriage has always gone intense opposition to abortion and restraint on human fertility; these principles will also be part of the spiritual culture of the new age. Another commendable stand of the Catholic Church has been its opposition to suicide and its low opinion of those feeble enough to take their own life. Its traditional opposition to homosexuality is also to be praised and will live on in the new age. The Catholic Church's traditional view on the status of women deserves to be applauded by the advocates of reaction, for it is a viewpoint which will once again find practical expression in the folkways of the new age. The ecumenical character of the Catholic Church at its zenith will be recaptured in the acceptance of the brotherhood of all members of the ruling class regardless of nationality. A place will also be found for the narrow minded attitudes which produced the dogmatic scholasticism of the Mother Church, in that the new age will be opposed to the progress of science and technology, as well as to freedom of thought, which produces ideas that disturb the status quo.

Not that the ruling class of the new age will have much need to suppress subversive ideas, for there will be very few of these. With the arrival of man's complete adaption to his environment, there will be no longer any need to strive for new interpretations of reality which would challenge the status quo. Intellectually, the mind of western man will at last be at rest; abstract theorizing and scientific investigations will no longer be of interest to him. As for those who believe a society lacking deep interest in science and technology would be an inferior civilization, they do well to remember the dictum that an unsubdued thirst for knowledge can lead to barbarism just as can extreme hatred of knowledge. This is especially so in an age such as ours when, unlike the ancients who were content with theoretical speculation, we have an unstoppable urge to apply our knowledge, regardless of possible consequences. One need only consider the development of atomic weapons with their awful destructive power, tests done in connection with biological warfare, and the development of defoliant agents powerful enough to destroy soil fertility for several years or longer. This may be the barbarism of the super technological state, rather than that of the primitive tribe, but it is barbarism nevertheless — a species of barbarism quite incompatible with the full development of the human spirit.

The material aspect of the Renaissance was its most visible achievement. Sculpture and painting were given a new lease on life, science and technology were viewed with renewed interest and commerce flourished (especially in the Mediterranean area) as never before. Faltering attempts were made to put science to work for man. The printing press was one of the most important inventions of this period and mechanical contrivances of lesser importance were also produced for the first time. Western man had broken away from the security of the middle ages with its well ordered social structure, to embark upon a search for a new world view. We, the heirs of the Renaissance, are nearing the end of this search. It is a search that will not find its conclusion in words, but in a new way of life. It is a way of life, we may add, that will exhibit many marked similarities to the lifestyle of the middle ages upon which the men of the Renaissance had turned their backs with such fanfare. In the new age all significant activities will be carried out in such a way as to call for the greatest possible expenditure of human labor power. This will mean that, for the most part, men will work without the assistance of machines. The artifices of simple technology will be sufficient to provide for man's essential needs. Commerce (in those places where it exists) will once again occupy its former subordinate position to agriculture as a means to an end and not an end in itself. Therefore, whatever commerce and industry may reappear in the new age will serve the social structure, but will never again be the dominant part of it.

The importance of the spatial changes which took place during the Renaissance are also of great relevance as indicators (i.e., by deduction) of the changes which will take place in the new age. Thus, the Renaissance was a period of great exploration; the discovery of the Americas by Columbus was, of course, by far the greatest achievement of western man's newly found desire to explore his surroundings with more courage than had been a feature of the middle ages. But there were other noteworthy manifestations of this spirit, including the great seafaring exploits of the Portuguese navigators who explored the coast of West Africa, sailed around the Cape of Good Hope to India and the spice islands and went on to discover Brazil, which was later colonized by that nation. It was during this period also that a circumnavigation of the globe was carried out for the first time by the Spanish explorer Ferdinand Magellan and his associates. The search for the Northwest Passage led to the discovery of Newfoundland and the establishment of commercial relations between Elizabethan England and Imperial Russia. All in all, this was a most expansive period, which called for a reorientation of western man's spatial horizons to encompass the new geographical discoveries and new contacts with foreign cultures, which were made with unbelievable regularity throughout much of this period.

The new age will be quite the opposite. The spatial outlook of the common people will be very limited and that of the ruling class only a little less so, just as was the case in the middle ages. The enterprising spirits of the new age will have no interest in exploring the world about them except for the purpose of conquest and colonization, once their homeland has become overcrowded, placing undue pressure on the availability of fertile land. Commercial contacts between different regions of the globe will be greatly reduced, for the social and economic circumstances of the new age will be unconducive to a high volume of international trade. And furthermore, most nations will be able to satisfy their essential needs with a minimum of foreign trade. Returning to the spatial reorientation that was brought about by the Renaissance, there is another factor which has some relevance to the future. This is that, although the spatial conceptions of Renaissance men were expanded in global terms, the towns also began to grow at the expense of the countryside, thereby increasing the numbers of those concentrated into a limited area and separated from the soil. We can expect exactly the reverse situation to appear in the new age, for although, geographically speaking, the spatial conception of the people will narrow so that they become inward looking, they will also have an overpowering urge to be surrounded by far more open space than would be possible if they lived in towns and cities. Thus, the population will be uniformly distributed, i.e., spread evenly throughout all parts of the nation and not thickly concentrated in a very limited area and thinly scattered in all other areas, as is now the case.

At this point, I want to remind the reader that when we speak about the transcendence of this age and the coming of a new age, we must include the People's Democracies of Eastern Europe along with the welfare capitalist nations of the West. The former countries have no more special claim to an indefinite existence than do the latter. One may add in this connection that both industrialized communist countries and industrialized non-communist countries spend roughly the same on social welfare programs. Furthermore, recent studies have indicated that the amount so spent has nothing to do with the countries' official ideology, but a whole lot to do with their economic prosperity (Harold Wilensky 1975). This is the main reason why developed countries, regardless of their ideology, are able to spend comparable amounts (as a percentage of their total budget) on social welfare, whereas less developed countries are unable to do as well, regardless of whether or not they are committed to socialism. We may also note that several non-communist countries of Western Europe spend proportionately more on social welfare than their East European counterparts, and that spending in other areas, such as education, is also roughly comparable for industrially developed nations regardless of official ideology (H. Wilensky: *The Welfare State and Equality*). The implications of this state of affairs should be quite clear. The most important one is that the industrially advanced nations, whatever their ideological complexion, have broadly similar aims with regards to public expenditure, and all are able to fulfill these aims much better than the economically less developed nations of the Third World.

Among the most important traits of modern industrial society are the commitment to economic growth, belief in the universal validity of causation, belief in the supremacy of science and technology and a commitment to increasing the material welfare of the people. These are the ideals which dominate both the developed countries and the less developed countries; these are the ideals which will be swept away by the arrival of the new age. For want of a better term, we may call this outlook the bourgeois world view since it originated in the West, and is still given its highest expression in Western Europe and North America. What I am saying is that the hegemony of the bourgeois world view will be broken by a new conception of reality. The dramatic quality which we would expect of such an event (i.e., the sudden transfer of hegemony from one world view to another) is brilliantly captured by Gwyn Williams as he describes to us Antonio Gramsci's concept of Egemonia. Williams explains that: "by hegemony Gramsci means a socio-political situation, in his terminology of a 'moment,' in which the philosophy and practice of a society fuse or are in equilibrium; an order in which a certain way of life and thought is dominant, in which one concept of reality is diffused throughout society in all its institutional and private manifestations, informing with its spirit all social relations, particularly in their intellectual and moral connotations."[5] It is such a "moment" that those who have lost respect for this age will be waiting for. Such a moment will come, such a moment must come, if mankind is to have a future.

THE RETURN OF CLASS RULE

One of the most regrettable aspects of the social structure of our age is that there is no clearly defined group of people who are respected by the vast majority of their fellows — who give to society its stability and serve as a counterweight to trends which could prove to be very disruptive, if allowed to proceed unchecked. In fact, no western nation has any longer a clearly defined ruling class from which the bulk of its administrators and statesmen could be drawn, a class whose members also possess an independent economic base. The younger western countries such as Australia, Canada and the U.S.A., have never possessed a clearly defined (i.e., traditional) ruling class, whereas the former ruling class of the Western European nations has long since faded out of existence. Among recent social theorists, only Joseph Schumpeter seems to have given consideration to the demise of traditional leadership. In his book *Socialism, Capitalism and Democracy,* Schumpeter comments on the decline in the quality of leadership in western society with the rise of mass democracy. This is a development which he believed would eventually cause all western societies to become susceptible to the socialist solution. To his credit, Schumpeter proposes the need for a recognized pool of talent — a social strata as he referred to it — that takes to politics as a matter of course and from which the leaders of the country can be drawn in order to maintain excellence. The novelty of this bold proposal has remained unappreciated, not surprisingly, in an age which is more concerned with the destruction of excellence rather than with its maintenance. The lack of a universally acknowledged ruling class is just one more nail in the coffin of modern industrial society.

In the days of aristocracy, it was the ruling class which made history, which directed the affairs of the nation and took personal command of its soldiery. Today, it is machines which make history. Troops are carried to the front by railway or armored personnel carriers; they are supported on the ground by tanks and field guns and in the air by bombers and jet fighters. Mechanized warfare has done as much as any other factor to rob man of his manhood. A ruling class is a warrior class above all else. Nothing gives its members greater pleasure than leading their followers into battle. Those who hanker after military glory in today's industrial society will attend a military academy to learn the science of war. But the very fact that the modern warrior must go to school to learn how to fight and how to lead, diminishes him in comparison with the ruling class of aristocratic societies to whom war was second nature. Nor is it an exaggeration to say that the modern soldier learns more about the peaceful application of his skills than he does about war. This fact is now looked upon as a plus by military recruiters, for regular warfare has become an anachronism in the nuclear age. Therefore, inducements like the gaining of experience in civil engineering, or training in electronics or picking up one of the many university scholarships offered to those of appropriate ability, must be stressed by the recruiters rather than the opportunity for military glory — for in truth this is no more.

While in training, the professional soldier is not taught to lead, but to be subservient to the will of his political masters, who in turn are subject to the whim and caprice of the electorate. Therefore, unlike the warrior aristocrat, the professional soldier, even though he may have the rank of five star general (or its equivalent) is not an autonomous individual, but must take his orders from the nation's democratically elected political leaders, who may be totally ignorant of military strategy. The sharp division between the political and military sphere limits the range of competence of those who compose the nation's political leadership as well as of those who compose its military leadership. For great generals rarely seem to make good politicians and great politicians have never made good generals (at least not in modern times). Be this as it may, the politicians have always had the upper hand, as would be expected in an economically complex and highly bureaucratized society such as our own. Georges Clemenceau's famous saying, that war was too important to be left to the generals, seems to aptly sum up the attitude of politicians to the military, and what's more, the military of western nations has generally accepted their subordinate position with little protest. When on those rare occasions (in western society) that the military have taken power they have appeared to be apprehensive and inept and usually end up by giving power back to civilian politicians and returning to their barracks, humbled and dejected. Perhaps this clear-cut division between political and military leadership is the only way in which a modern industrial society could work. But it certainly will not be the way in which the aristocratic societies of the future will work. Thus, although the future of western man is filled with many imponderables, there is one thing we can be sure of: the leaders of the new age will certainly not be supplied from among the ranks of today's military establishment. Not only is today's officer class totally unsuited by outlook and temperament to assume a commanding position in the new age, but also, at one stroke, the highly technical military organization and weaponry of today will become forever redundant.

Modern political leadership backed up by the awesome power of modern weaponry is no match for a warrior class in regards to ensuring social cohesion. Modern man has been taught to give high allegiance to the state as represented by its legitimately appointed political leaders. But these leaders have no independent standing among the people and, therefore, can expect to be brushed aside upon the arrival of the new age. The truth of the matter is that the modern state rests on very insecure foundations. Its guiding ethos embodies a number of false conceptions regarding the nature of man, his needs, and his place in the universe. Only a ruling class rooted in the soil could intuitively understand these things. When an aristocracy is in charge, the people know that it will act with ruthless vigor to crush all aberrant trends. Neither are the people intimidated by this fact, but tend on the contrary to feel reassured that there is someone around to keep them on the straight and narrow path of righteousness. They know also that the aristocrats are men of conviction who will seldom if ever change their opinion, and that those of noble blood will deal firmly with any commoner who steps out of line. Aristocrats have no scruples about the use of force to accomplish their will and are not subject to introspection, believing that they have been chosen by a higher power than mortal man to control the affairs of their fellow men.

A common man in an aristocratic society would never expect a noble to show weakness; neither could an aristocrat afford to show weakness, for the cohesion of his society would soon break down. Once the aristocrat becomes hesitant and indecisive, the common people also begin to have doubts about their way of life and customs. The aristocrats know all this, they are aware of the dangers to their ascendancy which come, not so much from excessive zeal in asserting their prerogatives, but more from a consistent failure to do so. Only an aristocracy is able to get the best out of the people under the most adverse circumstances — to demand large sacrifices from the people without being expected to make an equal sacrifice. In short, a well constituted aristocracy will be able to guarantee the continuation of western civilization. Only an aristocratic leadership would have the courage to turn its back on the cries of the suffering millions in other nations. Why should the ruling class of one nation attempt to care for the welfare of the people of another nation out of the goodness of its heart? Such a policy could only end in the ruin of both the receiver and the giver. Misplaced sentiment which is such a pronounced feature of our own age, will have no place in the new age — the ruling elite will see to that.

So far aristocratic leadership has generally been seen at its very best in regards to dealing with foreign affairs. This fact should not surprise us, for in the first place only an aristocratic ruling class could be absolutely certain of what is in the best interest of the nation, since this will coincide exactly with what is in its best interest as a class. Also, members of the ruling aristocracy can far better understand the complexities and long-term ramifications of foreign policy matters than the common people could ever hope to do. In this connection, we may note that many contemporary studies show that even the supposedly educated voters of the advanced industrial society understand little about the intricacies of foreign policy and care even less. Then again, once a decision has been made, whether it is to declare all out war or make a last ditch stand, an aristocratic leadership can be depended upon to undertake with vigor the actions called for. Should their early efforts meet with little success, they will keep trying until they have won a worthy victory or gone down to an honorable defeat. A democracy could not be relied upon to show such consistency, because of the undue influence of ordinary people who individually have little status but who collectively have a large voice. Their active resistance or disaffection could set at nought the best designs of a well qualified but democratically elected leadership — a rarity which does sometimes occur.

The history of two of the world's most celebrated aristocratic republics, Rome and Venice, shows how this type of government could be energetic and decisive in dealing with foreign affairs involving, say, military threat, diplomatic rebuff, or other threat to their sovereignty. Rome showed these qualities in the Punic Wars, in clearing the Mediterranean of infestation by pirates and in its dealings with the disrespectful Tarentines, while Venice showed them in dealing with the encroachment of the Turks and in its argument with Pope Paul V. The two examples given for Venice are particularly instructive of what one would expect of a self-confident aristocratic leadership jealous of its prerogatives, the first because of the enormously disproportionate differences in size and resources between the two antagonists, which turned heavily in favor of the Ottoman Empire; the second because, although Venice was a Catholic state and part of Catholic Italy, it stood up to the Pontiff of the day with resolute firmness rather than buckle under to his unreasonable demands — even though many ordinary citizens had their reservations about the wisdom of this course of action.

Some critics of aristocratic leadership may contend that this type of government has been far from successful on the domestic front and has often shown itself to be either vacillating or inflexible when dealing with legitimate demands for internal reform. Those who feel this way do not really understand the nature of aristocracy. For by its very nature, this type of government is the essence of traditional authority; it is the antithesis of social progress. It has almost no interest in promoting innovation or in bettering the lot of the majority, but only in the indefinite maintenance of the status quo. Nor must we forget that by no means all aristocracies have been resented by those who have had to live under them. For instance, historians tell us that the declaration made in the name of Napoleon Bonaparte to the citizens of Venice telling them that the Aristocracy which had ruled them for some eight hundred years without break was now dissolved, met with a great deal of public protest. By this we may reasonably conclude that Venetians were far from happy about gaining freedom from aristocratic rule. As we noted earlier, the presence of an all-powerful aristocratic ruling class provides a healthy restraining influence on the society, a fact that modern man should be easily able to appreciate. In fact, I am willing to predict that well before the curtain is about to fall on our age many will be crying out for an end to those bizarre and hideous expressions of the personal freedoms we now enjoy. They will be calling for the worst excesses of decadence to be eradicated by all available means. That is, assuming the rationalist perspective and modern man's almost total loss of faith have not already got the upper hand.

Only our age could be such a disgrace to the history of mankind; only our age could produce the material prerequisites for unlimited indulgence of every appetite. Only our age could degrade mankind by leaving such indulgence unredeemed, and glorify this fact. Valor, courage and honor have become strangers to us; war no longer has the central importance it once did because there simply is no longer the opportunity to win one's spurs on the battle field through one's own efforts. This is, after all, the push button age. In war, this means guided missiles with nuclear warheads stored in underground silos, and atomic submarines, all controlled by computers. Is this an age fit for man, man as we have always known him, or is it an age fit for computerized robots which have nothing to do with the glorious history which has been handed down to us by generation upon generation of noble and heroic men. This is, in fact, an age from which any self-respecting individual who has a modicum of feeling for history should shrink in disgust. It is an age which, if it were allowed to continue on its present course would eventually lead us to technological nihilism. Because modern industrial society has lacked a truly autonomous ruling class, the theorists of social equality were forced to invent one. No one has proved to be more adept at doing this than Karl Marx, whose seminal concept of class conflict was the basis of a most elaborate social theory, complete with predictions. The profit hungry investors, financiers and entrepreneurs of the nineteenth century proved to be the ideal group to cast in the role of villains. This image of a rapacious capitalist class, in league with the political leaders of the day, with the sole objective of maximizing their personal gain, seems to have made a deep impression on each generation of those who read the works of Marx and Engels. This image (i.e., a permanent struggle between two antagonistic orders) has in fact been so compelling that latter-day social theorists of Marxist persuasion have either propounded it almost word for word — especially the fringe revolutionary socialist groups — or have, like the late C. Wright Mills, spent a great deal of time looking for a ruling class that does not exist. When pressed on this point, the revolutionary socialists point to the enormous importance of giant corporations to the economy of the West and to figures which appear to indicate that wealth still remains highly concentrated, despite progressive income tax, inheritance tax and gift tax. But these are hardly convincing arguments for the existence of an all powerful ruling class, as were the patricians of ancient Rome or even more so the barons of feudal Europe.

The giant corporations of today certainly are a dominant factor in the economy of the West, but their ownership is highly diffused; their activities are closely scrutinized by government agencies and independent pressure groups working for a variety of causes. Finally, the managers and executives of these enterprises are probably more subservient to the general interest (as dictated by the government of the day) than probably any other comparable body of people. To refer then to the executives of large multi-national corporations as a ruling class is laughable; they have neither the freedom nor desire to act as such. More likely than not, they see themselves as part of the nation's economic effort to remain affluent and competitive and nothing more. Then again, they share many of the leisure interests of more lowly workers who are not decision makers, such as watching television and attending sports events. They also want the same things that the latter want, e.g., regular increase in their living standards and the opportunity to increase their material welfare without having to give up too much in order to do so. Neither does the fact that these executives are able to obtain special perks (such as car, home, business expenses) not available to the ordinary worker make them members of a select ruling class. Like everyone else they still have to obey the law and have only one vote. Similarly, by the criteria which we discussed above, the possession of great wealth alone does not entitle one to be called a member of the ruling class, even though it may set one apart from the majority of one's fellows.

In our culture, both the man who is a millionaire through inheritance, and the man who has become so by way of shrewd investment or by some other means, are greatly admired as paragons of success. But rarely are these people considered as potential leaders either by others or by themselves. More to the point, very few of them are fitted for such a role even if it were to be thrust upon them. Neither is access to great wealth restricted by one's class background, as it would be in a truly class conscious society, a fact that is especially true with respect to success in any of the many branches of the entertainment industry. The simple fact is that no matter how concentrated wealth may be, those who have great wealth do not rule and most of those who rule do not possess great wealth, that is, if anybody can be said to rule today's industrialized nations — a highly debatable question. Many attempts have been made by academics to discover the structure and power of today's ruling class. One of the most notable of these was C. W. Mills' *The Power Elite*. Mills and the other Marxist academics who have made investigations in this area have attempted to update the classical Marxist model of class conflict. In doing so, they have not only robbed classical Marxism of its appeal to those enamored of revolutionary causes, but they have also shown how totally irrelevant and outdated is such a concept in the analysis of contemporary society.

Just because certain business leaders, top government officials and military figures went to the same private school or university, and happen to regularly attend the same social occasions does not mean that they constitute anything approaching a ruling class or dominant clique. It should surely not be found surprising that even a legio-rational system of authority must draw most of its servants from certain traditional sources. For the type of career followed by the average individual will be determined mainly by his family's income, which will be largely dependent on his father's occupation. This will be found to be true of all advanced industrialized countries whether they have a market economy or a planned economy. Thus, in every developed nation there is a certain social strata whose children always seem to do better than those of lower social strata with regards to educational achievement and careers. This is true of the offspring of high party functionaries in the Soviet Union and most other East European countries, just as it is true in all western countries for the children of top bureaucrats and those whose father practices one of the more lucrative professions. But even so, people from an upper-middle-class background do not have an exclusive monopoly on the top decision making positions within western society, since there is enough upward mobility to ensure that lower-class children with sufficient talent and ambition can make their way to the top. Ironically, if a ruling class (i.e., the closest approximation to it) can be said to exist in this day and age in a developed country, we can do no better than point to the Soviet Union and her East European satellites.

In these countries, members of the Communist Party are the only people able to make decisions that will affect the lives of their countrymen, regardless of what the latter may think. Furthermore, since in order to gain official recognition for achievement in the arts or sciences, the individual must also be a member of the party or at the very least, toe the party line, the picture is complete. Of course, there are a number of reasons why the communist parties of Eastern Europe have produced a rather paltry ruling class. For one thing, the vast majority of Party members are nonentities, career bureaucrats who would gladly work under any system of government, provided they could be guaranteed job security. Many other members are not even bureaucrats, but hard working, docile manual laborers who may be highly productive economically, but can hardly be said to be more than a mere statistic in political terms. In fact, all major decisions are the sole prerogative of a power clique which was once known as the Politburo, and this select body itself may be dominated by the party chairman and two or three of his closest associates. Decisions emanating from the Politburo are final, the National Assembly is simply a rubber stamp. I suppose we could call this bureaucratic oligarchy, i.e., a corruption of the ideal model government for an industrialized nation which is plural democracy.

Even in the heyday of *laissez faire*, the bourgeoisie as a ruling class could not be rightly compared with the ruling class of previous ages, for one very good reason. The traditionalist viewpoint which dominated the thinking of the ruling classes of previous ages was gone. The ruling class of ancient and feudal times was especially concerned to maintain the status quo, i.e., their power and position in both the political and economic sphere, thereby guaranteeing their indefinite survival. The bourgeoisie which rose to power on the crest of the industrial revolution was quite different. Its only objective was to produce at the lowest possible cost and sell in the largest possible market at the highest possible price. It was not so much concerned with its continued existence as a class, believing, no doubt, as long as business was good, its own preservation would follow as a matter of course. The long term impact of this difference was to be profound, for it meant that from the very beginning of their shortlived ascendancy, the involvement of the bourgeoisie in politics was mainly with the aim of ensuring that they could have a free hand in business. Another factor which greatly contributed to the rapid decline in the supremacy of the capitalist class was the fact that contrary to what R. H. Tawney believed (see his preface to the 1938 edition of *Equality*), capitalism and democracy could hardly be said to have been incompatible. In fact, one could quite easily consider them to be complementary.

Thus, the early utilitarians led by Jeremy Bentham, supported universal manhood suffrage and two-year parliaments, both of which were considered to be very radical, even dangerous innovations by the political establishment of the day. Nevertheless, Bentham and his followers felt that this was the best way in which politicians could become responsive to the needs and demands of the people. On the other hand, the Benthamites, including James Mill, also favored the economics of *laissez faire*, believing that this was the best way in which the common man could satisfy his essential needs at the cheapest prices. Later on a political movement which was referred to as the philosophical radicals, and which included John Stuart Mill and the young Herbert Spencer among its supporters, also favored sweeping reform of the franchise to give all working men the vote, the abolition of the corn law and of religious discrimination, while reaffirming support for *laissez faire.* The same ambivalence towards the needs for capitalist development on the one hand, and the best interests of the workers on the other, was to be seen in the laws and decrees of the first French Revolution. On one hand, the revolutionary deputies promulgated laws which increased the freedom of trade, eliminating much of the cumbersome restrictions which had come down from the *ancien regime.* But on the other hand, they also promulgated laws which forbade strikes and the formation of unions, both of which became punishable offenses. One of the pair (i.e., laissez faire capitalism or popular democracy) had to triumph over the other. It seems that from the start democracy was assured of a magnificent victory, in England at least. It is true to say that it did receive some early setbacks, particularly during the first quarter of the nineteenth century. One thinks especially of Castleragh as Home Secretary, Peterloo, and the subsequent conspiracies to overthrow the government which only encouraged it to be yet more repressive.

But this was only a passing phase. Royal absolutism had begun to go into decline some years before the advent of the industrial revolution, the appearance of this phenomenon serving only to accelerate the process. Representative government for the industrial age meant bureaucracy and mass participation in politics, since this was the logic of democratic government. All the great political theorists after Burke would place themselves at the service of this ideal (i.e., political equality); all the great social movements, e.g., Chartists, would uphold it as their primary objective. Revolutionaries would make it their rallying cry and dynasties would topple before it. We may say that the first hundred years of modern industry were just as much the first hundred years of modern politics. During this period, the sway of the old ways and institutions was finally broken to make way for popular democracy. With hindsight we can say that capitalism was defeated by the very institution which it had done so much to promote, i.e., parliamentary government — just as feudalism before it had been defeated by centralized monarchy. Therefore, the fact that the greatest blows against the leading position of the bourgeoisie were delivered by members of this class serving in parliament should not be too difficult to understand, that is, assuming you follow all that I have said so far in regard to what constitutes a ruling class. Most of the great revolutions of the eighteenth and nineteenth century were, in fact, bourgeois led and inspired. Witness the American Revolution, which although led by the well-to-do, brought into being the first popular democracy to exist anywhere in the world since the days of ancient Greece.

This upheaval was shortly followed by the first French Revolution, which destroyed absolutism and opened the way for the eventual appearance of popular democracy throughout Western Europe. Few historians would deny the great influence of the American Revolution on those traumatic events in France which began thirteen years after the American declaration of independence. French soldiers fought on the side of the Americans, and one of the leaders of the French troops fighting for American independence was the Marquis de Lafayette, who was later to become a prominent figure in the early stages of the French Revolution. Later on Tom Paine, that literary firebrand of the American Revolution, was for a brief period a member of the Chamber of Deputies under the ascendancy of the Jacobins. The tendency for the ideals of popular democracy to overcome those of laissez faire capitalism — even though the link between the world of business and that of politics was closer than it would ever be again — became evident first in England from the 1830s onwards. It was during this period that the belief that the bourgeoisie constituted a compact and viable ruling class was shown to be a hollow sham, an illusion of the fevered-brain socialists whose writings were just beginning to appear. Thus, according to Marx, who should have known better, the only point of a bourgeois election is to decide which members of the ruling class should be elected for four or five years to represent the working class in parliament. If by this statement Marx meant to imply that members of parliament represented their own class interest — which he did — then he was clearly wrong. For the freedom of contract and all the other cardinal principles of *laissez faire* suffered setback after setback, e,g., the child labor laws, the institution of regular factory inspection, the granting of the right to strike and form unions.

Humanitarianism (standing in for popular democracy which had not quite come) was on the offensive and *laissez faire* capitalism was in full retreat. Although democractic socialism did not become a significant political force (in terms of parliamentary representation) until the 1890s, and then only in Germany, it seems that nothing could stop the onward march of popular democracy, a trend which can be said to have gradually brought about improvement in the status of the laboring masses whilst weakening the position of the capitalist class. All this was taking place under the auspices of governments which were dominated by liberal and conservative parties, both of which accepted the basic tenets of *laissez faire*. All the great social and economic reforms of nineteenth century England were championed in Parliament by those who would have been expected to stand up against these changes if they had any real idea of their class interest. Modern industrial society may have been capable of producing a ruling idea, i.e., the *primacy* of self-interest in economic affairs, but it was totally incapable of producing a ruling class. The breakdown of consensus among the traditional English political parties which began around the time of the split between Burke and Fox over the French Revolution, was to prove to be a most useful mechanism to push forward the process of reform. When the Liberals were not in the forefront of change (which they were for most of the nineteenth century), matters were taken over by the Conservatives. One remembers the case where Disraeli's Conservatives, having put Gladstone's Liberals out of office through fierce opposition to one of the latter's reform proposals in connection with the extension of the franchise, then went on to enact the very same measures which they had so recently opposed.

As Disraeli observed, the reform in question was inevitable and, therefore, why should it not be undertaken by the Conservatives instead of left to the Liberals who were always getting the credit in such matters? Not all members of the Conservative party went along with this about-turn, but enough of them did to enable Disraeli to get his way. It would seem that the cynicism of contemporary politics is nothing new, though with so little to argue about, consensus has once again returned to the political scene. When laws are made by individuals who are in theory at least accountable to the majority for their actions, then social reform, even if it proceeds at a slow rate, must be the order of the day — no matter what the ideology of those in power. This was the case throughout the last two-thirds of the nineteenth century (in England that is). There was no possibility of turning back the clock; the growing industrial work force had to be appeased at all cost, regardless of the views of the owners of capital. To anyone in politics capable of taking the long term view, the conclusion that the future lay with those who had only their labor power to sell and, hence, with popular democracy, must have been inescapable. After the law makers had done all they could to stifle individual initiative and freedom of action, the fledgling bureaucracy moved in to do what it could to make life miserable for the strong and independent, and comfortable for the weak and dependent. Welfare capitalism was the inevitable outcome of granting universal franchise.

The final blow to the leading position of the capitalist class came with the rise of the joint stock company during the last third of the nineteenth century. It is true that the early beginnings of each such company was closely connected with particular individuals, but in most cases, these individuals remained in a position of leadership mainly because they had the confidence of their stockholders, rather than because they were the dominant stockholders. No longer was the capitalist factory owner free to do as he pleased; he had to give a regular account of the company's affairs to his shareholders. His objective was still first and foremost to make the largest possible profit, but this now had to be done in a way which fitted in with the canons of rational decision making. In other words, he was not free to follow his own impulses to achieve the desired goal, but had to consider public opinion and rules and regulations laid down by the government. There were some men — as there always are — who would not allow themselves to be intimidated by the conventions of their age which counseled caution and prudence in business and the separation of one's political belief from one's business interests. One such man was Cecil Rhodes, who among other accomplishments was the founder of DeBeers, the monopoly diamond corporation, Prime Minister of Cape Province, founder of Rhodesia, which was named after him, and founder of the Rhodes Scholarship, which, by its original provision, was not open to women.

He was one of the few great capitalists ever to have combined preeminence in the business world with preeminence in the political world without making concessions to the weaknesses of his age. All his life was dedicated to just one cause, the improvement and expansion of the British empire; he was an unashamed imperialist who was totally indifferent to the business conventions of his day. Rhodes was, of course, a gigantic exception to the peace and prosperity ideals of his age. The more typical sentiments of the emerging corporate elite were expressed by Rhodes' fellow monopolist Barney Barnato, who felt that the purpose of the new corporation which would be formed from the combination of his company with that of Rhodes should be to obtain the highest rate of return for their shareholders and not as a vehicle to extend British influence Northwards. But the founder of Rhodesia got his way in the end. Rhodes is a significant figure in history, not only because of his accomplishments, but also as a demonstration that the exceptional individual can always break through the constraints of his age to accomplish great deeds. The exploits of Rhodes are also a useful reminder of the great heritage of western man, especially so since the age of modern industry has been dominated by an ethos which counsels that for success in both business and politics, caution, prudence and self-control are essential. But it is these same values which have led to the degenerate age in which we now live.

The excessive legal restraints which have come to characterize our age with its encouragement of "rational calculation" has given birth to an upper social strata composed of unimaginative hirelings who would be just as at home doing a simple clerical job as they now are directing the economic fortunes of their nation. This process, i.e., the separation of ownership from control has been referred to as the managerial revolution. I prefer to consider it as the last stage in the decay of modern capitalism. For just as the ancient Romans became enfeebled by shirking their military responsibilities, which were taken over by barbarians, so the propertied class has become enfeebled by their displacement from the management and control of the nation's industry. The metamorphosis of early nineteenth century *laissez faire*, first into monopoly capitalism and then into welfare capitalism, heralded the arrival of mass consumer society and the triumph of mediocrity, vulgarity and bad taste. One's background and social status no longer count for anything; all that is important to contemporary man is the ability to make a large amount of money. By this yardstick, entertainers are among the most prominent members of today's upper class. Who would have believed that the court jester would one day displace the king? It should now be clearly apparent that there was absolutely no substance to a comparison between the ruling class of pre-capitalist times and the bourgeoisie produced by the industrial revolution. The first had always combined economic and political power as a distinctive class, conscious of its class interest. The second had only briefly and imperfectly combined economic and political power and had never been really conscious of their class interest as distinct from their economic interest — something which is perhaps impossible for an upper class whose economic foundation is based on the productive powers of modern industry, and thereby the acceptance of consumer sovereignty in politics as well as economics.

With the rise of the joint stock companies to preeminence, we enter the age of bureaucratic rationalism in business. Although the aim is still to make a profit, great care must be taken to see that this is done in a manner which is strictly legal and compatible with utilitarian humanist values which had by that time taken full possession of the mind of modern man. The great industrialists did not immediately disappear but their days were clearly numbered. They had never been able to stamp their imprint on the political process as the great land owners had been able to do before them. The era of consumer sovereignty was not far off, as to complement this development the classical economics of Adam Smith and David Ricardo made way for the marginal economics of Wickes, Bohm Bawerk and others. The technocrat, the prudent administrator, was now the man in demand in industry, just as he would be increasingly demanded in the process of government. The ruthless capitalist entrepreneur prepared to take chances, to ignore the cries of the weak and defenseless, no longer fitted into the modern industrial age. By the beginning of the twentieth century the once proud captains of industry had ceased to be a social, political or economic force. In fact, they had almost ceased to exist. A few may have passed on the torch to the next generation, but most were succeeded by hired managers. Many small and medium sized companies were still owned and managed by one man who typically groomed his most capable son for succession — as remains the case today. But the economic importance of these companies pales into insignificance when compared with those companies run by hired managers and owned by thousands of faceless shareholders.

The joint stock corporation has absorbed the utilitarian-humanist ideals which arose along with mass democracy to guide our age in the right direction, a task which has been performed in a most "admirable manner," so much so that not only do we hear of companies being good corporate citizens by financing a bewildering variety of worthy causes, but something much worse than this has happened, that is, the wholesale corruption of values. Thus prudence, absence of emotion and pacificism are now taken as laudable qualities, whereas open hearted generosity, spontaneous reaction to insult, a high sense of personal honor and a willingness to risk one's life in combat at the first available opportunity, are frowned upon as archaic. But those qualities which breed effeminacy and a desire for ease and comfort are the same qualities which are supposed to be good for business. Many Marxist propagandists and even some well respected social theorists believe that the large corporations have taken over from where the captains of industry left off. This is a myth. Neither the directors nor the shareholders of the large corporations could take over the leadership of western society even if they wanted to, and all the evidence points to the fact that they do not want to. They are far more concerned with corporate profits and, of late, the corporate image. Understandably so, since in most cases involvement in politics by twentieth century industrialists has been for the most part hopelessly inept, from the days of J. D. Rockefeller and Henry Ford right down to the present time.

The same limitations apply to the unions; they have no inclination to aspire to the leadership of western society and are content to work within the legal framework of welfare capitalism. Economically, the bourgeoisie (a term which I am using here to cover exclusively those who derive by far the largest part of their income from the possession of stocks and bonds), is no longer the power it once was. Witness the fact that nearly half the total stocks listed on the stock exchanges of London and New York are owned by Pension Funds, Insurances Companies, Unit Trusts, Charities and many other types of institutions. Those who have inherited their stock holding (which is the majority of stockholders) rarely bother to take an interest in the management of the enterprise from which their wealth is derived or to actively defend the system which allows them to live the life of the idle rich — if they so choose. They are more likely to be defensive about their wealth, even apologetic, and fear most of all being stigmatized as a "coupon clipper." Inheritance then has done little to reinforce the position of the bourgeoisie, since most have no stomach for leadership and would gladly exchange their shares for government bonds. Moreover, we see that the capitalist class in Germany has long ago tamely accepted the introduction of worker directors and it will not be long before further laws are introduced to put worker directors in the majority. When this comes, the shareholders will cease to have even nominal control over the affairs of the company they are supposed to own. Similar measures are being introduced by other Western European governments.

Whilst the socialist government of Denmark has recently brought forward a plan that would force all limited liability companies to increase their share capital, so as to give the employees a larger share of the company than the original shareholders would have. This would, of course, lead to a massive dilution in the equity of the original shareholders, making their shares almost worthless, while at the same time depriving them of any control over the company whatsoever. But if the Danish government is insistent and the measure gets through their parliament, the shareholders will no doubt fall in line. In Volume Three of *Capital,* Marx seems to have foreseen that the descendants of the great enterprise builders would lose effective control of the means of production. What he did not foresee was how willing the property owners would be to participate in their own downfall. Joseph Schumpeter did foresee this and said as much, i.e., the socialization of private industry would be carried out right under the noses of the owners of capital. And this is indeed proving to be the case. As for capitalists making up a ruling class either now or in the past, this assertion belongs to the folklore of western culture along with belief in the existence of witches and the lost continent of Atlantis. In fact, the world's economy has become so complex and so interdependent that capital no longer has a master. Neither government, management nor unions are in full control and no one can predict with certainty what effects large changes will have on the economy in general. The only thing we can be sure of is that the profit motive remains in existence spurred on by the desire for indefinite economic growth.

Thus, it is the bourgeois ethos, and not the bourgeoisie as a special class, that has enjoyed a sustained period of dominance. The bourgeois ethos has been modified substantially since it first made its appearance, so we can probably best understand what it is and how it has changed by first discussing its economic origins. To begin with we must understand the pivotal status of the free market, for allowing the market place to play its central role was both an economic and a moral imperative for the early bourgeoisie. Thus, according to theory, unrestricted and competitive trade in the market place gave the purchaser what he wanted at the most favorable price, rewarding the efficient and industrious producer with a profit, while punishing the inefficient and slothful with a loss. All this became enshrined in the deceptively simple doctrine of *laissez faire.* Adam Smith in his book, *Wealth of Nations*, set the keynote of the new economic doctrine. "It is not from the benevolence of the butcher, the brewer or the baker that we expect our dinner but from their regard for their own interests." This was the foundation of classical economics which was to be subsequently elaborated and defended by David Ricardo and the later classical theorists. One of the major theoretical concerns of classical economics was the nature of value and the origins of profit. These two problems were to play a most important part in the development of Marx's economic theory. Marginal utility, which superseded the classical school, ignored these fundamental matters taking them as given, and turned its attention instead to aggregate changes.

Another aspect of early capitalism apart from its emphasis on self-interest as a positive quality, is also indicated by the above quote from Adam Smith — this is the work ethic. This desire to work hard, save and invest, then reinvest rather than spend, has also been referred to as the spirit of capitalism. Max Weber in one of his most provocative works, *The Protestant Ethic and the Spirit of Capitalism*, attempted to demonstrate a link between Protestantism (especially Calvinism) and success in business. However, it would seem fair to say that the work ethic is not confined to one religious group, but is to be found in all countries which are highly industrialized. Most people would agree with this, but the present day status of the work ethic is hotly disputed. Some of the top executives of major multinational companies like to list work as their chief recreation, but the commitment of those in the lower echelons of the corporate hierarchy and the workers on the factory floor is quite another matter. At least one minor car manufacturer in the U.S.A. has reported that absenteeism still remains high even in periods of recession. And there is also a tendency for the younger workers to walk off the assembly line. Apart from this decline in the work ethic, the bourgeois ethos has been modified in a number of other ways. For instance, government interference in the economy (e.g., price and wage controls) and government spending has come to play an enormous part in the economic affairs of the highly industrialized societies, although the market mechanism still remains the final arbiter.

But this greater degree of government involvement which was partly a result of increasing complexity of the modern industrial state and partly a result of increased political awareness among the enfranchised masses, gave birth to the concept of welfare capitalism, which has grown and grown. Moreover, for all practical purposes, Christianity, which had been struggling to find a home since the early days of the industrial revolution, became transmuted into an insipid utilitarian-humanist ideal. This process did not really get underway until near the end of the last century but has long since achieved its goal. The great advantage of the utilitarian-humanist ideal over Christianity was that with no trouble at all it has been able to provide the moral foundation for both reformed capitalism (i.e., liberal democracy) and reformed socialism (i.e., social democracy) so that there is no difference between them. As most people know, the terms liberal democracy (which has its origins in the late nineteenth century industrial society) and social democracy (which has its origins in the writings of the revisionist German Marxist theoretician, Eduard Bernstein), are now used interchangeably to describe any pluralistic parliamentary system of government which rests on the transfer of power by free elections. Furthermore, political parties within both traditions now compete frantically with each other in pandering to the desires of the majority for the better life. The fusion of capitalism and socialism in the contemporary modern industrial state has had far reaching implications for western man. In other words, the rise of the bourgeois ethos and its subsequent transformation has led to the displacement of spiritualism by materialism, a development which was extended into the realm of philosophy by nearly every notable philosopher of the nineteenth century. No philosophy has done more to encourage the development of the utilitarian-humanist ideal than Marxism, which ironically was said by its founders to be utterly opposed to the utilitarians, whose viewpoint Marx described disparagingly as that of a typical English shopkeeper. He and Engels also insisted time and time again that his views had nothing whatsoever to do with social justice for the workers, but were the outcome of a careful study of the logic of the capitalist system which clearly indicated that it would one day be superseded by a more rational economic system. No doubt Marx really believed all this, but since subsequent history has not paid close attention to Marx, it appears that no one else, not even his most ardent follower, could afford to. But the fact that history never followed the plot laid down by Marx has had only a minor effect on the career of his doctrine in the West.

To understand the reasons for this we must go over the strengths and weaknesses of capitalism and socialism. Now Heilbroner reminds us that "no capitalist nation or philosopher or economist has any grand design for the fundamental reshaping of society through capitalism,"[1] whereas our Marxist friends have always had such a vision, but their vision has been somewhat abstract, lacking in concrete reality. So what has happened, with very few people realizing it, is that the Marxist vision of a better society has been selectively absorbed into the contemporary bourgeois ethos and thereby become reified, whilst in turn it has imparted legitimacy to a system which is incapable of generating a grand design of its own, whereas the wilder aspects of scientific socialism were early taken out of the mainstream of western political theory and practice and injected into the whirlpool of Russian politics. It was a fortuitous occurrence, which meant that the fallacy of the economic interpretation of history was eventually laid bare for all to see. Returning to the West, the utilitarian-humanist ideal has served to promote tolerance, social and economic equality and freedom of choice.

But it has not been able to curb the excesses of these freedoms, which are now eating away at the very core of our society. Far from curbing these excesses, the utilitarian-humanist ideal has proved to be infinitely elastic. Every new trend, every new fad that is an insult to common decency and historic experience, is accepted as another healthy expression of modern society coming of age, when in fact it is nothing of the sort, but on the contrary, another example of the disintegration of an age which has lost contact with traditional values. The teachings of early bourgeois culture which were once thought to be essential success in the business world, as well as contributing to a properly developed character, no longer seem to matter. For example, there was a time when the children of the bourgeoisie were taught the importance of delayed gratification. But this is no longer the case; the younger generation of today do not believe in the virtue of delayed gratification and their parents no longer bother to teach them this value. The teaching of correct posture and dress which was a trait of the typical Victorian middle class family has also fallen into disrepute and hence neglected. The scions of today's middle and upper class have no special awareness of themselves as a distinct entity. The bourgeois ethos continues to exist, but having gone through so many changes and having experienced so much neglect, what remains of it is in a very poor state of health.

It wasn't so very long ago that bureaucracy could hardly be said to have existed, even though modern industrial society had clearly begun, when the highest positions in the governments of Western Europe were occupied by the toothless representatives of the class (i.e., the nobility) which had always traditionally supplied the candidates to fill these offices. But this is no longer the case. Political leadership exists today primarily as a coalition between unimaginative bureaucrats and lackluster politicians, with a sprinkling of so-called technocrats drawn from industry and the universities. Western society is to all intents and purposes leaderless and has been so for at least the last hundred years. Up until recently, this was not considered a very serious problem. The need for inspired leadership was thought to be a thing of the past. Peace and good will among men became the order of the day, war and political irrationality could finally be put behind us. All those industrialized nations that had to contend with the destructiveness of World War Two committed themselves to more of everything for everyone. Progress in technology and science (including the science of rational administration) was counted upon to make the dream of a better world become a reality. Well, the dream has turned sour; progress in just about every branch of science and technology has brought us nothing but trouble which threatens to get well beyond our powers of control, if we should continue to proceed along our present path.

Like Doctor Frankenstein's monster, modern industrial society threatens to destroy its creator — modern man. Nor does the almost universal preeminence of the utilitarian-humanist ideal give us much cause for hope. In fact, the values associated with this ideal are of decidedly secondary importance when compared with the possibility of mass destruction which is inherent in the organization of contemporary western society. This point is discussed with great insight by Robert Heilbroner in his book, *Between Capitalism and Socialism*, in which he tells us that, "Inevitably the technical capacities of a society come to exceed by an enormous margin its capabilities for exercising effective social control. The result is a technology that continuously escapes confinement, that develops in unforeseen directions, and that disturbs social systems by exerting its influences in unanticipated and unwelcome ways, such as the poisoning of the environment."[2] Not only has the utilitarian-humanist ideal promoted the disintegration of the fabric of western society, it has also failed to inspire the creative imagination of the younger generation. Many of the members of this generation have become disenchanted with the idolization of money, science and technology and the soul destroying routine of modern life. Some have taken up mysticism, others have become followers of obscure esoteric cults, while others still have set up communes as a way of demonstrating their belief in the viability of an alternative lifestyle. All of them are in their own way searching for a deeper meaning to life than is currently offered by the superficial and decadent values of contemporary western society.

Needless to say they are destined to be disappointed. Instead of turning their backs on the utilitarian-humanist ideal, they wholeheartedly accept this, but reject the materialism of their age. They do not realize that the ethical ideals of this age must be rejected along with the excessive materialism of our age. Both are in the long term destructive and totally at odds with what is necessary for the existence of a vigorous and healthy civilization. The great city-states of ancient times, Rome, Athens, Sparta and Carthage, had their own values, the most dominant of which was eudaemonism. This fitted in well with the circumstances of the period, such as the weak development of institutional religion, and also with the central importance of the city to the life of the people, a truth that was so eloquently stated by Pericles in his famous Funeral Speech. But an abstract ideal, no matter how noble, will never be sufficient to prevent a flourishing civilization from falling into decay, if those who profess it are not prepared to give it practical expression. Thus, the ruling elites of these ancient city-states were often on the offensive either against revolting slaves, or against the rabble who were always attempting to wrestle power from those who were born to it, or they were leading the city-state in the expansion of its sphere of influence. The latter could mean anything from entering into new military alliances to setting up new colonies overseas.

Members of the ruling elite could never be sure of their own personal safety or of the security of the city which had been built and cherished by their ancestors. The members of the ancient senates were not only statesmen but also warriors. One looks to Rome and plucks out the names of the Scipios, Caesar, Crassus and many others, or to Athens where one is greeted by the names of Pericles, Themistocles and Demosthenes, while Carthage can boast of the incomparable Hannibal and of Hano. Then again, Republican Rome was threatened on numerous occasions by hordes of fierce barbarians, as well as by more civilized adversaries, i.e., Hannibal and Pyrrhus. Athens had to be evacuated in the face of the advancing Persians under Xerxes. Carthage was twice defeated by Rome, each time arising once more to become an important commercial power before finally succumbing to the might of Roman arms on the third occasion from which there was no possibility of recovery. The people of this age lived under no illusions about the realities of their existence. The rules of war were simple; the victor was lord of all he surveyed, whereas the vanquished were sold into slavery. Rarely was there ever a middle way. How feeble is our age compared to that of antiquity, and yet we pride ourselves on having in common with the great western civilizations of antiquity an attachment to order, rational jurisprudence and a keen interest in culture and the pursuit of knowledge. Yes, we do share some of the trappings of these civilizations at their most developed (and, hence, most vulnerable), but very few of their redeeming features, such as a thorough application of the fundamental law of existence, i.e., when times are difficult the strong must survive and the weak must perish.

It should now be clear that an abstract ideal is not an adequate substitute for a class whose members can be looked to, to provide leadership and whose ideals are the ruling ideals, a class closely connected to all lower classes by bonds similar to those which unite a father and son. The demise of aristocracy left a void which the investor-proprietor class could not possibly fill. What they could do, and did do very successfully in Western Europe and North America, was to set their society on the path towards self-sustaining economic growth, thereby guaranteeing that future generations would automatically become better off materially than ever before. But even the bourgeoisie, as a distinct class wielding influence through their money and economic power, can hardly be said to exist any longer. What we have instead is a society in which a small and politically insignificant minority have a substantially higher income than the vast majority. The members of this minority are a heterogeneous lot, ranging from the owners and managers of industrial and commercial enterprises through to football players, comedians and pop singers. No wonder modern day Marxist theoreticians such as C. Wright Mills have had difficulty in convincingly depicting the ruling class of their society. We have now reached the point at which the absence of a clearly defined ruling class capable of providing sound leadership does matter. For as long as western society continues to exist without such a group, as long as it continues to be ruled by default, i.e., by the so-called will of the people, the closer it will come to irreversible ecological destruction.

One thing is certain: No matter how much longer we have to go before this age winds itself to an end, the re-emergence of aristocracy combined with a lack of inclination to rebuild and reactivate the ruins of modern industry will ensure that we never again encounter the problems which we now face. So far, the overthrow of advanced industrial society by human forces has appeared to be all but impossible. Western society has survived two great world wars as well as a period of massive economic depression, and there is now a powerful school of thought which believes that we can learn to live with the perils of nuclear energy, just as we have learned to live with the threat of nuclear war. But how would modern industrial society stand up under assault by superhuman forces? Not very well, I venture to guess. I will go further and say that the individual and collective energy which will be unleashed with the arrival of the new age will be far too great to be contained within the delicate arrangements of modern industrial society. Once western society has settled down and recovered from the traumatic events which will catapult it into the new age, its social organization and way of life will be entirely different from what it is now. For one thing, upward mobility will be absent. Family life will also make a come back. The ruling class of the new age will not need to be taught how they should behave; they will know this instinctively. They will have no interest in education for its own sake. They will be opposed to changes that would in any way reduce their power and status among the people. Thus, the ruling class of the new age will be a bastion of conservatism and tradition, and the ideas of this class will indeed once again be the ruling ideas of society as a whole.

Understandably, the question is asked how such an aristocracy would arise. It will arise quite naturally during the course of the economic, social and political re-orientation that will be discussed in the later chapters. Those who are successful in establishing supremacy within their area of operation (i.e., by keeping under the control of their family a relatively large area of land despite the difficulties this will entail) will automatically distinguish themselves as being fit to participate in the leadership of their nation. Those who decry the fact that western society is destined once again to see the return of aristocracy will be amongst the least important members of society in the new age. Such people (and this includes the vast majority) have been brainwashed into believing that the utilitarian-humanist ideal of contemporary western society is the zenith of the intellectual and psychological development of western man, when in fact it is nothing of the sort. It is only an intermediate stage in the onward march of western civilization. Those who long for an end to all strife, for the advent of eternal peace and friendship among men, are asking for the impossible. They want nothing more than the disappearance of mankind from the face of the earth. No one has put this better than Heraclitus when he says "Homer was wrong in saying, 'would that strife might perish from among Gods and men!' He did not see that he was praying for the destruction of the universe; for if his prayer were heard all things would pass away."

Without the rebirth of Aristocracy there could be no rebirth of western civilization. There would be no force great enough to galvanize a lethargic society into action. There would be no body of men able and willing to take advantage of the circumstances of the new age to rebuild western society into a virile and expressive culture. Only a regenerated aristocracy full of valor and ambition could embody all that is finest in the history of western man. Only under the patronage of such an aristocratic elite could art, music and culture once again flourish. Only under the leadership of such an aristocracy will the nation be able to mobilize the human and material resources under its control to undertake great works of construction or great military enterprise. Only under such an aristocracy will life recapture and retain the richness and variety which is the hallmark of all great civilizations. Only through the existence of such an aristocracy will the nation have a chance to maintain a large measure of cohesion and resilience in times of crisis. All these benefits surely out-weigh other considerations which would be opposed to the resurrection of aristocracy. An age in which everybody was more or less equal would be no age at all, for it would be distinguished by nothing of note except a drab, narrow-minded uniformity.

This type of backward, relatively uneventful, tranquil existence is most reminiscent of those societies which lack a literary culture and are destined never to develop one unless they come into contact with the culture of a superior society. Such a society is indifferent to most things except basic survival and seasonal rituals. If environmental conditions are favorable to its disorganized methods of agriculture, it will stay put. If not, it will become nomadic and wander from place to place. Typically, it would be led by a chief, perhaps assisted by a council of elders, but aristocracy as such is unknown to it. Great buildings, great construction projects, large-scale agricultural production (so as to produce a substantial surplus) and disciplined armies are foreign to such a society. It would have little interest in the pursuit of things unconnected with the provision of food and the other necessities of life. It would make no attempt to impress its character upon its surroundings, from which it would move away at the slightest setback. No one who has any feeling for western civilization and for the culture it has produced could possibly want to see it degenerate into the type of lifeless, aimless society characterized above. Personally, I find such a possibility totally unacceptable, and the very fact that there are differences in the capabilities of different individuals which would allow some to prosper while others perish under similar conditions, will ensure that this type of rootless, hopelessly fatalistic society will not be very common in the new age, either in the northern hemisphere or the southern hemisphere. It goes without saying that the differences between individuals in their ability to survive and prosper will be accentuated rather than lessened under the circumstances of the new age.

One of the key traits that distinguishes the nomadic tribal societies which we have outlined above from civilizations with which students of ancient and medieval history are familiar, is the non-existence of a literary culture. Although every civilization must be based on a literary culture, this does not have to be pre-eminent, and in fact, a society is best adapted when knowledge is the servant of the society and not its master. This was the case in ancient Egypt, in Sparta, and also throughout the medieval period. I am not saying that originality is necessarily always opposed to the best interest of a society, but what I am saying is that more likely than not it will be, even though at first sight it may appear to be beneficial. This opinion (i.e., conservation is to be preferred to progress) receives support from of all places, ancient Athens. Thus, one notable Greek sage commented that the present order represented the best of all possible worlds, since earlier generations had had plenty of time to try out other arrangements. Thus, he felt it was unlikely that anything of positive worth would be gained by over-ambitious social innovations. Also, the Athenian dramatist Aristophanes blamed Socrates for the decline of Athens which was shown up by the course of the Peloponnesian War.

Socrates' crime was to question the old beliefs and values of Athens and criticize them without offering anything of substance in their place. Since Socrates had no heroic values of his own, his idealistic teachings were bound to have a devitalizing influence on Athenian society. For to strip a courageous society such as ancient Athens of its heroic values and traditions is to leave it naked and defenseless, a prey to more aggressive societies, just as a predator whose teeth and claws are removed is unable to fend for itself. We should note in passing that Aristophanes also had a share in the decline of Athens, since his plays, especially those dealing with social inequality and the military impulse, also helped to undermine confidence in the traditional beliefs and values. A well constituted civilization must always rest upon the subordination of the many to the self-interest of the few. The taxes collected from the common people in ancient and feudal times were not spent on hospitals, schools or welfare programs for the indigent, but on the building of great monuments, paying standing armies, or one's military retainers, and on the patronage of artists and craftsmen. When not used for these or related purposes, they went into the coffers of the ruling class where they stayed until needed. This was the way in which history was made, i.e., by the decisions and actions of a ruling elite who drew their sustenance from the labor of the less privileged. Thus, historically at least, the ideal state is not, as has been believed by the devotees of Plato, a society in which each individual can find fulfillment in pursuit of the occupation he is best qualified to perform, for this is only part of the story. Far more than this, it is an entity for making history and does this by subordinating the welfare of the majority to the needs and passions of a minority. As for the place of literature in the new age, it will once again occupy a lowly position as it did in feudal times.

LEGALITY IN PERSPECTIVE

The man in the street generally thinks of law in terms of an organized body of rules, regulations and penalties. Then there are the institutions and special groups which give to the legal system of modern industrial society its awesome power, e.g., lawyers, judges, prosecutors, police and prisons. All this is daunting enough, and the average person is primarily concerned with staying on the right side of the law, rather than analyzing it to test its validity. But law and justice are in fact far more complex matters, when looked at from an historical point of view, than the average man can readily appreciate. For one thing, the society's complexity or level of civilization will have a significant bearing on its rules, regulations and penalties.

For many non-literate societies, a formal body of laws is unnecessary; time-honored customs are sufficient to maintain social harmony. But many such societies usually lack a hierarchial social structure presided over by a universally recognized leader. Instead, the elders will be looked to for leadership on occasions when this is felt to be desirable. But as a rule, each adult member of the society will think himself to be the equal of any other member. The Nuer of Southern Sudan, whose customs are well known to students of Social Anthropology though the pioneering work of the late E. Evans-Pritchard, are a good example of a large non-literate society with almost no legal mechanism whatsoever. Battles between neighboring villages leading to what is known as the blood feud are not uncommon. There is no force within Nuer society strong enough to inspire order and keep the peace, though disputes are eventually settled after sufficient time has gone by to allow the quarreling parties to get together and talk over their differences with the help of an intermediary if need be. The Nuer is what is known in social anthropological jargon as an acephalous society, i.e., a society without a recognized leader.

Those non-literate societies which do have a recognized leader tend to have a more highly developed system of rules and regulations than those that do not. Directives in regard to matters concerning the entire society emanate from the chief; all disputes of major importance would be brought before him to adjudicate. And unless part of the society is in a state of open rebellion against his rule, there are unlikely to be pitched battles fought between its members, as these would only serve to undermine the authority of the chief and lessen the morale of his followers. Thus, in such a situation, peace and justice can be seen as emanating directly from the chief. In many cases, he would strengthen his authority as did the Zulu paramount chief, by making himself high priest, i.e., spiritual leader, as well as political leader of his society. Obviously such a society would be much better placed to defend itself or to make war, as the case demanded, than would a society such as the Nuer with its lack of hierarchial leadership and consequent low level of discipline. Thus, while the Zulu regiments became great conquerors and empire builders in fact, the Nuer never went beyond raiding each other or the neighbouring Dinka tribe for cattle and whatever else they could carry off. It is also to be noted that, for a time at least, the Zulus were able to hold their own against first the advancing tide of Boer settlers, and later the regular British army, before succumbing to western technological superiority.

When we come to discussing law in the literate societies, especially those of western civilization, we are forced to embark upon a rather more detailed analysis. Two themes run throughout the history of law in western civilization. One is the quest for justice, i.e., just laws, and the other is the close connection between law and the exercise of power. These two themes are almost inseparable, cropping up again and again from the earliest times right down to the modern era. The debate over the nature of law and justice can be said to have begun with the pronouncements on the subject attributed to Socrates and set down in the immortal dialogues of Plato. It is often said that one of the weaknesses of the ancient Greeks as pursuers of knowledge was that they were so committed to theoretical deduction that they tended to ignore the practical aspects of many of the studies in which they were involved. This would seem to be just as true of much of their social and political theory as it was of their natural science. Thus, although they were the first to discuss the nature of law and justice, they could never come to terms with the fact that justice emerges from the possession of power and not the other way around. In one of the most famous of Plato's dialogues dealing with this subject, several characters attempt to define the nature of justice. The most enduring definition, that of Thrasymachus, namely that justice is the right of the strong, is immediately taken to task and discredited. The next definition follows; this is that justice is treating everybody equally. But objections are again raised to this definition on the grounds that one man may be incapacitated while another may enjoy good health, and to treat them equally could be an injustice. But we are much closer to the idealistic definition of justice. All that needs to be done is to introduce the idea of equity, i.e., weighing all available facts before a decision is made. Thus, we arrive at the Socratic definition of justice, i.e., justice is giving to each man his due.

From Socrates onwards, the Greek philosophers tended to idealize justice, as if there was one standard applicable to every age and society. Aristotle, not to be outdone by his great mentor, was also generous in his praise of the just society and stressed the central importance of law. But, not being as original as Plato, we can hardly be too hard on Aristotle for his limited insights.

Thus, he tells us that, "law is reason free from all passion." It was not until some two thousand years later that David Hume came along to remind us that "reason is and ought to be the slave of passions." Neither is Aristotle content to leave matters here but wants us to know that law and justice are what gives to a society its superiority over non-human communities, maintaining that "man, when perfected, is the best of animals, but when separated from law and justice, he is the worst of all." Here I think he was letting his enthusiasm for the just society get the better of him, for he is talking as if the existence of law and justice was some kind of magical formula which could guarantee the perfection of man. We now have enough experience to know better. Plato came much closer to the essentials of human society, i.e., when he desisted from thinking as he thought Socrates would and instead applied his own insights and experiences. For he correctly perceived that when perfected, man would have little need for law and what was just would be decided, not by the average man, but by the one who was in a position to know best.

Be this as it may, the post-Socratic Greek philosophers appear to have been mesmerized by the appeal of deductive logic and the power of reasoned argument, whereas in truth, justice has always involved not only the power of the opposing arguments but also a large number of other factors, such as economic constellations, the status of the accused and that of the accuser, the nature of current trends in the society as a whole, and so on. The Athenian philosophers, true to the middle class ideals of their city, saw moderation as the essence of justice but failed to see that even under optimum conditions passion and personal preference is never far below the surface. Who, for instance, can forget the fact that one of the first things that the Athenians did with their newly restored freedom was to place Socrates on trial for his life. Thus, not even a democracy is above taking decisive action against those who seem to have no other ambition in life than to demoralize their fellow citizens. Nevertheless, Socrates' misguided search for virtue was to leave a lasting impression upon the moral philosophy of all those thinkers who came after him, right down to the present time. The influence of the Socratic tradition is apparent in the famous quotation of the great jurist of Republican Rome, Cicero: " We are servants of the law in order that we may be free." Whatever else we may say about the origins of this quotation, it certainly did not accurately represent conditions as they existed in the Rome of Cicero's time.

Cicero was well aware of the fact that, outside the municipal courts of Rome, it was force and not freedom which was the dominant factor. He knew that it was not a committee of Roman jurists that crushed the Catilline conspiracy, but the arms of the Republic. He witnessed the defeat of Pompey, Cato and the other Senate stalwarts by Caesar, and the overthrow of the Republic in all but name. He knew all about the proscription lists issued by those who had the city under their control, e.g., Marius, Sulla, Anthony, Octavius. Neither could the law protect him from the assassination squad sent by Anthony to dispatch him. Perhaps Cicero did not fully appreciate that the extra-legal activities which were waged intermittently in Rome were not transient aberrations but came from the same source as did rational jurisprudence, i.e., the exercise of power. Of course, whether power is exercised tyrannically or constructively is quite another matter. The enduring fact of life, then, is that law has always been the servant of man and must always remain so.

Though depending on the circumstances operating at the time, law may be administered in the name of an individual, a special group, a particular class, or simply the majority. Rule by an individual could mean an absolute monarch or tyrannical usurper or a military despot, whereas rule by a special group implies that those who exercise power are united by certain commonly held beliefs (sometimes codified) which represent what they feel to be in the best interest of their society. More often than not this special group has no traditional roots within the society, but comes to power upon the overthrow of the old status quo, believing itself to have a mission of regenerating the nation. This was the case with the Puritans who came to power under Cromwell, with the Jacobins and the Bolsheviks. But the two types of rule we are here particularly concerned with from the point of view of their legal structure are the last two of the above four. The first of these two, i.e., rule by a particular class, implies aristocracy, whereas the second (rule by the majority) implies democracy. Both have in common the fact that the law must reflect the dominant ideals of the society. Thus, in an aristocratic society, the law (as far as it can be said to exist) will clearly favor the interests of a distinct minority over those of the majority, whereas in a democratic society the law will tend to reflect the egalitarian ideals of the society.

This seems simple enough as far as it goes, but while there can be little dispute as to what constitutes an aristocratic society, there has been a great deal of debate (much of it needless) as to what constitutes a democratic society. Some have felt that the right to vote in the election of a parliamentary representative is not enough, but only direct involvement by the entire population in deciding major issues would be sufficient to classify a nation as democratic. Others are not so much concerned with the exact arrangements of the voting system, but with greater economic equality. The most radical of these do not believe that popular democracy, as now constituted, could bring about greater economic equality with the speed and thoroughness they would like to see. We need not waste too much time over the second of these two issues, since with regard to this matter, I have already stated my belief that there is no contradiction between democracy and the desire for economic equality. They have been getting along quite comfortably and will no doubt continue to do so.

With regard to the call for the direct involvement of the populace in political affairs, this has ceased to be anything other than the fanciful dream of romantics. The modern origins of this movement go back to J.J. Rousseau's concept of the General Will, according to which he imagined an ideal community in which all adults participated freely in political deliberation before taking a vote on the matter, all having agreed before hand to be bound by the result regardless of the size of the majority. By Rousseau's reasoning, whether it was a large or a small one the majority represented the General Will which would probably be the best course of action for the society as a whole. On the other hand, the minority more probably than not represented those who did not properly understand the issues involved, or were perverse and recalcitrant or just wanted to vote differently from the majority for the sake of doing so. Thus, there would be no need for elections or political parties since the General Will would guarantee a fair decision was reached on every occasion. The minority could reasonably be expected to fall in line once the issue had been decided. In theory, it must be said that this does not sound to be a bad idea, provided that the society is of a reasonable size and differences in wealth are not too great. But as a concrete reality, and especially considering the lessons that history has taught us about the true nature of civilization, such a society would appear to have strictly defined limits.

Moreover, Rousseau himself admitted that the General Will concept would not work in a modern state, but was in fact a description of how an ideal non-industrialized democratic society should be organized. Nevertheless, Rousseau has always had his admirers, and even today they are still around. Thus, we hear talk of replacing the large modern cities of today with small face-to-face communities which presumably would be small enough to allow the operation of the General Will. A more viable trend in the movement to increase the involvement of the people in the political process was begun by Marx with a few sentences in his book entitled *The Civil War in France.* In this work, for the first and only time, he sketched the outline of the possible political organization of a future socialist state. The basic unit was to be the democratic commune and each commune would send representatives to the provincial assembly and each provincial assembly would send representatives to the national assembly. Marx probably felt that the national assembly would not meet very often and then only long enough to deal with the few pressing problems of national importance. This idea was not particularly original and was certainly more cumbersome than a straightforward national election by district, but it kept alive the ideal of the community, rather than the individual, as the sovereign political power.

With late-nineteenth-century industrial society confronted by the growing realities of industrial power, split-level systems of representation such as that elaborated by Marx, fell into disfavor and were replaced by more activist ideas. Thus, by the end of the first world war, anarcho-syndicalism and democratic pluralism had arrived on the scene. The former involves the violent takeover of factories by the workers and their management as autonomous entities under worker committees. The French engineer and political propagandist, Georges Sorel, wrote in support of this doctrine and propounded the myth of the general strike to go along with it. Anarcho-syndicalism did enjoy fairly widespread support among revolutionary groups on the continent in the early part of the twentieth century, but was not heard from again until it experienced a brief revival during the hectic events that occurred in France in May 1968. Democratic Pluralism on the other hand is associated with the name of H.D. Cole and several other noted British social democrats. Its supporters have certainly been more restrained than the proponents of anarcho-syndicalism. Although one of the main planks of this doctrine when it first appeared was support for worker control, its most consistent principle has been the belief that the democratic process should pay greater attention to the interests of the occupational groups into which the modern industrialized nation is divided, allowing each group to be represented roughly in proportion to its numbers.

By this means, the various interests of different groups could be accommodated by a process of give and take, though the majority group would always retain the upper hand. The weaknesses of this type of political arrangement are so obvious as to hardly need comment. For example, the various groups could become bogged down in an irreconcilable conflict of interest which would threaten the nation's stability. Then again, what about those interests not represented by one particular group but are all the same of great importance to the entire society — how effectively could they be represented within such a system of government? But most of all, such a blatant gerrymandering of the political representation within a modern industrial society would set up a permanent majority of limited outlook, and this would certainly not be in the best interests of the nation as a whole. From what little I am able to understand of their political philosophy, it would seem that both anarcho-syndicalism and democratic pluralism live on the ideals of the International Socialists. As for conventional politics, we do regularly hear the suggestion that a little decentralization would be a good thing, but even if this could be done, it would hardly affect the realities of present day life.

Still, there was at least one place where the people did govern themselves directly and did so very well when under the guidance of highly capable leadership — this was ancient Athens. Athens was unique in being a complete state — not just a community within a greater sovereign entity — which was also a model democracy, by the standards of the time. Also, its aristocratic class appears to have been neither very large nor very powerful; at least that was the situation after the reforms of Solon. This fact, combined with the ingenious arrangement of their compact body politic, ensured that the average individual had a greater say in decisions of state, as well as matters that would affect him directly, than has ever again been the case. Athenian democracy produced many great statesmen who were also fine orators and men of outstanding courage, e.g., Aristides, Pericles, Thucydides, Themistocles and Demosthenes, but there was also another side to it, i.e., popular democracy gone out of control. It is something which occurred when capable leaders were not at hand and their place was filled by demagogues born of the rabble. This aspect of Athenian democracy is also captured for us by the historians of ancient Athens and makes ugly reading. So much so that one is almost tempted to sympathize with the periodic attempts made to reassert oligarchy.

We are told that in proportion, as the popular assembly or large portion detached from it for the exercise of judicial functions, drew all the branches of the sovereignty more and more into their sphere, the character of their proceedings became more and more subject to the influence of the lower class of the citizens which constituted a permanent majority. And thus the democracy, instead of the equality which was its supposed basis, in fact established the ascendancy of a faction which, although greatly preponderant in numbers, no more represented the whole state than the oligarchy itself, and which was more prone to yield to the impulse of the moment, more easily misled by blind or treacherous guides, and might just as frequently trample, not only on law and custom, but on justice and humanity. This disease of a democracy was sometimes designated by the term "ochlocracy" or the dominion of the rabble. The historians tell us that a democracy thus corrupted exhibited many features of a tyranny. It was jealous of all who were eminently distinguished by birth, fortune or reputation; it encouraged flatterers and sycophants; it was insatiable in its demands on the property of the rich and readily listened to charges which exposed them to death or confiscation. We are further told that the class which suffered such oppression, commonly ill satisfied with the principle of the constitution itself, was inflamed with most furious animosity by the mode in which it was applied and regarded the great mass of its fellow-citizens as its mortal enemies. In the *Republic* (Book IV) Plato confirms this experience with the observation that "any city, however small, is in fact divided into two, one the city of the poor, the other of the rich."

Republican Rome was quite a different proposition from democratic Athens. The aristocracy of Rome was powerful and deeply entrenched; it was not going to allow itself either to be legally reformed out of existence (as happened in Athens) or to be violently overthrown by the majority. To this end, the Senate tried to ensure that, although it shared certain of its powers with the popular assembly, it would always remain the dominant partner. The Senate was so successful in this objective, that it was only after several centuries of artistocratic leadership that the Roman masses began to get restless and demand a greater share of power. This short but intense period of class strife is very revealing, for it indicates how deeply the principle of aristocracy was ingrained in Republican Rome. The Gracchi brothers are the first ones to make an assault on the principle of aristocratic leadership, and both pay with their lives for betraying the class of their birth. Two issues are at the center of the great class conflict which racks Rome during this period. The first is a diminution in the power of the Senate in favor of the popular assembly and the second is the granting of full political rights to Italians who are non-Roman. This reform, if carried out, would have tended to put the Senate under greater pressure to reduce its involvement in national affairs.

If Rome's democrats had got their way, the power of the Senate would have been gradually whittled away in a manner similar to what took place in Athens and the other ancient Greek democratic cities. Perhaps the Senate might have served the purpose of supreme court like the Areopagias in Athens, though even this body was abolished by Pericles on the grounds of its being incompatible with Athenian democracy. It was such a fate that the Roman ruling class intended to avoid at all costs. Fortunately, they had the determination and the leaders to ensure their survival. The next enemy of the Senate proved to be far more successful than the Gracchi brothers were. This was Marius, the illiterate Roman General, a great soldier whose heart was with the people. He actually succeeded in taking over Rome, and for a brief period Rome enjoyed something akin to popular democracy, although it was all rather chaotic and essentially held together by the faith of the people in Marius. This brief flirtation with non-aristocratic leadership was swiftly crushed by Sulla, who set himself up as dictator and proceeded to institute a series of conservative reforms reaffirming the powers of the Senate before returning to private life. By this time, the Republic was fast approaching its end, but at least the coming battle would be between aristocratic forces rather than between the aristocracy and the masses led by rogues and demagogues.

In comparing the judicial organization of Athens and Rome, the thoughtful observer is struck by the fact that despite their great intellectual preeminence in the ancient world, the Athenians were never able construct the basis for a rational legal system, unlike the Romans who were generally much inferior in most other intellectual pursuits. The answer to this puzzle lies, I believe, in the differences in social structure of the two city states, the first one dominated by small farmers, traders and artisans, the other by large land owners and wealthy merchants. In other words, Rome was a society dominated by men of substantial property holdings who stood well above a moderately wealthy middle class and the propertyless rabble. The class structure of ancient Athens was never so distinctive, and of course, was never effectively mirrored in its political structure (except during periods of oligarchy) after the reforms of Cleisthenes. The relationship between the law and the society's social and economic organization was a matter which attracted a great deal of comment from Karl Marx.

I am inclined to believe that he was right in seeing a link between the social structure and legal structure of a society. A rational system of law can be a most useful instrument in helping to maintain the status quo of aristocratic dominance (within a Republican framework of government) while at the same time appeasing the propertyless masses with the thought that they have recourse to the law which protects their interests along with those of the very wealthy. An added advantage of a well organized legal system to such a highly disciplined society as Republican Rome was that it helped to prevent recourse to more drastic modes of settling disputes among the patrician class. In feudal society, on the other hand, this was the normal way of settling disputes rather than recourse to the law courts, at least until the arrival of the Renaissance and the subsequent development of the centralized state. No more will be said about the legal structure of feudal society, although it is a subject to which we shall be returning at a later time.

Right now I am more interested in post-Renaissance developments in legal and political thought, since it is these which have largely determined the shape of present-day legal theory. When one talks about post-Renaissance legal theory one immediately thinks of Natural Law and the name of one of the greatest exponents of this school of thought, Thomas Hobbes. Hobbes is the first author of note to give us a clear indication that the days of aristocratic leadership are no more. He reduces life to a competitive scramble, the war of all against all. He talks about the struggle for power but he is really talking about the drive to obtain security by way of material success. He makes this quite clear by stressing that the only way a man can avail himself of power and the means to live well is to acquire more of these things. We can thus be sure that this is not an analysis of an aristocratic way of life, for the aristocracy already have the means to live well. So Hobbes is in fact addressing himself to the spirit of nascent capitalism which was then emerging in Northwest Europe. According to Hobbes, there is a natural tendency for man to maximize his self-interest. Therefore, he further observed that security depends upon the existence of a government having the power to keep the peace and, if necessary, to apply sanctions in order to restrain man's innately unsocial inclinations. He also felt that fear of punishment was one of the most effective agencies by which men are socialized and that the authority of law extends only so far as its enforcement is able to reach.

We can already see the difference between the way in which the legal order of Republican Rome served that society and the way in which the emerging legal order of capitalist England would be serving its society. In the first case, the law was structured in such a way as to maintain the power and privileges of a plutocratic elite. For all intents and purposes, membership of this body was fixed by birth so that wealth, power and prestige were automatically handed on from father to son. A small degree of upward mobility did exist, but this was not sufficient to alter the most fundamental aspect of the society, i.e., the leadership exercised by an hereditary elite. The Roman middle class, though it existed in far great numbers than the nobility, was almost a cipher, politically powerless. With Hobbes, the situation is quite different, for he is speaking about the newly awakening middle class. The aristocracy, which has already lost most of its political power, had its day; it was now the turn of members of the middle class to struggle amongst themselves for supremacy. Although these mainly economic struggles among the middle class could never be a threat to the integrity of the state, as the power struggles among the aristocracy had been, Hobbes nevertheless believes it best that a powerful figure in the form of an absolute monarch (or failing this a sovereign parliament) should be on hand to lay down the rules and give a final decision on all matters of major importance. Obviously, Hobbes had taken his own words too much to heart, since there was hardly need for the level of government involvement which he advocated. It was left to John Locke to improve upon the insights of Hobbes. He did this so well that nearly some three hundred years later his ideas are still basic to the legal and political creeds of the western world, especially so in the United States of America.

Like Hobbes, Locke also recognized that the age of the capitalist individual had arrived and this required a political theory which captured the spirit of the age. But Locke's approach to the problem was far more sensitive to bourgeois prejudices than that of Hobbes and it was this which was to endear him to future generations of liberal theorists and politicians. The most important group of them would, of course, turn out to be the founding fathers of the United States constitution. The essence of Locke's viewpoint is expressed in his *Second Treatise on Civil Government:* "The freedom of man, and liberty of acting according to his own will, is grounded on his having reason, which is able to instruct him in that law he is to govern himself by." According to Locke, then, man's natural reason should be near enough in complete accordance with the laws by which he is governed. This is, of course, a species of natural law, a concept which was eventually to be discredited by the writings of David Hume and others. But the liberal ideas which emerged from Locke's writings were destined to stand the test of time, even though they have been stretched well beyond the original intention of their author.

Thus, Locke held freedom of speech and freedom of association to be just as important as the right to property which a man had acquired through his own efforts. Therefore, it was the duty of the government to protect the individual in the enjoyment of these rights. But Hobbes appears to have considered these rights to be expendable should they ever threaten the unity of the whole. Then again, Locke favored religious tolerance for all groups save atheists, whereas Hobbes appears to have been indifferent to religion and upheld the right of the monarch to insist that the nation subscribe to the same religion as he did. As well as his discussion on civil government, Locke gives a most eloquent defense of the right to property, something which would hardly have been considered necessary when aristocracy was the leading principle of social organization. Locke argued that the right to private property arises because by labor a man extends, so to speak, his own personality into the objects produced. Private property, then, is a right which each individual brings to society in his own person, just as he brings the physical energy of his body. According to Locke's reckoning, society did not create the right to property, but both society and government were nevertheless under an obligation to protect it.

In the days of aristocracy, naked force, and not legalistic restraints, confirmed one's right to property. Therefore, protection of property rested with those who possessed it. The nobles were quite capable of keeping by force what they had taken by force and hence did not need to appeal to the goodwill of the common people. Further, since they also had control of the government, their position was never seriously threatened from below. With the passing of the middle ages, all this began to change. The rules of the game had to be rewritten to accommodate a different type of society, one in which the ownership of great wealth would neither guarantee political power nor cause one to act exclusively in one's class interests if one gained political power. Also the non-agricultural enterprise was just beginning to take its place next to the traditional land-based enterprise as a significant component of the nation's economy. It was against this background that Locke wrote his treatise *On Civil Government* and his other major works. Anyone who closely scrutinizes with an open mind Locke's defense of the right to property cannot help coming away with the opinion that it is rather weak and unconvincing.

For instance, he believed that, except within the most narrow limits, society could not justly regulate this right, but on the other hand, he expects government to protect this right with the full support of the society as a whole. Such a position is untenable, since it expects too much wisdom to be shown by a popular democracy. For while Locke would agree with the owners of property that sizable differences in wealth are essential to a well-constituted society, there is no guarantee that a popularly elected government could maintain these differences even if it also believed them to be necessary for the society's well being. Thus, once responsibility for protecting one's birthright is handed over to the representatives of the majority, one has no right to expect that such a government will be sparing with regard to its claims upon the property of the rich. Evidently Locke did expect it to be, and here he turned out to be wrong. Moreover, relying on a democratically elected government as protector of one's rights and arbitrator of one's disputes tends greatly to diminish the individual relative to the state, no matter how great his personal wealth or economic power. This subjection of the individual (i.e., every individual) to the will of an all-powerful impersonal state first appears in the writings of Hobbes (*Leviathan*).

Admittedly, Locke attempts to make the idea more palatable by the attention he gives to individual freedoms, but the net result is the same. The individual is subordinated to the state with a thoroughness that would have been impossible in an aristocratic society, for the simple reason that the nobility was the state. A similar case of weak, muddle-headed thinking arises in connection with Locke's views on individual rights, i.e., they failed to live up to expectation. George Sabine tells us that "He (Locke) conceived all natural rights on the same lines as property, that is to say as attributes of the individual person born with him, and hence, as indefeasible claims upon both society and government. Such claims can never justly be set aside, since society itself exists to protect them; they can be regulated only to the extent that is necessary to give them effective protection."[1] But since these rights only had meaning within a social context, and since both society and its government were to be superior to any one individual, it follows that government acting under a desire to serve the interests of the greatest number, could curtail any right without serious challenge.

Alternatively, it could extend individual rights to such an extent as to seriously imperil the integrity of the nation as a whole, while disregarding the protests of the small minority who are staunchly opposed to the changes. This can ultimately result in the license to act as one wants, a process which is already leading to the destruction of all worthwhile values and their replacement by a state of anarchy, as each individual sets his own standard of behavior. This is certainly not what Locke had intended. But without the stabilizing presence of a well-entrenched and politically powerful aristocracy, government and individual freedom were bound to grow at the expense of individual responsibility. Likewise, with his belief that "life," "liberty" and "estate" of one person can be limited only to make effective the equally valid claims of another person to the same rights, Locke set the stage for the equality of opportunity doctrine which has done so much to penalize those who would rather stick to custom and tradition than give in to progressive trends, something which should be their right according to Locke's original views on the matter. But the truth is that within mass-oriented modern industrial society, the small minority with noble views have no voice in national affairs and hence no influence on the direction taken by their nation.

Lockean liberalism still remains today the most enduring trait of our political and legal institutions. Although the late eighteenth and entire nineteenth centuries were remarkable for producing a vast amount of original political and social theory, very little that was new was added to legal theory. In fact, the English jurist John Austin, although considered to be the most eminent legal theorist of his time, and an important influence on the utilitarian school, produced nothing that was original but for the most part restated truisms which had been known to legal theory well before his time — no wonder his lectures at London University were so poorly attended. For example, he agreed with Hobbes to the effect that if a law could not be enforced then it cannot be valid, a most practical observation which carries the force of common sense as well as legal theory. In addition to this rule, there are several other criteria of sound law making.

One is that a law should be general in nature rather than pertaining only to a specific person or thing. This rule can be set aside on special occasions to allow the nation's legislative body to display a touch of individuality in decreeing the preservation of an historic landmark or acknowledging the meritorious services of a particular person, or for some other reason. Also, in times of national or local emergency when martial law may be declared, the authorities have the power to act outside the law and ignore altogether the rule of generality. Another rule of sound law making is that of permanence, in other words, law must be used to regulate a state of affairs which is not simply a transient phenomenon but one which can be expected to remain a serious problem well into the future. All this having been fairly said, we must not make the mistake of believing the existence of a logical legal system to be the most important feature of a civilized society. In fact, I venture to assert that a literate but well adapted society can exist quite happily with very little in the way of a formal legal structure. Note the fact that lawyers only came back into prominence after the middle ages had come to an end.

Thus, the fundamental question of this chapter is whether or not a civilization radically different from and psychologically superior to the present one could exist without a legal order. Civilization and legality seem almost to have gone hand in hand, ancient Greece and Rome providing us with a good illustration of this fact. In those pre-industrial societies where a legal tradition was not strongly developed, religion and custom always played an important part in determining what was right and wrong. The Old Testament of the Jews and the Koran of the Muslims are notable examples of what I mean. There have, in fact, been few civilizations worthy of note which did not rely on either legal restraints or religious authority (separately or in combination) to assist with the maintenance of social cohesion. Thus, at first sight, the prospects for the existence of a dominantly secular civilization unencumbered by formally organized legal or religious institutions does not look too good. But on closer examination, quite a different picture emerges. To begin with, we may note that the earliest legal codes, which have been the models for all later ones, were based on time honored customs, rather than rationally deduced propositions.

It was only later that these codified customs were elaborated and rationalized to produce a coherent body of law which could assist with the adjudication of the most complex disputes to the satisfaction of both parties. Judicial precedents were later added as a way of providing consistency in the interpretation of the more obscure parts of the law or its application to a rather involved case. This is probably the way in which Roman law developed, and it is most certainly the way in which English Common Law developed. The latter is a body of law which has been the basis for the legal system of many nations, including the U.S.A. The importance of custom in shaping law was fully appreciated by the German jurist Count Savigny, who was the foremost theorist of the German Historical School. Although this line of thought remained influential for quite a time, many later jurists came to believe that the German Historical School had over-emphasized the importance of custom in shaping law. If one considers the development of jurisprudence since the industrial revolution began, this criticism may indeed be valid.

Expediency rather than custom has been the dominant factor of jurisprudence over the last two hundred years as our law makers have struggled to keep up with the rapidly changing nature of industrial society. Judges have tended to take increasing latitude in regards to interpreting statutory laws, in setting new precedents, and applying previous ones. With an increasingly complex society has come an increasingly complex legal structure. Our law schools are turning out more and more graduates each year. With more and more laws and detailed regulations having the force of law, litigation has become the rule rather than the exception. In fact, it is fair to say that the modern industrial age is the most legalistic age that has ever existed, easily surpassing Republican Rome in this respect. Having a family lawyer has become almost as essential as having a family doctor. To help with civil law problems, the individual has the Citizens Advice Bureau in England and an assortment of semi-official and private bodies serve the same purpose in the United States, while in connection with the administration of criminal law all western countries make provision for the defendant to receive legal aid if his means are insufficient to pay the costs of his own defense. But with all this attention to due process, and equality before the law, and despite all the money spent on law enforcement, the legal system of contemporary western society is falling apart at the seams.

The morale of the police has suffered greatly over the last few years for a number of reasons, all of which are well beyond their control. Thus, we find that they are nobody's best friend and everybody's punching bag. They are suspected by the poor of being biased against the underprivileged and by many of the rest of us, at various times, of being incompetent or venal. They are caught in the middle of the argument between those advocating more law and order and an altogether tougher approach to the criminal, as opposed to those who are calling for lighter sentences for all forms of crime and more emphasis on what they refer to as the constructive aspects of the penal system such as parole and probation. The average policeman is no doubt more inclined to the former position, but he cannot be too vocal in expressing his viewpoint in this respect for fear of laying himself open to censure from his superiors or from one of the numerous watchdog groups on civil liberties which now abound in most western nations. The police are often the specific or unintended targets of fanatical terrorist groups and deranged individuals or simply people who want to gain public attention for what they believe to be a worthy cause.

They are regularly placed in situations (especially in connection with crowd control) in which confrontation becomes inevitable, resulting in serious injury and perhaps loss of life, all of which might have been avoided if their superiors had shown greater consideration in their deployment. They are not responsible for devising the laws which they have to enforce, yet they must accept at least part of the criticism when it appears that these laws cannot be effectively enforced. They have absolutely no power to alter and very little to influence the society which relies upon their dedication to duty as its first line of defense. Like most other groups of public employees, they have recently become seriously discontented with their working conditions and levels of pay — discontent which has broken out into open rebellion, including disorderly demonstrations and refusal to deal with minor traffic violations. But unlike most other groups of public employees, they are not permitted to take strike action in pursuit of their demands, as this would be a breach of contract leaving them open to instant dismissal without compensation and without the possibility of again rejoining the nation's police force.

Surrounded by all these contradictory pressures, it is not surprising that the police are sometimes over-zealous in carrying out their duties and then lash out wildly at their critics, or are often accused of over-reacting in situations where tact and patience would have achieved better results than the employment of force, not to mention the large number of what can only be called "questionable arrests" for petty crimes made by all metropolitan police forces of Western Europe and North America. All these things are indications of the strain under which the police are now working. It is no coincidence that in the urban centers of many western nations the police force is seriously understaffed, owing in part to lack of applicants of suitable calibre. Also, the rate of attrition through personnel leaving the metropolitan forces for the less demanding police duties of rural areas or smaller towns has become a serious drain on the manpower of the big city forces — the place where police are most needed. Neither must we forget the increasing tendency of disillusioned personnel at all levels to leave the police force altogether in search of more satisfying or more financially rewarding and less dangerous work. Underlying all these problems is the intense frustration which must be felt acutely by the upper echelons of the police force as well as by the men on the beat, in regard to their inability to check the crime rate. Crime seems to have embarked upon an upward spiral with no foreseeable end in sight. Day-to-day police work appears to be powerless in the face of such stark reality.

On top of the malaise within our law enforcement institutions, there is increasing disenchantment with the legal order itself, especially among a growing number of the young and the more articulate members of western society. We may note in this connection the reported unwillingness of some young people to serve on juries. Many of the elder generation, on the other hand, believe that the courts are far too lenient, especially in regard to their treatment of young offenders. We often hear how a young person is brought before a court on what most would consider to be a serious charge only to be placed on probation and released into the custody of his parents, so that the next day he is free to walk the streets and able to commit more crimes like those for which he was originally brought before the court. More than a few people have asserted that such lenient justice is not justice at all. Others take the opposite viewpoint that the courtroom is not a suitable place for dealing with delinquent youngsters, regardless of their arrest record.

The same people say that only those convicted of violent crimes should be imprisoned and that community service should play a bigger part than it does now in the treatment of wrongdoers. There are also complaints being heard in regard to the increasing number of crimes which go unsolved. One of the reasons for this, the experts tell us, is lack of manpower, and another is that the allocation of resources to law enforcement has barely been able to keep pace with the skyrocketing crime rate. But even if the arrest rate were to be greatly increased we would still encounter serious problems since our beleaguered system of criminal justice is already in a state of near breakdown, with delays getting longer and longer. Admittedly, few western countries have yet reached the situation which prevails in Italy, where someone who has been charged but not convicted can spend up to several years on remand before being finally convicted and sentenced, or in some cases, acquitted and set free.

Nevertheless, all the indications are that this is the direction in which all other western countries are heading unless something very dramatic happens. For the courts are being called upon to handle far more than they can cope with, hence the extensive use of magistrate courts in England and plea bargaining in the U.S.A. to deal with what would have been at one time considered as very serious crimes. The intricate system of appeals which can begin once the lower court has given its verdict may have been a useful adjunct to the basic judicial process at an earlier time, but today this is no longer the case, since it serves only to raise another time-consuming hurdle to the execution of what may be a very worthwhile judgment, e.g., in connection with environmental matters or with the commercial exploitation of sex.

Our legal structure is continuing to survive, but it does not take too much thought to realize that this is no guarantee of the continued good health of modern industrial society. Our legislators are only capable of doing more and more to undermine the legal order, since it would be impossible for them now to desist from introducing each legislative session an infinite variety of bills, most of which are petty, futile or just plain silly, but some of which are bound to be passed into law, though these new laws will have absolutely nothing to do with the most urgent problems facing modern industrial society. This is what the increasing complexity of our lifestyle is doing to us: it is turning our legislators into morons. Or to paraphrase an old Roman saying, the more bankrupt the government, the more the laws are multiplied. And the laws of modern industrial society have been multiplying at a phenomenal rate.

We now have to consider what would be the situation in an age in which the ruling ideals were those of a ruling class, in which town had given way to country, in which mass production had been superseded by small-scale production. Under these circumstances, would not custom once more come to dominate social relationships; would not the need for third party interference greatly diminish? These seem to me to be reasonable assumptions. To understand how we can have a civilization in the new age existing without the guardianship of laws or institutional religion, the nature of the key differences between this age and the new age must be kept in mind. I have already stated that our only hope for a renewal of the human spirit is a period of cataclysmic change which will shake us out of our lethargy and foolish misconceptions as nothing else could ever do. The collapse of the present status quo would undoubtedly be more far-reaching than any previous collapse of a civilization which has so far been recorded in the annals of world history.

It would culminate inevitably in the demise of modern industry as the leading factor in social and economic affairs.

Great changes would follow such an event, and these would shape the new societies, not in years, but almost immediately, i.e., before the people had a chance to realize what was happening. Along with the changes mentioned above, the rhythms of our modern industrial lifestyle which we now take for granted will become foreign to the people of the new age, whereas the slower rhythms of a simple rural lifestyle will become as natural to them as urban existence now is to contemporary western man. Needless to say the political and legal institutions and practices which characterize this age would automatically cease to be relevant. In fact, we can expect the bolder spirits, those who are destined to be members of the regenerated ruling class of the new age, to renounce the authority of the political institutions and laws of their society as soon as it becomes apparent that we are about to see the dawn of a new age.

The main preoccupation of this new breed will be the reestablishment of their ancestral links with the countryside. We may also expect them to begin to extend their dominance in rural parts of the nation, at first stealthily, but later openly, as the old institutions begin to lose their grip on the allegiance of the people. A formal legal structure would be of no use under these circumstances, for it would only serve to impede the rapid establishment of the new status quo. Instead, it will be left to these men of ambition to set their own standards and to set limits to their area of dominance through mutual agreement with like-minded individuals who have also been successful in bringing a sizable area of the countryside under their control. Out of this situation will develop certain conventions and practices which will help to minimize unwanted conflict and promote the existence of civilized social relationships, especially between members of the ruling class.

There will not be any need for a central authority to be reestablished, through members of the ruling class may meet on a national or regional basis to clear up outstanding problems as to areas of dominance. What has already taken place will be sanctified and any nation-wide decrees will be made with the interests of this new ruling class as the most important consideration. Each member of the new ruling class will have absolute responsibility for administering the affairs of his area of dominance. If a noble should ever need military assistance to deal with an external or internal threat to his position he will request it from those of his allies who are closest at hand. Other than this contingency, there will be no interference in the internal affairs of one noble by any other. There will probably be a superior and an inferior rank among the nobility.

Those of superior rank will be distinguished by their higher qualities of leadership, by their consistent success in battle, by their effectiveness in administering the affairs of their domain. Thus, the inferior nobles of a particular region will look to the acknowledged superior nobles of the region for advice and leadership, especially in times of crisis. At national gatherings (should these ever need to be held) a particular region would be represented in the main by its superior nobles, with perhaps a small number of inferior nobles from the region to act in support. Since a superior noble would be well-known and generally respected throughout the region, he could be called upon to arbitrate in disputes between lesser nobles if both parties so desired this. This is something which could only happen if the superior noble in question was not allied with either party to the dispute, for if he were he would have already given military support to his ally.

Although a superior noble would be expected to be among the largest land holders in the region, the main source of his strength would be that a sizable number of his fellow nobles would be prepared to give him their loyalty at a moment's notice, so that whatever course of action he may decide to undertake, he knows that he can rely on their full support. This unqualified support would only last as long as the superior noble was able to show himself second to none in those qualities expected of leaders within a warrior society. This is why the position of superior noble (for a given locality) would always have to be held by someone not only respected for his shrewdness and sagacity but also for his military powers and success in dealing decisively with his enemies on the battle field. Since, for the most part, the common people will be expected to look after their own affairs, there will be little need for the massive apparatus of government which has come to characterize the legio-rational system of authority that we now have.

As to exactly how the new status quo will be established, I can only say that the following comments are offered more in the way of educated speculation than as a definite prognosis. There are two things we can be certain of. First the struggle leading to the establishment of the new status quo will take place in the countryside among those men who have the greatest desire to dominate all around them. Secondly, the vast majority will be bewildered and insecure; they will have enough problems coping with the difficulties of adapting to rural life. They will hardly be in a position to participate with confidence in the struggle which will determine who shall become members of the new ruling class. Only the members of this class will have any say in the governing of the nation. Thus, for the most part the vast majority will be simply bystanders, passive observers of the great drama which will unfold within their very midst.

But this does not mean that the struggle will involve no one except the family and friends of these men of ambition, since their collective desire to dominate will set in motion enormous military forces the like of which will probably not have been witnessed for a very long time. Ordinary men will be prepared to follow them in large numbers and subordinate their will to that of their chosen leader, knowing that he and all he stands for represents the future which no one can escape, so the choice will be to conquer or be conquered. Whilst only a relatively small number of men (compared to the population as a whole) can become conquering leaders, a great many more can avoid being conquered by joining up with a potential conqueror. And this is what they will do in their thousands and tens of thousands as soon as the new age gets underway. The land titles of the old age, the laws and values of the old age, will mean nothing to the men of the new age. All will be wide open country waiting to be divided up and pacified by a new breed of conquering heroes. All stratagems will be permissible; no one will be able to consider himself safe from assault on his position until his area of dominance has been officially acknowledged by all those who are able to threaten his ascendancy.

There is nothing strange or shocking about a future characterized by the free play of the unfettered ambitions of some men to dominate their fellows. The struggle for power which may even begin before the great transition has come about, will ensure that only men of superior ability attain a position of dominance and leadership in the new age. Further, the rank of superior noble will always be there for an exceptionally ambitious noble to aspire to — an honor he could obtain either by mounting a challenge to one of the superior nobles of his region or by some other equally impressive means. Thus, the leadership of the nation would always be in the hands of the most capable men in the nation and as soon as any one of them (among the superior nobility especially) showed signs of weakness or incompetence he would quickly lose his influence and prestige and may be threatened with displacement by a more able relative or other member of his class. This competitive struggle for power and prestige will be one of the most abiding features of the new age.

We might also note that competitive struggle is the mark of a vigorous society and this aspect of the new age can be compared to the free enterprise system in its heydey, i.e., before monopoly capital came to the fore. But the aristocratic ethos of the new age will be far superior to the capitalist ethos of the days of laissez faire. For one thing, the bookkeeper mentality which dominates the mind of the capitalist whether of the early variety or the much weaker contemporary breed, will be entirely absent, more so because industry in the new age will be kept to a minimum so that only what is most useful will be produced. Although members of the ruling class will employ artisans and make use of manufactured products (made in workshops, not factories) they will not concern themselves in any way whatsoever with the management of industry or commerce as it would be beneath their dignity to do so. Competitive struggle will be the redeeming virtue of the new age; it will prevent the societies in which it is most energetically pursued from slipping into the languid condition so common among those peoples in whom the traits necessary for military greatness are absent. It will also prevent our newly reborn civilizations from once again sinking into decadence and effeminacy. What all this will mean in regard to the status of law in the new age should be readily apparent — justice will once again be the right of the strong!

Equality before the law will have no meaning in the new age, for in the first place there will be no statutory laws. There will be edicts issued from time to time in the name of the ruling noble, but these will be mainly to tell the people what is expected of them in response to an abnormal situation of temporary duration, rather than to lay down permanent rules as to how they should live. Thus, for the most part, social affairs will be dominated by custom and tradition, which the ruling class could conceivably interpret at any time to suit their own convenience. And in the second place, there will be no equality. The relationship between a noble and a commoner residing within the boundaries of his domain will be on a similar level to that of the relationship between an absolute monarch and the humblest of his subjects. The noble man would have the right to treat a commoner residing within his patrimony just as he pleased. Relations between individuals in the new age will be based exclusively on rank, not on the principles of law equally applicable to all.

There will be no popular tribunal to protect the rights of the common people, since the latter will have only those rights granted to them by their ruling lord. This is one area in which the new age will differ from Republican Rome, and other aristocratic societies in which the position of the ruling class was bolstered by law, a factor which could on occasions work against them as well as for them. Thus, the Roman Senate regularly found itself in the position of having to punish members of the patrician class much against its will for misdeeds committed against members of the lower order. Moreover, it is a fact that the general populace was able to wring concession after concession from an aristocratic body (the Roman Senate) which relied to a large extent on the trappings of legality to maintain itself in power. The aristocracy of the new age will have no desire to meet democracy even half way.

A full-blooded aristocracy or nothing will be the cry of the men of destiny in the new age. Although a ruling noble will be absolute master within his own domain, this does not mean that the nobility of the new age will indulge in cruel atrocities against those who look to them for protection and leadership, since the very fact of their natural superiority will generally be sufficient to restrain all but the most vile nobles from abusing commoners. We will have a return to the aristocratic code of *noblesse oblige.* Adherence to this code by all nobles will ensure that the common people do not suffer unduly from the great power wielded by members of the ruling class. The ruling noble of the new age can be likened to Plato's philosopher king in his concern for his society and his knowledge of what decisions would be in the best interest of his subjects.

In regard to justice at community level, it is better to talk about social cohesion than law and order. My belief is that the unfettered instincts of the common people will bring about a viable status quo at community level without too much difficulty, one involving a high degree of tolerance, but also with the inherent potential for severe action to be taken against any member of the community who offends against community standards or who threatens to seriously disrupt its cohesion. Their ideas of right and wrong will be based not on the principles of rational law or some other artificial construction, but on what contributes to adaption and hence survival, and what behavior detracts from adaption. The former will be right and enshrined in custom, whereas the latter will be wrong and suppressed. Murder and theft for example would not as a rule promote adaption since if practiced regularly they would produce a great deal of dissension and generally make members of the community distrustful of each other. Therefore, we can expect those who showed a tendency to indulge in either of these activities to be firmly dealt with by the community as a whole in order to protect its integrity.

We may note in passing that, with regard to the balance of opinion on capital punishment, this is one issue on which the instincts of the masses are much sounder than the anti-capital punishment sentiments of the supposedly enlightened minority. For vengeance against one of their number (which is what capital punishment is in effect) will always remain the prerogative of the people. It will always be part of their emotional make up. The attempt to deny vengeance through the legal process is one more denial of man's basic humanity — another futile attempt to purge man of all passions and strong feelings, except those which tend to make him meek and mild. This anti-historical idealism is bound to fail. If the death penalty is not restored in this age, then it certainly will be in the new age. But it will be the sole prerogative of a ruling noble to order the execution of anyone within his domain, i.e., the common people will not have the right to do this. It will be the duty of the dominating noble to do the best he can to protect his subjects from the activities of brigands and freebooters. Non-conformity to community norms is likely to be relatively rare. Those individuals who persistently offend against community standards will probably be early recognized for what they are — irretrievable troublemakers — and permanently expelled from the community.

THE END OF MODERN IDEALISM

Upon the collapse of this age will arise a breed of men with such ambition to dominate their fellow men that in comparison with men of the preceding age they will appear to be superhuman. These men — destined to become lords of the land — will gather around themselves lieutenants and followers. They will push outward across the land until their progress is checked either by natural barriers: forests, rivers, deserts, mountain range or by an equally ambitious individual coming from another direction. The meeting point between two such individuals will be the boundary of their respective domains. The Great Lord will divide much of this conquered land among his most faithful lieutenants. The latter will in turn hold this land as vassals, paying homage to their lord and swearing fidelity to him. In this way will feudalism once again be established in the western world.

With the arrival of the new age will come a new economic structure more human and less emotionally demanding than the one that went before it. Craftsmanship will make a return and will be practiced with such easy fluency and grace shortly after the new age gets underway, that one would hardly realize that it had been an insignificant activity throughout the entire duration of the previous age. The relative importance of agriculture and industry will be transformed at a stroke to something resembling what it was before the separation of town and countryside had occurred. In other words, no matter wherever they may happen to live the vast majority of the people will spend more of their time working on the land than on any other pursuit. Yet such things as cutlery, cooking utensils, drinking vessels, and furniture will still have to be made, often by specialists who may not have much time left to devote to agricultural activity. But since unselfish cooperation will be the basis of community life in the new age, this should present no difficulty. There will also be corresponding changes in the way we produce and distribute the products of the land. Gone will be the use of complex agricultural machines and artificial fertilizer. Instead, simple agricultural implements will be employed of the kind that can be made by the community's blacksmith and repaired without too much difficulty. Instead of using chemical fertilizers to replenish the soil, the process of crop rotation will be re-introduced. Furthermore, large tracts of arable land will be left fallow from time to time to ensure that the soil does not become exhausted through excessive use.

All land throughout the nation, regardless of its nature, will be held by members of the nobility, though it will be farmed by the common people, who will raise poultry and livestock as well as grow those food crops best suited to the nature of the soil. The traditional procedures will ensure that work on the land is organized in such a way as to derive the largest possible surplus of grain and other commodities. All surpluses would be under the control of the ruling noble. After he has taken what he requires to satisfy his own needs, he would be free to apply the remainder to other purposes or to put it into storage. One of these purposes could be for exchange of commodities with other ruling nobles. Alternatively, part of the surplus can be sent to the lands of a ruling noble who has experienced a poor harvest. Should the entire nation produce an exceptionally good harvest, then grain would be available for dispatch abroad in return for foreign produce or other precious commodities. But owing to the nature of the changes in climate and soil texture that will take place in the new age, no society will be certain of being a regular producer of large agricultural surpluses. This is why it will be important for the nobles to keep a large quantity of grain in storage, to help the society get through periods of food scarcity.

The only ways in which an individual will be able to acquire land in the new age will be through unchallenged inheritance, family dissension leading to the displacement of a ruling noble by another member of his family, or by way of boundary adjustments, which will inevitably be to the advantage of the stronger party, perhaps after an extended period of hostilities. Under no circumstances will land be bought and sold in the new age. The domain of a ruling noble will consist of many widely scattered communities. For the purposes of cultivation, land will be divided up into communal fields, and domestic plots on which each family of the community could grow some of its food. Communal fields would be cultivated by the entire community and the bulk of the produce from these fields would be divided among the people according the custom and decisions made by the community's elders; the remainder will be turned over to the appropriate officials of the ruling noble. In times of a poor harvest, the ruling noble would be expected to make supplies of grain freely available to the destitute throughout his domain.

Should he not have sufficient reserves on hand then, he would be expected to make arrangements with the nearest ruling noble in surplus to dispatch additional supplies to him. The wealth of the nobility will come from all manner of agricultural produce and livestock, as well as minerals and timber within their domain. But the factor which will convert all this natural wealth into the trappings of an aristocratic civilization, will not be money but rather the diligence of the common people and their devotion to the interests of their noble lord. Thus, the lifestyle of the nobility will include fine clothing, exquisite furniture and fittings for their palatial homes, frequent journeys to distant parts of the nation accompanied by a large retinue, and lavish entertainment, including great fetes and banquets. A large number of servants will also be necessary to the maintenance of such a lifestyle. In addition, the nobility will use some of their great wealth for the patronage of artisans and talented entertainers. Each member of the nobility would also be expected to maintain a body of military retainers whose number could quickly be augmented from the garrisons within his domain and from contributions made by his allies. In addition, he would be expected to have his own armory so as to keep himself well supplied with the tools of war.

This is as good a time as any to discuss the circumstances surrounding the decline of feudalism, since only by understanding this will we properly understand why the reversal of present-day ideals will bring into existence an aristocratic society far less subject to economic social or political change than was feudal society. One of the most important aspects of the decline of feudalism was that the nobility gradually became more concerned with increasing their stock of monetary wealth than with retaining their power over the lives of the people. Thus, they began to concern themselves more with the management of their estates and less with affairs of state. They eagerly accepted the introduction of new methods of farming and husbandry which required the use of less labor but led to the production of more crops, so that excess labor was forced off the land. Also, they sold land to the up and coming yeomen farmers (in England) and peasant proprietors (in France). Social relations on the land came increasingly to be dominated by legal arrangement and less by custom and tradition. Since the efficiency of capitalist farming was greater than that of traditional farming in which social relations predominated over monetary relations, the status of the latter was bound to suffer in competition with the former. The aristocracy (or at least the more innovative members of it) was cutting the ground from beneath its feet.

To add to this, the inexorable tendency towards centralization of government was reducing the traditional role of the aristocracy to that of mere spectators. For instance, Henry VII of England, its first Tudor monarch, promulgated a law forbidding members of the nobility from settling their disputes by way of military conflict. Instead, their arguments had now to be brought before a special court presided over by three of the highest officials in the king's government. So the once proud English nobility were by degrees reduced to the role of humble plaintiffs petitioning a court for justice which not so very long ago they would have obtained for themselves in a manner worthy of their heritage. It was therefore no coincidence that, from about this time onwards, capitalist farming, whether undertaken by members of the aristocracy or by the rapidly rising yeoman class, began to displace traditional farming. By the late eighteenth century, the process was all but complete. An early sign of the effects of capitalist farming was the institution of the poor law in the reign of Elizabeth I, which was a response to the problems of impoverished agricultural laborers who had been displaced from the land. Without a well developed class of independent capitalist farmers, the commercial and manufacturing classes of the town cannot make headway.

It therefore seems reasonable to assert that the rate of industrialization in the earliest days of industrial society depended to a large extent on the hold that capitalist farming had taken in the countryside. Thus, the more developed the profit motive in agriculture, the greater would be the tendency for mass production to develop in the towns. It was probably this factor more than any other which determined the order in which nations industrialized and the time taken for them to do it. For instance, this could help to explain why Belgium followed England to become the world's second industrialized nation, rather than France or Holland. Then again, the fact that Germany's landowning class made the transition to capitalist farming practices in the latter half of the nineteenth century without too much difficulty helped to get that country's rapid industrialization underway. On the other hand, the indifference of Russia's landowning aristocracy towards the financial advantages of capitalist farming helps to explain the slow progress made in efforts to industrialize that country and the failure of sufficient impetus for this task to be generated from within Russia itself — i.e., rather than having to rely on foreign investors and entrepreneurs.

As well as tending to stimulate increased productivity (i.e., output per man) capitalist farming means in effect that the legitimacy of buying and selling land as if it were just another commodity as grain or wool is accepted. Thus, land is tended for profit rather than as an inherited obligation befitting one's rank. Capitalist farming is not concerned with social status as such, but accepts the pre-eminence of the cash nexus. Once it becomes widely established, the way is open for the rapid emergence of modern industry. By this time, the aristocracy will have long since ceased to be an important force in national affairs. It goes without saying that capitalist farming is always favored by the existence of a strong central authority which can guarantee protection under the law, and equal justice to all. This is especially important in view of the fact that capitalist farming facilitates the emergence of the small family farmer who uses his own labor as well as employing others for wages when he can afford to do so. A class of such farmers could not possibly survive in all-out competition with large landowners, but fortunately for them the large capitalist landowners are never free to act as they want. The small farmers will usually have enough political representation to protect their interests against encroachment by the great land owners.

The situation in the new age will hardly be conducive to such a state of affairs. The nobility will hold onto power at all costs. They will have absolutely no inclination to displace people from the land. In fact, they will always be seeking for ways in which they can increase both the number of people and the amount of fertile land under their control, since the greater the number of people owing allegiance to them, the greater will be their power and prestige. Their wealth will be counted in bushels of corn and not in bars of gold. As for the sale of land, this will be impossible. Ownership of land will be a priceless possession, inalienable except under the circumstances mentioned earlier.

What I am saying, in effect, is that the aristocracy of the new age will forsake the pursuit of objectives such as better production techniques and getting more from their land for less input of labor. Their one and only interest will be in the pursuit of power, something which they could not do effectively if they embarked upon capitalist agricultural practices. Once land is looked upon solely as a source of wealth rather than as a source of wealth and power, decadence and decline are bound to set in. It is my belief that although this process has happened once before, it will never happen again.

Having briefly considered what the coming transformation of modern industrial society would mean in economic terms, we are now in a position to make a detailed investigation of the idealist tradition, i.e., in relation to the search for the principles of organization of the ideal society. Like so much else about western society, its idealist tradition really begins in antiquity with the achievements of the great lawgivers. These were people who could solve social problems with a combination of intellect and imagination, and could do so in such a simple and decisive manner as to leave their contemporaries dumbfounded. The ancient world seems to have abounded with such men. Thus, Rome had its Numa, who is said to have helped the Republic to organize its affairs with better precision than had been the case up to his time. And ancient Greece can boast the names of several of these extraordinary men. One of the earliest was the tyrant Draco, who attempted to deal with a serious breakdown in law and order in his native Athens by the institution of a series of stringent laws, which included the death penalty for idleness.

Another was Solon, who flourished at a later date. His great achievement was to bring peace to an Athens which was at that time the scene of bitter strife between a small number of wealthy creditors and their poverty-stricken debtors. He introduced a new system of repayment, so giving the poor more time to discharge their debts. But it seems that the new arrangements did not satisfy everybody, for Solon was continually requested to interpret his rules in regard to specific cases. In the end, he left

Athens to go in search of wisdom in other lands, but also no doubt to gain peace of mind. Before Solon died, he witnessed his beloved Athens fall under the dictatorship of the Pisistrades, which enjoyed a great deal of popular support during the period of the first Pisistrades. The man who did more than any other to re-establish popular democracy was Cleisthenes, who also laid the political foundation for the Golden Period of Athens which lasted up until the beginning of the Peloponnesian War.

Among the most important of Cleisthenes' reforms was extending the franchise to all Greek citizens of Athens, since it had previously been restricted to the four original Ionic clans whose ancestors had founded the city. To facilitate this, he organized the inhabitants of Athens and its surrounding territory into ten new clans, such that clan affiliation was primarily based on area of residence as opposed to blood ties, as was the case before. From these fundamental reforms proceeded all other changes in the reconstruction of Athenian democracy, which was to serve Athens so well when working at its best. There is one other Greek lawgiver who deserves our attention. This is Lycurgus, who was not an Athenian. His name is associated with the founding of Sparta's timocracy. He is profiled in Plutarch's *Lives of Noble Greeks and Romans* and mentioned in other ancient texts, but all the same, many modern historians have doubted whether such a person ever existed. This is not surprising when one considers the vast amount of wisdom embodied in his reforms. The possibility of the existence of anyone with such a perfect understanding of what would be best to produce a warrior society like Sparta seems almost to be beyond the bounds of credibility.

Many of his reforms and beliefs which have come down to us are marvels of clear thinking. We could, in fact, consider him as a model for future lawgivers of the new age. He carried out a number of limited but sensible reforms of Spartan's political institutions, the nature of which need not concern us, before proceeding to deal with the problems of Spartan society as a whole. To understand the logic behind his social reforms one must realize that Spartan society, especially its ruling class, had sunk into a low state of degeneracy. Lycurgus set himself the task of correcting this situation and restoring Sparta to health. He replaced gold and silver coins by iron coins making very heavy coins of little value, so that a large number would be required as being equivalent to a gold or silver coin of former times. He did this so as to decrease the excessive indulgence in luxury of the wealthy few, and also to reduce bribery and corruption. He also introduced a law which commanded all (including the wealthy) to eat in common the same meat at a public table. At the same time they were forbidden to eat at home, upon expensive couches and tables, to call in the assistance of butchers and cooks, or to fatten like voracious animals in private. It is most unlikely that we will ever need to go this far in the new age, but should indulgence get the better of the ruling class then they can expect the remedy to be painful.

Lycurgus left none of his laws in writing. It was observed in one of his edicts that none should be written, for what he thought most conducive to the nature and happiness of a city, was principles interwoven with the manners and breeding of the people. As for smaller matters, it was better not to reduce these to a written form and unalterable method, but to suffer them to change with the times, and to admit of additions or retrenchment. He resolved the whole business of legislation into the bringing up of youth. This is probably one of the most brilliant of Lycurgus' perceptions, for a well adapted society would have little use for written laws, something which will be verified in the new age. When they were seven years old, Spartan children had to be enrolled in companies where they were all kept under the same order and discipline, and had their exercise and recreation in common. They learned only what was absolutely necessary. All the rest of their education was calculated to make them subject to command, and to use sharp repartee, seasoned with humor — whatever they said was to be concise and pithy — the famous laconic discourse. Lycurgus towers above all other ancient lawgivers in his understanding of human nature and the requirements of a vigorous society. All the lawgivers mentioned above worked within societies which did not have the social and economic complexity of modern industrial society and neither were they undergoing rapid changes in science and technology.

On the other hand, the period with which we are most concerned, i.e., from the beginning of the industrial revolution to the present time, has been a period of rapid changes which have produced a highly complex society. The lawgivers of ancient times could not have done much with a society such as this. But the spirit of the lawgiver was not to be entirely lost to western man of later ages. It was superbly captured in a way that would be appreciated by generations to come by Greeks who were theoreticians rather than men of action. The most notable of these was the great Plato. For with regard to ideas for the construction of the ideal society, Plato is preeminent among the ancients. Furthermore, it is fair to say that although the creative genius for the ideas set out in the *Republic* and his lesser works was Plato's alone, he drew much of his inspiration from the tradition of the great lawgivers to which he was heir. The result was a very special type of idealism which, for the sake of convenience, we may call Platonic Idealism, and which has drawn both praise and criticism from generation after generation, right down to the present time. One of its earliest critics was Aristotle, who felt that Plato had allowed his fertile imagination to get the better of him. In more recent times, Plato has been classed along with Marx and Hegel by Karl Popper as one of the enemies of the open society.

At this point, we should make clear exactly what is meant by the term modern idealism, since it will be a subject with which we shall be concerned for most of the rest of this chapter. We can conveniently date the appearance of modern idealism with the beginnings of early capitalist society, i.e., in the sixteenth century. More precisely, we can say its advent was marked by the publication of Thomas More's *Utopia.* But just as there is a period of early capitalism which began at about the time of the

Renaissance, and late capitalism which began with the industrial revolution, so we also have early modern idealism and late modern idealism which span corresponding periods of time. In both periods, there were talented individuals who were often critical of their society and resorted to the theoretical construction of a new type of society in order to establish their claim to be considered as enlightened thinkers. These people included Thomas More, whom we have already mentioned, as well as Francis Bacon and James Harrington, in the first period.

There were many, many more such people in the second period, some of the more important of whom we shall be discussing. There is one key difference between the two periods which is worth mentioning; this is in regard to the intensity of conviction felt by the writers. Radical books of the first period had in common the fact that their content was never taken too seriously by their authors, since their main purpose was to draw attention to a few simple ideas which their author wished to make more widely known rather than bring about wholesale social change. This has not been true of most books of the idealist genre written in the second period. Their quantity has been vast and their authors have been in earnest. They have wanted big changes and have sincerely believed these changes to be possible.

Before moving on, a review of the distinction between Platonic Idealism and Modern Idealism is in order. It seems fair to say that the former was basically elitist and always had a more limited view of the possibility of human perfection than did the latter. Most modern idealists believed that perfection could ultimately be achieved by everyone, whereas Plato believed it to be achievable only by a few. Thus, whereas modern idealism has almost reached its end, the essentials of Platonic Idealism (especially as set out in the *Republic*) are still relevant to the future of Western man. It is of great interest to note that the beginning of the second period of modern political idealism should be almost coeval with the beginning of philosophical idealism as founded in Germany, and whose origins and development is associated with the names of several well-known German writers and philosophers, including Immanuel Kant. This trend of thought was destined to receive complete fulfillment in the writings of Hegel and Marx. The essence of the German Idealist position was that the mind was the most dominant force within the universe; all reality was subject to the perception of the mind. Thus, knowledge came to us not solely from the senses, but more importantly through the progress of the mind. The political implications of this should be readily apparent for it meant, in effect, that as the mind of man grew in knowledge and gained a better understanding of his surroundings, he would be able to make changes for the better.

One should hardly find it surprising, therefore, that over much of the last two hundred years, the most persistent builders of new societies have been those motivated by some kind of belief in the equality of man. This was certainly true of Morelly and J.J. Rousseau, two of the very first. The interesting fact about the idealist writings of these two authors is that although the industrial revolution was just beginning to get underway during the period that they wrote, neither of them made it central to their scheme of things. Morelly seems to have envisaged an agricultural commune in which absolute equality of condition would be the glue that would hold things together, and said nothing of consequence about the place that industry would have in his ideal society. Rousseau, in contrast, was positively hostile to industry and praised the simple rural life as best, arguing that progress had not been such a good thing as most people believed. Neither of these writers could have been expected to be anything more than passing curiosities to future generations and this is how it has turned out, especially so in the case of Morelly.

Most of the later writers who felt that society ought to be reorganized along egalitarian lines looked upon industry and technology as two very positive forces for the betterment of mankind. This was true of men like Saint Simon, Charles Fourier and Robert Owen, who were referred to by Marx as the utopian socialists, as it was for Marx and his disciples. The three utopian socialists were highly imaginative and sincere men, but their programs for the organization of new societies based upon voluntary cooperation and national distribution of the products of the community's labor, did not come to terms with the realities of their day. All the same, as far as the later socialists were concerned, each of these utopian theorists had their good points which could not be overlooked, and which made them important figures in the annals of the history of socialism.

Saint Simon was in some ways the most original and most perceptive of the three. He saw that modern industry was destined to be a force of great importance, and felt strongly that it should be organized in such a way as would be to the benefit of the entire society. He did not advocate class war, but felt that a rational organization of industrial society would come about when people began to appreciate how wasteful and chaotic was the present organization, with its large number of unproductive bureaucrats, small number of idle renters living on the backs of a large number of toiling ignorant workers, not to mention the large standing army of the modern state which was concerned only with the destruction of capital and having nothing to do with the creation of wealth. It was Saint Simon who first coined the now internationally famous socialist slogan, "to each according to his need, from each according to his ability," which completes the central passage of Marx's *Critique of the Gotha Programme.*

Charles Fourier was constantly busy with plans for communal societies, "phalanstries" as he called them, in which manual labor would be obligatory for everyone. Although he was a typical exemplar of modern idealism, Fourier considered himself more in the guise of the lawgiver of ancient times. Such a grand delusion could only end in a lifetime of frustration and disillusion. Despite this, he could often be a sharp and discerning critic of his society, a fact that was not lost on Marx. The latter relished Fourier's comments on the bourgeois family and also noted with approval Fourier's statement that like all other civilizations before it, bourgeois civilization would also come to an end. Obviously, Marx was blind to the full implications of this statement. Robert Owen was possibly the most single-minded of our three theorists. He firmly believed that personality was molded by the environment, and that if children were brought up in a good environment, they would grow up into pleasant, well-adjusted adults.

He put his beliefs into practice at New Lanarkshire and achieved such a high level of success in combining a profitable industrial operation with the formation of good character among the work force, that his textile mill attracted visiting dignitaries from all parts of Great Britain, as well as from abroad. Later on, Owen's idea took a more radical turn after disagreement with his partners in the New Lanarkshire venture. He took part in the founding of a commune in the United States, which ended the way all such attempts have ended, i.e., in dissension among the members. Although two of his sons decided to remain in America, Owen returned to England an embittered man. He now advocated the total overthrow of the political and economic system as the only way to bring about the far-reaching changes he believed to be essential to build a better society. He gave encouragement to the more radical movements of his time, but was not looked upon as a leading figure in radical politics of the period. The best that can be said for Owen was that he was sincere but ineffectual.

As we saw earlier with the case of Morelly and Rousseau, not all of those motivated by egalitarian ideals idealized industrial society. Another one of those who did not was Pierre Proudhon, an antagonist of Marx who had a substantial following in his native France. Proudhon was a supporter of peasant proprietorship. He was against the capitalist class only inasmuch as they undermined the position of the land-owning peasant. He was not against private property in land as long as it was under the ownership of those who worked it. He had little of substance to say about industrial society or its future. Marx bitterly resented Proudhon for his attachment to the small peasant farmer. For

Marx and Engels, the future lay with mass production under the control of the workers. They also felt that agriculture would have to be scientifically organized and run like an industrial enterprise to make it as productive as possible. The distaste which Marx had for the peasant proprietor is clearly shown in that well-known passage of "The Eighteenth Brumaire of Louis Bonaparte," in which he disparages the peasant's way of life as backward, and a serious obstacle to progress.

Another egalitarian thinker who relegated modern industry to a very low place in his views of the ideal society was William Morris. He saw socialism as the key to a happy, peaceful, idyllic life. This is what counted for Morris far more than the common ownership of industry. In a way, his ideals are very close to those set down by Marx in his 1844 Economic and Philosophical Manuscripts. Thus, according to Morris, the foundation of life in the new society would be a free and unfettered animal life. In fact, he demanded "the utter extinction of all asceticism." But whereas Marx was often longwinded and confusing in his 1844 Manuscripts, Morris is simple and straight to the point. For instance, in elaborating his views on the better society, Morris treats us to the following pronouncement: "If we feel the least degrading in being amorous, or merry, hungry, or sleepy, we are so far bad animals, and therefore miserable men."[1] There is not much connection between this outlook and the rational organization of industry and agriculture to produce the highest level of productivity which seems to have been such an obsession with Marx and Engels in their later years.

Despite its numerous shortcomings, scientific socialism has lasted longer than any other idealist construction of the modern era. We have already discussed several of the reasons for this. For present purposes then, all we need do is to note those special features which put it in a class by itself as an outstanding example of modern idealism. For instance, it not only gave us a new interpretation of the past, but also made definite predictions about the future. No lesser commentator than Joseph Schumpeter has stated that "the so-called Economic Interpretation of History is doubtless one of the greatest individual achievements of sociology to this day,"[2] an assertion with which I will not argue. But Marxism also achieved what had been a rare triumph up until then, i.e., an acceptance of the realities of the period, and their successful incorporation into a grand design for the future. Thus, Marxism was by far the most engaging of all schemes for the reorganization of industrial society to those among whom it first appeared, and has remained so ever since.

The complete rationally organized community which had been drawn up just as a draughtsman draws up a blueprint, became an anachronism overnight, though this did not stop people from continuing to produce them. Another factor which has enhanced the staying power of scientific socialism is its protean nature. It is so amenable to change as to have been the inspiration for both Social Democracy of the West, and the events leading to the reign of terror that characterized Stalinist Russia, not to mention the multitude of revolutionary fringe groups which have also adopted the message of Marx as their own. Then again, since the beginning of the Renaissance, western man has been striving to discover his place in the universe, and his ultimate destiny. Scientific socialism has helped in this respect, since although it did not provide all the answers, it appeared to indicate that there was some sort of plan to the unfolding of reality which could be fathomed by the human intellect.

In still other ways, Marxist theory has filled a need; it has given a goal to the intellectual strivings of those who are critical of the organization of modern industrial society. Suitably modified, it appears to be the ideal instrument for the modern day lawgiver who attempts to solve the problems of industrial society within the framework of that society. It can also be employed in various ways by those who are turned off by the progress of modern industrial society, as well as by those who believe that the workers still do not get sufficient reward for their labor. A body of social theory so versatile as this is bound to enjoy a long career, and Marxism certainly has done so — even though belief in the Marxist millennium was long ago renounced by such able Marxist theoreticians of the old school as Bernstein, Kautsky and Korsch. Nearly every contemporary Marxist of note has seen fit to jettison at least some of the most radical propositions and concepts of classical Marxism. Moreover, it seems that Marx himself was, in his less sanguine moments, not above entertaining doubts about a future based on the productive power of modern industry. On one occasion, he states frankly that, "There is one great fact, characteristic of this our nineteenth century.... On the one hand, there have started into life industrial and scientific forces, which no epoch of the former human history had ever suspected. On the other hand, there exist symptoms of decay, far surpassing the horrors recorded of the latter times of the Roman empire. In our day everything seems pregnant with its contrary."[3]

Having reviewed the high points of modern idealism, it is only fair to say that not all preceptors of the better society have been socialists and egalitarian in their thinking. Some have been inspired solely by that closely related and similarly misguided ideal of belief in progress along a straight line. It is an ideal which has proved to be almost as potent as belief in equality, in bringing out the most far-fetched schemes and getting people to believe in them. No group is more blindly addicted to this fallacy (of indefinite material progress) than those who laud every development in science and technology as a plus for human advancement. The belief that an increase in scientific knowledge, and our power to apply this knowledge, contributed to the welfare of man, and so to the progress of the human race was most prevalent in the latter part of Victorian England. Beatrice Webb, in her book, *My Apprenticeship*, attempts to convey the mood of the period, which was first highlighted by tremendous optimism, but this later gave way to bitter disillusionment. Writing in the early 1920s, she tells us that her generation has learned, by the bitter experience of the Great War, to what vile uses the methods and results of science may be put. With hindsight, she comments how hard it is for her to understand the naive belief of the most original and vigorous minds of the seventies and eighties, that it was by science, and by science alone, that all human misery would be ultimately swept away. She further underlines her point by quoting passages from Windwood Reade's *The Martyrdom of Man*, published in 1872. The fulsome praise this writer gives to scientific and technological progress has to be read to be believed. Reviewing it from the vantage point of the late twentieth century, Reade would seem to have taken his belief in the powers of man to ludicrous proportions — idealism gone mad! As a salutary corrective to the worship of material progress, I quote the relevant passages in full:

"His triumph (the triumph of man regarded as pure intellect) indeed is incomplete; his kingdom has not yet come. The Prince of Darkness is still triumphant in many regions of the world; epidemics still rage; death is yet victorious. But the God of Light, the spirit of knowledge, the Divine Intellect, is gradually spreading over the planet and upwards to the skies.... Earth which is now a purgatory, will be made a paradise, not by idle prayers and supplications, but by the efforts of man himself, and by mental achievements analogous to those which have raised him to his present state. Those inventions and discoveries which have made him, by the Grace of God, king of animals, lord of the elements, and sovereign of steam and electricity, were all founded on experiment and observation.... When we have ascertained, by means of science, the methods of Nature's operation, we shall be able to take her place and to perform them for ourselves. When we understand the laws which regulate the complex phenomenon of life, we shall be able to predict the future as we are already able to predict comets, and eclipses and the planetary movements.... Not only will man subdue the forces of evil that are without; he will subdue those that are within. He will repress the base instincts and propensities which he has inherited from the animals below him; he will obey the laws written in his heart; he will worship the divinity that is within him. ... Idleness and stupidity will be regarded with abhorrence. Women will become the companions of men, and the tutors of their children. The whole world will be united by the same sentiments which united the primeval clan, and which made its members think, feel and act as one.... These bodies which we now wear belong to the lower animals; our minds have already outgrown them; already we look upon them with contempt. A time will come when science will transform them by means which we cannot conjecture, and which if explained to us we could not now understand, just as the savage cannot understand electricity, magnetism, steam. Disease will be extirpated; the causes of decay will be removed; immortality will be invented. And then the earth being small, mankind will emigrate into space and will cross airless saharas which separate planet from planet, and sun from sun. The earth will become a Holy Land which will be visited by pilgrims from all the quarters of the universe. Finally, men will master the forces of Nature; they will become themselves architects of systems, manufacturers of worlds. Man will be perfect; he will be a creator; he will therefore be what the vulgar worship as God."[4]

We must be grateful for the fact that these days scientific progress and human welfare are no longer automatically linked together as they once were. For I do not think mankind will ever be ready to play God, not now or in the future. But the old beliefs linger on, and not only among technocratically oriented social theorists. Listen to Ernest Mandel as he discusses the reorganization of the World's economy along socialist lines: "... a world plan of economic development... would make possible a rationalization of the use of the world's resources going far beyond the boldest dreams of mankind. Gigantic projects which even today are too great to be accomplished by the most advanced countries — the irrigation and fertilization of the Sahara; the transformation of the Amazonian Jungle; the settlement and industrialization of Sinkiang; the organization of expeditions to the planets — would be put into practice by a joint effort of the human race, so as to increase the wellbeing of all men."[5] This sounds like Windwood Reade all over again, though it was actually published in 1968, almost one hundred years later. One would think we ought to know better by now. A new age is certainly in the offing, but it will be nothing like that which Mandel sketches for us above.

Having selectively reviewed the idealist tradition from its ancient beginnings to modern times, I now intend to do the same for ethics and morality, that is to say, ideals seen as a body of belief which will help men live better lives, rather than as a way of reorganizing society, since this will enable us to better understand the making of history in the new age. For men of the new age will make history with a greater understanding of themselves and the place occupied by their society in the onward making of mankind than was ever possible before. Up to the present time, historical acts have usually been judged as good or bad, if not by the historian, then by his reader. Several historians have stated that it is not the business of the historian to make such judgments, but they have been doing so for so long now that it is hard to see how they can stop. One of those who maintains this position is E. H. Carr, one of the better-known modern historians, who is justly praised for his multi-volume study of the history of the Soviet Union beginning with the 1917 November Revolution. In his little book entitled *What is History*, Carr tells us that the primary job of the historian is not to make a moral judgment about historical events, but to allow the reader to come to his own conclusions.

This is the way in which he went about his task of writing the history of the Russian Revolution and its aftermath. But despite the best efforts of Carr and others, history has generally been seen as a process of moving towards the better society, or more specifically the good society. Democratic Athens was our earliest model of the ideals and political organization we would expect to find in such a society. The tradition of popular democracy and freedom of inquiry places ancient Athens in a class by itself. But there was one aspect of Athenian society which rather spoiled it for us moderns of tender conscience. This was the existence of slavery, admittedly not on a massive scale, but there all the same, and what's more, taken for granted with very little, if any, condemnation of it to be found in the writings of the great philosophers of ancient Greece. In fact, they either tended to ignore its existence altogether, or accept it as a natural fact of life that some men were born to live as slaves all their lives, just as other men were born free and remained so. The better life continued to be central to the writings of all post-Aristotelian schools of Greek philosophy. But its character took a different turn. No longer was the city state seen as the center of the world. The city state ideal which had been so loftily praised by Pericles: "We alone regard a man who takes no interest in public affairs, not as a harmless, but as a useless character;" and defended so valiantly by Demosthenes, first in his three Philippics and then on the battlefield of Cheronea, had almost by now become a thing of the past. Instead, Hedonism, Cynicism and Stoicism came to the fore. Their appearance corresponds to a period of decline, a time which Sabine aptly refers to as the twilight of the city-state — when Athens and the other city-states of the Hellenes had lost those heroic qualities which had once been present in so much abundance.

Hedonism was founded by Epicurus. He and his followers preached that instead of involving themselves in public affairs, men should seek to retreat from such matters to concentrate on their private affairs and the enjoyment of those pleasures which were available to them. Vernon Bourke,[6] in his book *History of Ethics* (Vol. I), gives us a balanced discussion of Epicurus' doctrine. Bourke tells us that Epicurus believed that most men live in terror of death and in fear of the gods. Hence, he taught that there is no personal survival after death and that the gods are not concerned with human affairs. He further held that study and personal effort will enable a man to acquire the virtues that lead to the equanimity of the sage. Epicurus may not have been the teacher of allout indulgence of the appetites, as many have made him out to be, but this fact is not sufficient to redeem his philosophy from the oblivion it richly deserves. For nothing of lasting value can be accomplished by a philosophy of non-involvement and retreat from the world of affairs. Our worst fears are confirmed when we are told by Bourke that Epicurus believed that the goal of morally good activity was peace of mind and freedom from mental perturbation. This is not the sort of outlook that one would expect to find among a hardy race of warriors.

The Cynics were a group of philosophers who were more extreme in their views than the hedonists in that they despised all involvement in public affairs and all attempts to gain knowledge, believing both to be meaningless time-wasting activities. Bourke tells us that the Cynics' ideal of virtue became simplicity of living, a renunciation of wealth, pleasure, adornment and ambition — the less said about this philosophy the better. Stoicism was probably one of the most influential life-style philosophies of the Greco-Roman world. It originated in Athens but did not receive its full development until introduced into republican Rome. Basically, stoicism preached attention to duty as one's foremost obligation. It also counseled self-control, especially in the face of adversity, and the curbing of the desire for gratification of one's appetites. It further taught acceptance of one's place in society with good grace.

In one way, it had a far greater impact than either hedonism or cynicism, because it taught that the universal community of reason could be entered into by all men regardless of whether free or slave, oriental or occidental. The universal appeal of stoicism is often said to be illustrated by the fact that it was elaborated by a slave (Epictetus), a Roman patrician (Seneca), and a Roman Emperor (Marcus Aurelius). It also had a positive effect on world affairs in that the granting of Roman citizenship to all peoples living within the boundaries of the Roman empire was a direct outgrowth of the teachings of stoic philosophy. The ideals encompassed by it have never entirely died out, but then again they have never again been a force within society as they were in the glorious days of ancient Rome. Stoicism seems to have experienced something of a revival at the beginning of the

Industrial Revolution, and gained strength throughout the nineteenth century with adherents such as General Gordon and Cecil Rhodes, only to fade out again in the twentieth century. If modern industrial society was proceeding in such a way that the moral ideals of its members complemented its "technocratic and economizing mode of operation" (to quote Daniel Bell), then stoicism (or some version of it) is the type of ethos that we should expect to be prevalent. But this is not so.

Feudal society had no use for such a restrictive and reductionist ideal as stoicism. According to the theocratic Feudal outlook, medieval society was complete, there was no need to strive towards a better or fairer society, since in Feudal society each class had its purpose, and its status in relation to all other classes. The characteristics of this period are well-known, and therefore do not need to be elaborated in detail. They include the elimination of slavery and its replacement by serfdom; the weak position of the monarch relative to his nobility, who usually acted as autonomous rulers over the land under their control, while giving nominal allegiance to their king; and finally the wealth, power, influence and prestige of the Catholic Church completes the picture of a society in which there was very little upward mobility (outside the Church), and in which the countryside dominated the towns. There were numerous serf revolts during the middle ages, all of which were eventually crushed with little mercy shown to the vanquished. The ancient authors who attempted to sketch the ideals by which a man could live the most satisfying life as a citizen, were concerned with matters such as aristocracy versus democracy, and whether or not a well-off and well-educated individual should even bother to take part in public affairs.

These issues were foreign to the feudal age, for although there was an immense cleavage between lord and serf, and the periodic frustration felt by the serfs often erupted into open revolt, strife between nobility and peasantry was not really important as far as the development of ideas on what constitutes the better society. Those who are interested in this aspect of feudal society have to look to the conflict which took place between church and state. It was a situation by which the monarchs of Western Europe continued to treat the Papacy with deference while at the same time attempting to extend their power over the clergy within their domain. A celebrated example of the latter struggle was the argument between Pope Boniface VIII and Philip the Fair of France over the right of the King to tax church property on French soil. This was the dispute which eventually led to the so-called Babylonian Captivity of the Papacy by which a succession of Popes resided in Avignon instead of Rome for a period of seventy years.

The Babylonian Captivity did much to undermine Papal authority in the courts of Western Europe, and ensured that the Papacy was never again going to attain the ascendancy it had in European affairs some hundred years previous to its relocation in Avignon. When this great battle was at its hottest, both sides employed propagandists to get their views across to the uncommitted. For the Papal side, one of the best known of these was the Franciscan friar, William of Ockham, who is also noted for his rule of the razor, which, put simply, states that, all things being equal, the simplest explanation should always be accepted in preference to the more complex alternatives. He also contributed to the debate over Universals, the only other controversy that seriously disturbed the medieval scholastics. Universals were concepts such as truth, love and justice. The main point of contention centered around whether they had only the meaning ascribed to them by a particular society at a particular time, as the nominalists believed, or whether they had a meaning which was unchangeable, transcending time and place as the realists believed. The importance of this debate was not that it established the correctness of either school of thought — this is not possible — but rather, it kept the medieval scholastics harmlessly occupied instead of troubling themselves with more worldly matters.

Returning to the social conditions of medieval society, since violence, an early death, and impoverishment among the masses, and the superior position of the nobility and clergy were accepted by the common people as part of the natural order of things, original views of the better society were not a feature of this era. Particularly so, as nearly all men of letters came from the ranks of the church. Thus, the status quo was generally defended rather than attacked. The most common line of defense was the reinterpretation of Platonic Idealism. Now, according to Plato, "All things are produced more plentifully and easily and of a better quality when one does one thing which is natural to him and does it at the right time and leaves other things."[7] To put it another way, man can only fully develop in a *polis* which allowed him to contribute according to his abilities, as say a farmer, artisan, teacher or statesman. The theological sages of medieval society proceeded to interpret this as suggesting that the social order of the time performed exactly the role that had been allocated to the ideal city-state by the Greek authors, since each of the principal orders of clergy, nobility and serf — had their proper function, i.e., saving souls, ruling and fighting, producing food, while the monarch was given to the nation by God's divine grace to see to it that each order lived in harmony with the others.

Thus, the ideal city-state of antiquity had been at last achieved in the social structure and lifestyle of the middle ages. If one considers carefully the view of the schoolmen in taking their society to be the personification of Plato's ideal society, one will see that it was not simply an empty boast, or a misguided assertion, but on the contrary, was very close to the truth. As a matter of fact, in writing done near to the end of his life, Plato actually stated the view that man required spiritual guidance and gave religion a much higher place than he had done in all his previous writings, going so far as to prescribe specific penalties for atheists and heretics. But the position taken by the establishment clerics did not go unchallenged, especially by those who resented the temporal power of the Catholic Church.

For instance, Marsilo of Padua attempted to undermine official doctrine by pointing out that if the ancient city-state is taken as a model to justify the hierarchical structure of medieval Christendom, one comes up against the problem that such a community was not considered by its members to need theological guidance, at least not in the form as it existed in the middle ages. The people of antiquity believed their cities to be quite self-sufficient in the spiritual as well as the secular sphere. But this is not really a discrepancy of consequence, for the fact is that a highly developed hierarchical religious institution did exist for almost a thousand years, side by side with an hierarchical political structure, and what's more, served its society very well. No modern writer puts this better than Erich Fromm when he tells us, "The Reformation broke down the complex medieval network of social, economic, and religious institutions, rituals and beliefs which combined to give the individual some material security and much spiritual security. The ordinary man in the middle ages knew where he stood, had so to speak to make, to a minimum extent, the kind of decisions that put a strain on him."[8] The poverty of medieval philosophy is a tribute to the fact that this period represents the highest level of the adaption of western man achieved to date.

On the other hand, the period following the demise of feudal society stimulated new theories in just about every area of social life, which eventually culminated in the French Enlightenment and the advent of popular democracy. The literary outpourings of the French Enlightenment ushered in a tremendous period of optimism in intellectual circles, which lasted without a break all the way up to the First World War. The last vestiges of feudalism were victoriously shaken off so as to make ready for political freedom and economic competition. Most of the onerous restrictions which had been placed upon Europe's Jews were lifted out of respect for the spirit of the age. As for religion, the Enlightenment effectively destroyed the lingering remnants of sincere belief in the Christian faith, which had come down from an age in which life and faith were indistinguishable, replacing it with a scientifically rationalized humanism. To add insult to injury, Auguste Comte, the highly original and flamboyant French sociologist, attempted to found a new religion of humanity complete with philosopher priests.

The attempt never succeeded, but was in any case hardly necessary, since such a religion had already come into existence in all but name. So there was really no reason for western society to go to the trouble of breaking its historic links with Christianity. The way was now clear for the full-scale degeneration of western man to begin. And begin it did, in great earnest. The hedonism of Epicurus and his followers was transformed into the doctrine of utilitarianism, whose origins are associated with the name of Jeremy Bentham, though he did not invent the term. Bentham had been greatly influenced by Helvetius, one of the more authentic contributors to the French Enlightenment. Stated in the simplest possible terms, the utilitarians believed that the greatest good was to be found in providing the greatest happiness for the greatest number. The principle of the 'greatest happiness' has proved to be one of the more enduring social ideas to have come down to us from the early days of modern industrial society. This despite a critical reappraisal of it by John Stuart Mill, who was early converted to this doctrine by his father and Bentham, and later coined the term 'utilitarianism' as an aid to its propagation. In his critique of the doctrine, Mill reminded his readers that the feelings of the minority had always to be considered and not just the desires of the majority. He further maintained that with regard to happiness, not all pleasures were of equal value, and that the higher pleasures were generally enjoyed by a minority as opposed to the lower pleasures which tended to be enjoyed by the majority. When there was some doubt as to which was the higher and which was the lower pleasure, Mill felt that a person of sound intelligence who had experienced both, would be the best judge. How far we have descended from the lofty ideals of Plato's *Republic!*

Karl Marx was another stinging critic of utilitarianism, but I suspect mainly because it summed up the psychology of modern man better than he could ever hope to do, despite his remarkable brilliance and the astounding insights of his theory. For utilitarianism has succeeded, even though it had nothing comparable to the Economic Interpretation of History to bolster it. It is rational, practical, and above all democratic. When necessary it can be tempered by humanitarian concerns, a sentiment which allows consideration of the feelings and interests of the majority to take second place to the rights and welfare of a minority. If the greatest happiness of the greatest number (suitably tempered when necessary) was the ideal capable of producing the best adapted society, then all would not be well with modern man. But the truth is that it is not, and could never be. Despite our enormous material gains and the promise of still more to come, contemporary industrial society is discontented, bored and not a little insecure. It still does not feel satisfied. This is not really surprising, since those who believed that the welfare state could alter the abiding truths of the human condition have been deluding themselves and their followers.

The arrival of the new age will confirm the truth of this statement. No more will judgment be made on whether an act was morally right or wrong. No more will we look at past events from the perspective of progress towards the better society. For we will be living in the best possible society, one which corresponds exactly with the essentials of human nature. As for the past, the only people who will have any interest in history, in the new age, will be the aristocracy and those who serve them as advisers. Thus, all future history will be written by the aristocracy and looked at from their point of view, and not from the point of view of the "reasonable man." The reasonable man has generally been an individual devoid of power, and hence constrained by his circumstances to applaud moderation, self-respect and similar traits, whereas those strong-willed, independent-minded individuals who have shown indifference to the fears of the weak, and used them only to further their own ambitions, have often been roundly condemned as insensitive monsters. In making this assessment, I readily exclude all history written from the death of Boethius to the time of Dante, which although written by clerics, showed a much better appreciation of the nature of man and the realities of a vigorous social life than much of the history written either before or after this period.

In saying this, I also readily admit that there are certain historical texts which, although not falling within this period, were written exactly in the way that good history should be written, i.e., from the warrior point of view. We may include here Caesar's narrative of his Gallic Campaigns, Xenophon's account of the retreat of the Ten Thousand, and in modern times, Napier's account of the Peninsula Campaigns. It is to be noted that all these writers took part in the events that they recorded, and this is probably why their writings show very little sentimentality and make no concession to those of tender conscience. It is just as Goethe once said, i.e., the man of action cannot afford to have a conscience; that is a luxury he leaves to the observer. In the new age then, history will no longer be written, or made for that matter, as if man is on his way to a future of happiness for all. Instead, it will once again be written as a straightforward chronicle of events which future members of the ruling class may use to further their own ambitions.

BEYOND POLITICAL MAN

In this chapter, we will be primarily concerned with discussing the political organization of the new age. Most of us are familiar with Aristotle's famous saying to the effect that man is a political animal. This gives us our first clue to the nature of political man. That is, the term "political man" describes the average individual who uses the political process to maximize his personal welfare. But for him to do this effectively, he must live under a democratic government or one that is almost democratic. Hence, political man as we know him today was a child of the *polis* of antiquity, especially ancient Athens. So far so good, but the real question is whether or not being a political animal is natural to man, or whether it is a role he is required to accept by force of circumstance. The latter would appear to be closer to the truth, for history shows that man has not always been a political animal, and neither did he fret unduly when he was not allowed to play an active part in the political process.

The average man does not crave for political freedom when he has not got it, he does not resolve to leave his society rather than live without the right to vote, and he rarely commits himself to work all-out for the overthrow of a tyrannical dictatorship. Like so much else about the human condition, the establishment of democracy and its maintenance has generally been the work of a relatively small minority. The story of the reestablishment of Athenian democracy by Cleisthenes is a typical example of this. The foremost concern of the majority is to survive under the least possible stress. If they can also have democratic government, all well and good; if they cannot, they are not too bothered. On the other hand, a restless and aggressive minority is always looking for a challenge, their ambitions are easily kindled, their heroic feelings always present. These are the people who are ready at a moment's notice to overthrow a dictatorship and set up a democracy or vice versa. These few are the pathfinders; where they lead, the majority will follow — especially so once victory seems assured. The same is true for the major political struggles for supremacy between legitimately competing groups. Although the majority will be interested in the outcome and will give their support to one or other of the participants, only a small minority have a say in how the contest is fought and only a small minority will gain most of the tangible benefits that are to be derived from the result.

Not surprisingly, the average man has more often than not been the willing or unknowing tool of those greater than himself, often sacrificed to further fanciful dreams and wild ambitions which stand little chance of fulfillment. Hence, the ascent of western man to his present level of political awareness has not been smooth or uniform, but rather checkered. So much so, that we would do better to consider him throughout much of his history as a political pawn easily susceptible to manipulation by others, than as a freely acting individual fully aware of what is in his best interests, and determined to pursue this at all costs. In his role of political pawn, western man has had to adapt to a number of political environments, some better suited to his nature than others. In most cases, he has had no trouble understanding what was required of him, and acted accordingly, although on occasions political differences have been totally obscure (at least to later generations), as were the battles between the reds and the greens which racked the Byzantine empire at the time of Justinian the Great. But even those cases in which political differences were far from obscure — at least to begin with — can degenerate into petty squabbles and local rivalries, most people having lost sight of the original points of contention. This is exactly what happened to the conflict for dominance of Italy between the Ghibellines and Guelfs, led respectively by the emperor of the Holy Roman Empire, and the Pope. This conflict waxed and waned for many years, so that eventually participants were no longer guided by historic precedent, but changed sides when it suited them to do so, and generally strove to advance their own interests rather than those of the figure to whom they gave nominal allegiance.

Thus, the latitude allowed to the common man to act as a self-seeking individual (as far as he is capable of doing this), depends on the age, the nature of the society and its historical traditions. No one needs to be reminded that the re-emergence of political man to enjoy something resembling the status he enjoyed in democratic Athens is a relatively recent phenomenon, dating from the late nineteenth century in England and several other Western European nations. The ballot box is of course the symbol of political man, along with the town hall meeting, and the principle of one man one vote. But what the common man may consider to be a good thing is not always best for his society as a whole. Nevertheless, the democratic ideal has taken such a hold over modern man that nearly every country in the world, regardless of its system of government, considers itself to be democratic, though democracy does not always serve a nation as well as its people expect it to, and for their part, the peoples of democratic countries are capable of doing the most absurd things at election time, or when called upon to vote in a nationwide referendum.

They have elected vicious, unscrupulous tyrants to power, and they have countenanced the persecution of minorities. Both Napoleon and Hitler used the referendum to good effect in gaining overwhelming support for their dictatorship and for the constitutional changes which they desired to make. It has been established by repeated examples that if an individual or group is bold enough to subvert the democratic process to their advantage, then the vast majority of the people will go along with them rather than oppose them. I am not the first to make this observation. Bertrand Russell has said the same thing on more than one occasion, a fact that can be verified if one reads his collected essays. It seems fair to say that the mere existence of a popular democratic political system offers no guarantee of good government. Perhaps it was this thought that was behind Lord Bryce's assertion that "men desire to be governed well more than they desire self-government." It certainly was a point Aristotle had very much in mind when he depicted democracy, i.e., rule by the majority, as a degeneration of polity, i.e., rule by the sober and frugal middle class.

Since democracy has for long been considered as the high point of a nation's political and social development, let us take a close look at what happens when democracy breaks down. The breakdown in democracy has usually led to the setting up of a dictatorship as the first stage in the society's political rehabilitation. The ancient world, especially ancient Greece, gives us numerous examples of democracy replaced by dictatorship and the latter in its turn eventually replaced by revived democracy. For example, the dictatorship of the thirty (in Athens), which resulted from discontent with the conduct of the Peloponnesian War after the death of Pericles, was overthrown after a short period of time to allow the return of democracy once more. The conduct of the Peloponnesian War was not much improved by this event, but at least the attachment of the Athenian people to democracy had again been tested and once again a small minority, led this time by Thrasybulus, had successfully risen to the challenge.

The Roman republic institutionalized the office of dictator so that in emergencies the incumbent Consul who was elected for one year only, could step down and be replaced by one whose abilities were widely acknowledged and who would be entrusted with the powers of a dictator for six months. Under these conditions, the consul could not be brought to account for his actions at the end of his consulship. Although democratic Athens did not recognize the institution of dictator in a legal way, as did republican Rome, we may note that the people of Athens, having regained their democratic institutions after the overthrow of the thirty, did not immediately set about taking revenge on every member of the dictatorship they could get their hands on, but on the contrary, forbade vengeance to be taken against these individuals or their families. They recognized no doubt that, although the dictatorship might have gone astray, the original intentions of its leaders were not so much to enslave Athens as to set up a better political structure for the conduct of the War.

Thus, from the point of view of the ancients, dictatorship could be seen as a corrective measure which might not always be popular, but whose legitimacy was almost unquestioned; rarely did it lead to a drastic break with the past, but only that the number of people able to influence policy was greatly reduced. Even down to the seventeenth and eighteenth centuries dictatorship could still provide a useful service to the nation. For instance, the dictatorship of Oliver Cromwell is a noteworthy chapter in British history, and he has been praised as a soldier and statesman by no lesser figure than Lord Macaulay, whose attachment to the principles of democratic government hardly needs elaboration. Hampered as it was by sectarian division and political dissension, the dictatorship of Cromwell was still notable for the advances that were made by England in commercial and military affairs — advances which could not have conceivably been made under the incompetent and corrupt monarch whom he displaced. For the first time, England was able to challenge the maritime supremacy of the Dutch, while taking Jamaica from the Spaniards during the same period, a conquest which was never to be returned to Spanish hands. A very important event during Cromwell's dictatorship was the passage of the Navigation Act, which at one blow greatly reduced the pre-eminence of the Dutch in sea-borne trade, while laying the foundation for England's maritime prosperity... though the full benefits of this act were not to be reaped until England's industrialization was well under way.

It may also be remembered that England went to war with Holland over the Navigation Act. The remarkable fact about the naval battles which followed was that the British navy, led at sea by men who had been officers in Cromwell's model army, and which up to that time had no great tradition of seamanship, established its superiority over the Dutch navy in a manner which forces us to return to the history of the Roman republic to find a parallel. By the time of the Napoleonic wars, England had established herself as the world's foremost maritime power. Surely it is a remarkable tribute to the spirit that Cromwell enthused into every branch of state machinery. But whereas in pre-industrial society, a dictatorship could come to be looked upon as a blessing in disguise, if not by the people subjected to it, then by later generations, the same cannot generally be said for modern dictatorships, especially those of this century which have shown a fanatical commitment to an ideological goal. As far as western countries are concerned, the consensus of opinion is that dictatorships have outlived their usefulness and are only a hindrance to progress and peaceful coexistence.

Then again, dictatorship as an institution for the restoration of order, is now seen as a positive evil, a cure which is worse than the disease, an office which gives the dictator far too much power over his fellow men. So striking is this difference felt to be, that the word "totalitarian" has on occasions been used to characterize a dictatorship when found in a modern industrial nation. I would tend to agree that the modern dictatorship, by whatever name it is called, is quite a different creature from the dictatorships of any era of pre-industrial times, although some students of political science have attempted, wrongly in my opinion, to characterize ancient Sparta as a totalitarian state. As we shall later be discussing, it is not an easy matter to make a valid judgment on a particular system of government, since a number of complex factors are involved. But nevertheless I feel justified in attempting to make some sort of distinction between a modern day dictatorship and a modern day democracy, so that we may at least have some idea of what we are talking about when we say that the modern dictatorship is a unique institution which shares nothing in common with the dictatorships of pre-industrial times, except the same name.

Thus, possession of all or most of the following four features would appear to distinguish a modern dictatorship from a modern democracy: (i) the absence of free elections and the exclusive monopolization of political power by a particular group; (ii) total government control of all media of communications; (iii) the absolute supremacy of the executive branch of government; (iv) a specific ideology which all must accept and the continuous call for permanent mobilization against internal or external threats to national security. The last mentioned feature is usually sighted as being characteristic of a totalitarian dictatorship, which is supposed to show a higher degree of ideological commitment than non-totalitarian types. Be this as it may, I am not at all certain that the term totalitarian serves a useful purpose in regard to political analysis. I have the distinct feeling that the term is an anachronism carried over from the days of the Third Reich and Stalinist Russia, two horrendous dictatorships, the likes of which the world will never see again. It is much too crude a term to encompass the complexities of modern politics, and neither is it able to reflect changes in a nation's political and legal organization, such as those which have taken place in the Soviet Union since the death of Stalin to the present time. Quite frankly, it does not belong in the vocabulary of the political scientist, and should be dispensed with. As for the place dictatorship may have in the future of western society, I too believe that this type of government has had its day, and is unlikely to become a significant factor in the affairs of western man. But I also believe it not improbable that many western nations which are now plural democracies may move towards a more strictly regulated type of society as social breakdown comes closer. But this will not be sufficient to prevent modern industrial society from undergoing a tremendous transformation.

Just as social and political breakdown in earlier times has led inexorably to dictatorship, so the circumstances of the new age will demand the resurrection of aristocracy. The quantity of fertile land will be greatly reduced from what is available at the present time; far-reaching climactic changes will be another factor which will affect present-day patterns of population distribution. Only the emergence of exceptionally capable individuals will be able to check the subsequent disruption and bring order out of chaos. Rather than being left alone to fight each other for the right to make use of a small patch of fertile land, the people will be led by these exceptional individuals to appropriate a large area of fertile land which will be divided up in the best possible manner so as to enable the common people to work in harmony, produce food and bring up children without living in fear of neighboring communities, as would be the case without the existence of a superior source of authority. It is such a source of authority which will be embodied in the new ruling class.

It is important to understand that there will be absolutely no relation between the dictatorships of ancient or modern times and the organization of society in the new age, for the individuals who form the dominant class in the new age will automatically have earned the right to maintain this position in perpetuity. This is one factor that unites all aristocracies regardless of time or place, i.e., membership of a highly exclusive group which is designated by one's birth. Typically, members of this group can expect to be among the wealthiest members of their society, they can expect to hold all the important positions in government. They will be the military leaders of the nation; the officer ranks of the army and navy will be composed entirely of scions of the aristocracy. Most of the nation's religious leaders will also originate from the aristocracy. All forms of artistic creativity in such a society, are undertaken with the objective of catering to the prejudices, preferences and vanity of the aristocracy. To please the aristocracy is the ultimate goal of all those of lesser rank. In fact, all that is finest in the society will be concentrated in and around this group. Only once in history have the lower orders absorbed the virtues of aristocracy and used these to build a rich, diversified and energetic culture — these were the ancient Athenians.

In a well-constituted aristocracy, no one questions the leading position of the aristocracy. For their part, the members of the aristocracy accept the responsibilities of their exalted station. Members of the aristocracy do not live in fear of the lower orders; they are sure of their position, a self-confidence bred by generations of leadership. Aristocracy thinks on a grand scale; it is not inhibited by considerations of cost or time. A project which will take many decades to complete is nonetheless considered worthy of construction. Aristocrats are by nature generous people, they think nothing of spending great sums to entertain their friends and followers in regal splendor. They pay for the cost of public works and fine statues, not because they want to reduce their tax liability, but because they require great monuments to remind future generations of how high they stood above their fellow men in greatness. Members of the aristocracy are punctilious in regard to the respect that should be paid to them, i.e., as befits their rank. When insulted, they react not with disguised resentment, but with open anger, which they may appease straight away, or save revenge for a more convenient time — that is, when they are in a better position to strike back. They will not stand for any encroachments being made upon the power they hold, but on the contrary, are always looking for ways in which they can extend this power to ever greater heights. Membership of the aristocracy will encompass all individuals who are the most aggressive, the most courageous, and the most virtuous members of the society.

But all aristocracies are not the same. Some aristocracies have given far more freedom of action to members of the nobility than others. As far as the history of western civilization is concerned, there have been basically two types of aristocracy, feudal and non-feudal. The distinctive feature of feudal aristocracy is that it is based more on military power than legalistic arrangement, and as a corollary to this, members of the aristocracy often fight among themselves. Non-feudal aristocracies, on the other hand, are characterized by the legalistic nature of the organization of power according to which laws are passed by a Senate in which members of the aristocracy are expected to take part in debate and discussion in order to settle their differences. Two further features distinguish the non-feudal type of aristocracy from the feudal type; the first is the close association of the former with commercial interests, and the second is the fact that this type of aristocracy is always centered in the city rather than the countryside, as is the case with feudal aristocracy. The Roman nobility, it is true, were overwhelmingly landowners, but membership of the Senate also included wealthy merchants, well-connected lawyers, and other highly successful members of the middle class.

The non-feudal type of aristocracy is, needless to say, more restrictive than feudal aristocracy. For power is highly centralized in the capital city, the army is raised on a national basis, rather than by locality, and its commanders are appointed by the Senate instead of each noble leading his own contingent into battle. Provincial governors are appointed by the Senate and can be dismissed at the pleasure of this body. Instead of nobles acting as administrators of these provinces, they must accept the appointment of a lackey of the Senate, and restrict themselves to the management of their estates. The aristocratic Senate must move carefully, since more likely than not there is a highly developed middle class looking over its shoulder and watching its every move. Moreover, as we earlier observed, members of the middle class will probably be found sitting alongside nobles or perhaps even plotting the complete overthrow of this class. One is reminded of the class wars which took place in ancient Rome, and much later in several of the Italian city-states. While aristocratic Venice had to employ a special police force — the sbirro — to deal with the threat from revolutionary elements within its society. Under these circumstances, a nobleman's home is not his castle, but his country retreat. He is an eagle with clipped wings, a thoroughbred born to race the wind, but hemmed in on all sides. As well as being the form of government exhibited by the Roman republic, Carthage and other ancient city-states, non-feudal aristocracy was also represented by the Swiss aristocratic republic, e.g., Berne and Geneva, and by the Italian city-states, e.g., Venice and Genoa.

The non-feudal aristocracy, then, channels the energy of its nobility into the service of the state; they are not free to pursue their own personal aggrandizement, except in the most sordid and underhanded manner. John Stuart Mill, in his *Considerations of Representative Government,* attempts to convey the flavor of aristocratic rule in the Roman republic when he likens the Senate to an hereditary bureaucracy and describes how the individual pledges himself to serve the state:

> ...the Senate was in general exclusively composed of persons who had exercised public functions, and had either already filled or were looking forward to fill the higher offices of the state, at the peril of a severe responsibility in case of incapacity and failure. When once members of the Senate, their lives were pledged to the conduct of public affairs; they were not permitted even to leave Italy except in the discharge of some public trust; and unless turned out of the Senate by the censors for character or conduct deemed disgraceful, they retained their powers and responsibilities to the end of life. In an aristocracy thus constituted, every member felt his personal importance entirely bound up with the dignity and estimation of the commonwealth which he administered, and with the part he was able to play in its councils. This dignity and estimation were quite different things from the prosperity or happiness of the general body of the citizens, and were often wholly incompatible with it. But they were closely linked with the external success and aggrandizement of the state.[1]

In feudal society, on the other hand, service to the state is of secondary importance to increasing one's own power and glory.

In fact, the state itself is simply a loose confederation of autonomous provinces. It is the nobility acting as sovereign individuals who lay down the law of the land and not a governor acting at the behest of a distant Senate. Another point to note is that there is no such thing as a standing army within feudal society. Troops are raised locally throughout each province and led into battle by the highest ranking noble of the province. Further, the grip of the nobility on society as a whole is more complete under a feudal aristocracy, since the middle class is very small and totally dedicated to the needs and interests of the aristocracy. Therefore, it is in no position to make an effective challenge to either the political or economic supremacy of the ruling class. So weak is the state under the feudal system of political organization, that some provinces may be held by nobles who live in other countries. This would mean that the lesser nobles of these provinces would owe their first allegiance to a foreign lord rather than to their king. Among the nations of western Europe in the middle ages, France, Germany and England showed the feudal spirit to perfection.

For example, throughout this period, France can hardly be said to have existed as a nation state, so fiercely independent was its nobility. Several of the greater nobles were in military terms more powerful than the French king, if their possessions in other European countries were taken into account, e.g., Charles of Burgundy. The nobles who helped William of Normandy conquer England thereby became large land holders in both England and Normandy. The marriage of Eleanor of Aquitaine to Henry II of England brought a huge portion of French soil under the personal control of the King of England. Whereas in the non-feudal type of aristocracy, the state is represented by a corporate gathering of the nation's nobility, the state in feudal aristocracy is represented by the person of the monarch. In theory, the king need not consult with his nobility before making a decision, but in practice he must do so if he is to have any chance of gaining meaningful support for a particular measure.

But those whom he consults are entirely of his own choice. In recognition of this fact, those nobles who were regularly called together to consult with the King of England became known as the privy council, i.e., those who were privy to the thoughts of the king. Not that nobles who were not confidants of the king considered themselves to be at a disadvantage, for if necessary they were prepared to meet their king on the battlefield to settle serious points of disagreement. Thus, in the non-feudal type of aristocratic society, the state is highly regarded, whereas in feudal society it is not.

It is important to grasp this point, because societies of the new age will be characterized by the disappearance of the nation state. The changes in climate, soil conditions and physical features of the land that will take place in the new age, will lead to a breakdown of national boundaries, as large numbers of people leave what was the country of their birth in search of a hospitable climate and fertile land. The reaction of the indigenous population to newcomers of different cultural background may be hostile to begin with. But any attempt made to preserve cultural purity will be doomed to failure. Either the indigenous inhabitants must accept the newcomers, or they must move elsewhere. No one will any longer give much thought to his nationality, only his survival and that of his family will count. New societies will be formed by an amalgamation of peoples of different national origins, and will be separated from other societies by physical barriers, some of which may be impassable, but most of which will be accepted by common agreement as rough boundaries.

These new societies will not become new nations, but rather new groupings of the populations of what were neighboring nations in the previous age. The land occupied by these new societies will be the property, not of those who farm it, but of those who have shown outstanding military leadership in conquering it. The new age will resemble feudal society in that the state will not be of much significance in the reckoning of the leading men. But in a number of important ways, societies of the new age will go beyond feudal society. The most important of these is in regards to the institution of monarchy. Feudalism was originally brought into existence after the mainly Germanic tribes of Northern Europe overran the Roman empire. Each of these tribes had long since held the position of chief to be hereditary, thus it was not long before the office of king was made hereditary with the transfer from father to son just a mere formality.

In theory however, the king owed his elevated position to consensus among the nobility, any high ranking members of which had the right to challenge the competence of a successor to the title, a right which was, in fact, rarely if ever exercised. The result of this was that not only was the king often one of the least courageous men of the land, but by the same token a weak and incompetent monarch usually survived to hand on the scepter to a son who was not worthy of it. The institutionalization of power of the feudal monarchs, and its subsequent fossilization in the hands of one family, led also to loss of vigor among the nobility. As a succession of weak but cunning monarchs sought to reduce the independence of their nobility by slowly centralizing power while reducing the nobles to ceremonial nonentities. This course of events will not take place in the new age. For one thing, the leading figures of the new societies will not be tribal chiefs but individuals who have displayed exceptional skill in gaining a large following and leading it to victory. These men will start off then as equals, and that is more or less how it will remain. No one family will be elevated above all others to represent the unity of the nation. This will not be necessary.

Leadership within the ruling class will not be entirely absent, but it will be based on what we may term oscillating hegemony rather than on the institution of kingship. Thus, one noble will distinguish himself from most others in his region by his efficiency in dealing with his enemies and the way in which he manages the affairs of his domain. This individual would be expected to gain the following of not only lesser members of the nobility, whose lands form part of his domain, but also of other nobles whose lands do not form part of his domain, but who are members of the same society that he is. These other nobles could come to him for advice and assistance, and in turn would be available to assist him in any way he required. Hegemony may remain with this individual for a fairly long period of time and even be taken over by another member of his family, but he would not be a king, since no such office would be recognized. He would have no authority to enforce his wishes, except within his own lands, though he would also have great influence on the policy followed by those nobles within his domain who were faithful to him.

Once his prestige begins to wane through old age or other cause, e.g., a succession of defeats, then a noble whose star appears to be on the ascent would be expected to gain a following as a result of defections from the followers of the established leader. This following may be small at first, but could eventually surpass that of the established leader whose fortunes appeared to be fading, and with whom he was in competition. In the event of such a situation, what remained of the alliance built around the person of a fading Seigneur would probably dissolve upon his death. On the other hand, if he managed to maintain his allies in awe of his power right up to the time of his death, there would be a good chance that leadership of the alliance would be taken over by his son (perhaps without opposition), assuming the latter was experienced enough to take on such a demanding responsibility. If he were not, then other members of the alliance could bring forward their claim to leadership. Thus, hegemony within a particular region would shift from one family to another and back again, and so it would continue. There would be no room for weakness, incompetence or misjudgment, if one wanted to maintain hegemony. Societies of the new age will have no capital city; instead, the homes of those individuals who are exercising hegemony at a particular time will be the nerve centers of the society. The nobles will meet at the homes of the leading men of the region, to whom they have given their loyalty, to give or receive advice and to discuss matters pertaining to the affairs of the society as a whole.

The individuals exercising hegemony will not have any special insignia apart from their family coat of arms, since their superior standing will be known to all nobles throughout the society, though the superior status of a particular noble may be grudgingly accepted by others in his region as only a temporary state of affairs. It would seem reasonable to assume that superior status will not be easy to attain, and once attained, it would not be lost suddenly, but gradually over a fairly long period of time. Thus, instead of national states with centrally located seats of government and clearly defined boundaries, the societies of the new age will consist of a combination of contiguous territories ruled over by competing nobles, any one of whom could (in theory) assume hegemony over a large number of the rest at any time. An important factor in determining the limits of hegemony for a particular society would be distance, since the influence of a leading (i.e., superior) noble, no matter how well thought of throughout the society as a whole, would obviously decrease as distance from his power base increased. This would mean that others, perhaps of less ability (but with just as much ambition) would have the chance to amass an equally large following among the nobility. It should be clear to all by now that what we are talking about is a society whose social organization is based on pure aristocracy. The power of the nobility will be diluted neither by the existence of a representative assembly, nor by the institution of monarchy. It is the competition for power which will give the society its identity and coherence, rather than the suppression of this tendency, which has been the hallmark of the nation state.

Political man, the man without power, has always feared those who did have power and who would increase this power at the slightest opportunity. He (political man) works rather through compromise and shabby backroom deals. The greater the number of those involved in the political process, the more he likes it, for that means the caucus and the committee become all-powerful, since we know that an assembly of four or five hundred persons cannot possibly conduct legislative business as efficiently as a committee of ten or twelve persons. This also allows the clever floor manager and the good orator to use their skills to greatest advantage. Without proper leadership, envy, vacillation, bigotry and narrow-mindedness are the marks of political man. He is envious of those who are better than he is, and seeks ways to reduce their pre-eminence. He is incapable of sticking to a course of action and seeing it through to the very end, especially if it calls for heavy sacrifices. He is always ready to make a scapegoat of some religious or ethnic minority as a way of compensating for his own impotence. He is incapable of thinking up bold sweeping designs which in one giant leap can change the present state of affairs. He must look over his shoulder at his colleagues, he must weigh the claims and counter-claims of various pressure groups and special interests.

The political man of today cannot even be realistically compared with the political man of the ancient city-state. Political man of that age knew no other reality than the right of those men of good family to rule over him. He accepted without question the right of these men to require him to make sacrifices for the good of all. One remembers the fact that if the Roman republic suffered a serious military reverse, such as occurred in the first battle with Hannibal, the wives, daughters, sisters and mothers of all soldiers who died were instructed by the Senate not to cry or go into mourning, but on the contrary, to look happy for their husbands, fathers, brothers and sons, who had died nobly for a worthy cause — the preservation of the Republic. The same instructions were issued by Sparta's Senate after its army had suffered a crushing defeat in the battle of Leuctra at the hands of Thebes, which was led at that time by the soldier-statesman Epaminodas, one of the few great men of ancient Greece who was not an Athenian. He died as a result of wounds sustained in this battle, though not before his goal had been accomplished, which was to break the military power of Sparta. This noble spirit of self-sacrifice (shown by the ancients), which permeated the entire society, was called forth by the nobly born and could only have been called forth by those whose ancestors had always led the nation as a matter of duty.

Political man of today, on the other hand, participates in national affairs for no other reason than the fact that we no longer live in an heroic age as were antiquity and feudalism. Political man was without voice in the middle ages, a person of no account; he was the man whose re-emergence was signaled by the writings of Thomas Hobbes. The course of politics from Hobbes' time onwards has shown that the greater his (political man's) involvement in political affairs, and the more the involvement of established families declines, the more diminished the leadership of society becomes. Nothing is more nauseating than to see those who have taken upon themselves the duties of leadership striving desperately to demonstrate their equality with those whom they are supposed to lead. Not only is leadership diminished by this, but the society as a whole derives little benefit from the exercise, whilst many of its more perceptive members become depressed, insecure, skeptical, and unequal to mighty undertakings. Contrary to popular misconception, aristocracy does not depress energy, but actually promotes it, though keeping it within bounds and ensuring that it is channeled into the right activities at the right time, so that it does not become a threat to good order and the society's long-term chances of survival. Many supporters of democracy have not been unaware of its limitations in this respect. Thus, Freud in his *The Future of An Illusion*, tells us that the masses must be led by men of superior virtue if a new civilization is to be built or an old one is to be maintained. In his words, "It is just as impossible to do without government of the masses by a minority as it is to dispense with coercion in the work of civilization."[2] A similar message is to be found in his book *Civilization And Its Discontents*. Then again, the reverend Jeremy Belknap is credited with the following observation: "Let it stand as a principle that government originates from the people; but let the people be taught that they are not able to govern themselves." This is becoming every day more apparent. Whereas political man is often base and conniving, a nobleman is straightforward and honest. For the nobleman in an aristocratic society does not need to manipulate from behind the scenes, he is not a floor manager, he has no interest in maximizing his personal welfare — he is born to the good life. But what he must be interested in, if aristocracy is to be kept alive as the leading principle of social organization, is holding onto and increasing the power he already has.

Mankind went from barbarity to civilization, not by the way of one man one vote, but by the strongest free spirits being allowed to realize their ambitions and desires. Once the majority is given a share in deciding upon the affairs of their society, no matter how small, it becomes weak, vulnerable and insecure. In the ages of aristocratic leadership, war had its proper place in the scheme of things, and did a great deal for the health of the society. But as soon as the common people obtain a share in political power, one of their first demands is to participate in all matters relating to the declaration of war and terms of peace. No longer does the aristocracy have a free hand in these matters. The position of the bureaucracy grows stronger and military affairs become centralized. The standing army officered and led in the main by professional soldiers displaces the nobility from the area of activity in which they excel above all others. Attitudes to war within the nation as a whole also change. Both the common people and degenerate nobility look upon the making of war as something that should be avoided at all costs. The paranoid attitude to war that characterizes modern man is yet another reason why he is so inferior to pre-industrial man. On the one hand, having witnessed two devastating world wars, contemporary man craves for peace. But on the other, he continues to design and manufacture weapons of enormous destructive potential. War and the threat of war no longer does anything for the moral fiber of the nation. It does not inspire virtue and a strong sense of family commitment, but only fear, despair and hopelessness. Like most other aspects of contemporary society, military affairs have gone beyond man and have become an invisible but heavy burden upon his existence.

A society which is not fully imbued with military virtues is a society whose long-term survival is imperiled. And a society which does not look forward with relish to the prospect of going to war is a society which is incapable of cultural improvement and in a state of decline. The only real interest contemporary man has in war is the impact that the manufacture of armaments has on the economy. Huge standing armies which have no purpose and very little to do apart from going on training exercises are maintained by all advanced industrial nations. How these armies can possibly be trained to withstand all-out nuclear war I have no idea. Enormous quantities of sophisticated weaponry are produced every year and turned over to the military establishments of both well-to-do countries and to those which can least afford them. Such weapons are unlikely ever to be used by most of the purchasing countries; in some cases the latter do not even have sufficient trained manpower to operate and maintain these sophisticated armaments. But the industrialized nations do not care, since foreign sales of weaponry help bring in foreign exchange, keep many thousands of people in productive employment and generally add to the all-round health of the economy. Military affairs have become just another branch of the welfare state. As for those who control the production of armaments, they think in terms of profit not power. Our perspectives and values have been totally distorted. The idealism which bids us to believe in the possibility of permanent peace, while arming for all-out nuclear war, is a great disservice to western man.

The exercise of power in the new age will bypass representative institutions, something which will be an anathema to the ruling class. Each noble will be responsible for administering the affairs of his own domain. In addition, the leading nobles of the society would be expected to exercise considerable influence on the policies that the lesser nobles follow throughout their domain. The senior officials of the noble's household would also advise their lord on the administration of his patrimony as well as undertaking their regular duties. Matters of great importance may involve consultation of several nobles before a definite decision is made. One of the most important administrative tasks in the new age will be ensuring that in times of poor harvest all available food is distributed according to need. Another is that of ensuring that the territory's military requirements for weapons, manpower and supplies can be satisfied at short notice. Therefore, the territory's military organization would have to be kept up to scratch at all times. Some might believe that no society living in a more or less permanent state of war could for long survive the cost in destruction of people and property.

But we are not speaking of the technological warfare of industrial society, but the warfare of pre-industrial society, which was not at all as destructive of life and property as is the modern kind. As a matter of fact, war was a positive good in earlier ages, for it helped to keep the population in balance with the amount of accessible land which could be productively brought under cultivation by the agricultural techniques available. It also promoted a higher degree of circulation among the nobility than would have been the case if war was a relatively rare event. As for the destruction of property, this was not a matter of great account and war could be of positive value here, by promoting industry among the general populace in replacing their losses, such as they were. The long period of hostilities between France and England which goes under the name of the Hundred Years War, hardly troubled the economy of medieval France, although it was fought entirely on French soil. Similarly, the War of the Roses, which went on in England for some thirty years, barely touched the life of the common man throughout its entire duration. And internecine warfare among the nobles in these and other European countries was a daily fact of life.

In the new age then, the welfare of the common people will not be promoted by the pursuit of peace and prosperity, but by the desire of the noble lord to increase his power and influence. For if ever a ruling noble should show himself to be weak in his dealings with neighboring nobles, his subjects would be the first to suffer from incursion upon his domain. Thus, all matters brought to his attention with strategic military implications, must be given the most careful consideration. The nobility will also act as judges in disputes involving two or more communities within their domain. The decision of the ruling noble will be final and binding on all parties. The common people will be informed of decisions affecting them by messengers of the ruling noble. A community which has a special problem could, if it so wished, make contact with its ruling noble through a delegation of several persons, nominating one to act as spokesman for the rest. This delegation would return to its community after having visited the residence of the ruling noble and talked to the noble himself, or to one of the senior officials of his household. Provided his subjects have faith in him, a noble will be able to do great things. A noble will have the right to instruct the common people to undertake any task he so desires without receiving any sort of recompense for their services. The common people will take absolutely no part in the political affairs of the society as a whole, except as camp followers in the service of their lord. Each village will have a headman who will deliberate with a council of elders when the need arises. The first and only duty of the common people as far as politics will be concerned, will be unquestioning loyalty to their lord, and prompt compliance with his wishes as indicated to them by their headman, his messengers or other officials in his service. All else will be of secondary importance.

Power over the land and people will pass from father to son. The son in question need not be the eldest, but will probably turn out to be in most cases. If a noble lord should die without legitimate sons, then his lands would go to his eldest daughter or a son of his brother or sister, or alternatively to whomever he may desire, provided that the person is of full-blooded noble lineage. The uppermost thought in the mind of a noble who has no legitimate sons will be to prevent his lands from falling into the hands of someone who already has a patrimony of his own or is the certain heir to one. For should an individual who already has a patrimony of his own gain more land by inheritance, this could create a particularly difficult situation, especially so if the inherited land was not contiguous with the ancestral lands of the inheritor. For the physical presence of the noble in a traditional seat of power will be indispensable for maintaining the integrity of its surrounding lands. In other words, a noble will have a difficult time keeping order in lands willed to him by a deceased noble, unless he lives there permanently and renounces all other claims or allows one of his sons to establish an independent patrimony in this land. Blood ties between members of the nobility can be expected to be a factor of some importance in the politics of the new age, a factor which will cut two ways: On the one hand, there will naturally be a tendency for related families to enter into alliance for mutual benefit in times of external aggression or internal unrest. But there will probably also be a tendency for conflict to develop between closely related nobles, especially over matters of inheritance which will probably be a significant source of strife in the new age.

We may note in this connection, that no one will want one particular family to be in control of an exceptionally large amount of land, especially when their possessions are not widely spread out, but concentrated in a specific region. This would tend to give its members a specific advantage over and above their individual abilities, which could facilitate their dominance of the region for an indefinite period of time. The news of the accession of a new ruling noble and the death of the old one, would be announced throughout his territory and carried by messengers to other territories whose rulers had been faithful allies of the deceased ruler, in the hope that they would continue their friendship towards his successor. The civil and military officials of a ruling noble's household would be drawn mainly from two sources: in the first place, from the ranks of the landless of noble birth, and in the second, from among the children of these officials. But a son would not automatically assume the position of his father, if his abilities appeared to be unsuited to the duties which his father had performed. These civil and military officials will live a lifestyle much above that of commoners. Since, although landless, they will still retain their membership of the nobility as will their descendants, provided that they do not participate in any way in either trading or farming. The noble family of the new age will, as in ages gone by, be a corporate entity with its own coat of arms and titles of nobility. Once established, a noble family will not change its coat of arms, as the proud defense of its original coat of arms will be one of the most important things linking generation after generation of noble sires.

By now the reader should be aware that the leading societies in the new age will be warrior societies. War and aristocracy are inseparable and indispensable for a vigorous and healthy society. Once the aristocracy begins to prefer a life of ease and comfort to the rigors of a military campaign and sends subordinates to lead their troops into battle, instead of taking the lead themselves, degeneration is at hand. Such degeneration has happened in the past and led to the decline of the nobility and the rise of the unified state, but it will not happen in the future. Armies will always be led by members of the nobility, and not by professional soldiers, just as the administration of every part of a given territory will always remain in the hands of the noble families and not abdicated to officials with executive power. In other words, there will be no such office as governor in the new age. Rule over a territory will not be by appointment, but by right, and needless to say, in the new societies — might will make right! There will, hence, be no intermediaries between the people and their ruler, except the civil and military officials of his household.

Should a general call to arms be issued throughout a noble's domain, it will be obeyed swiftly and enthusiastically, for the common people will be only too happy to share the rigors of campaign with their noble lord. They will be inspired, by his bravery and courage, to overcome his enemies and return home victoriously. If they fail, but fight well, they will still be able to go home as proud survivors of a battle well fought. The right or wrong of a particular conflict will be of no interest to the common people, no pamphlets or manifestos will be written by their lord to explain his point of view. It will be sufficient for a noble to believe that he has been wronged for him to give orders for a war of vengeance. Or he may decide to take advantage of the weakness shown by one of his neighbors to increase his power at their expense. Alternatively, he may respond to the call of one of his allies for military help and mobilize his forces. These are just a few of the possibilities that could bring about a general call to arms. The fact that more or less any of the noble families of a region may be able to assume hegemony in this region given enough time, and if sufficiently ambitious, will make the new age one of greater vitality than any that has gone before it.

I willingly admit that it is most difficult for modern man to understand the essence of power in a truly aristocratic society. We moderns think of politics in terms of give and take, compromise and tolerance, pressure groups and interest groups. Political scientists conduct surveys on how people vote according to income, age, sex, occupation and location of residence. All so very trivial! Heads of state have taken to dining with a typical family or asking the people to send suggestions as to what course of action should be followed in the formulation of policy. How any leader can do these things and still call himself a leader is beyond me. This is the idealism of political man carried too far. The possibility that there are some people alive today who are disgusted with modern politics and long for a stronger age, must seem incredible, but it is no more incredible than the fact that they not only exist, but their numbers will increase as time goes by. It is these people to whom we must look if we have any hope left regarding the future of western man. These are the people who are so appalled by the degeneracy of the present age that they look forward to its disappearance and the opportunity to take their chances in the stronger, cleaner age to come. As the problems faced by the advanced industrialized nations become more and more pressing, only those who have completely written off modern industrial society as a viable way of life will be able to face up to the realities of the situation. All other people will be hopelessly confused, indecisive in thought and action, still clinging desperately to the ideals and lifestyle of a dying age.

Of course, simply standing up and publicly declaring oneself to be in favor of an end to this age will not be enough to guarantee one a place of honor in the age that is to come. One's standing in the new age can only be determined after this age has arrived and the land has been divided up among those who were the most successful competitors for power and prestige. Sharp debate, fiery speeches and flaming oratory will not be of great significance in the new age; deeds rather than words will be the deciding factor, deeds unrestrained by any code of conduct other than the desire to obtain for oneself and one's family the maximum possible amount of power. Attempts will be made by nobles from one generation to the next to decrease the power of the most powerful among them, while he will strive to maintain his power and if possible increase it. Rarely will disputes among the nobility be settled by discussion or arbitration. Either a noble is strong enough to have his own way and gets it with or without a battle, or he realizes he is not strong enough and so does not press the issue. The mark of politics in the new age will not be a debate followed by a vote, but — action! Fast, furious, military action. Only those who can live with this state of affairs will be members of the ruling class. Those who cannot, i.e., the vast majority, will be commoners with no hope of achieving a higher status.

During the course of discussing the relevance of his philosophical outlook to the political doctrines of his era (especially to the contract theory of government), David Hume noted that no political system was superior to any other; what counted was viability, rather than rule according to the ideals of popular democracy, which were rapidly coming to the fore at that time.

He reminded his readers that although England had a political system which came as close as any to approaching the ideals of popular democracy as then understood (i.e., restricted franchise), many other societies, for instance, all nations controlled by the Ottoman Sultan, lived under circumstances in which the very concept of popular democracy was foreign to them and had never existed at any period of their history. But still these nations had their own traditions and culture and their peoples showed no particular inclination for the institution of some form of representative government. Although, for the most part, Hume's philosophy is negative and uninspiring, he has a valid point here which has not been properly appreciated until quite recently with the arrival of detente; for no one political system is right (or possible) for every nation, considering differences in history and traditions.

This point is important because there is a tendency in the West to confuse a nation's political system with its lifestyle when attempting to assess it in comparison with the system of another nation. Thus, the political organization of Eastern Europe may not allow as much personal freedom as that of the West, but this fact by itself does not make it inferior. For one thing, it works; for another, it is superior to the political organization of the West in several ways. For instance, it is better at mobilizing national resources to complete gigantic tasks, it greatly reduces opportunities for corruption, and eliminates much time-wasting debate and party posturing. But on the other hand, when judged by contemporary standards, the lifestyle of the West is decidedly superior to that of Eastern Europe and the Soviet Union, as is evidenced by its greater economic, social and cultural vitality. Perhaps because a superior material lifestyle for the majority has been generally associated with democracy, it has been considered superior to all other forms of political organization. But even this is not necessarily always true, as Jacob Burckhardt reminds us in connection with Renaissance Italy: "Political impotence does not hinder the different tendencies and manifestations of private life from thriving in the fullest vigor and variety."[3] The truth of the matter is that as long as a political system works it must be accepted in its own right, fit to take its place alongside currently operating systems or those which have existed in previous ages.

One of the most important features of a fully developed aristocracy is that the political system and the lifestyle of the nation fuse into one, they become inseparable. The aristocracy not only make all decisions relative to the larger affairs of their society, but also dominate in other areas such as being the arbiters of good taste in fashion. The highest ideals of such a society will be all that is noble. And though some of the common people may possess and exhibit on occasions a few noble qualities, only members of the aristocracy will possess these qualities in abundance and exhibit them regularly. It is this factor, i.e., the supremacy of noble qualities which will cement the societies of the new age in a way that would be impossible under any other form of social organization. But the supremacy of noble qualities as the dominant ethos of the society can only remain for as long as all members of the aristocratic elite maintain their ascendancy. Thus, they have every right to take whatever action is necessary to keep the common people in their place. This may at times mean physical repression or restriction of freedom. It will all be for the good of the society. One of the sad failings of modern man is that he does not properly understand the benefits of restricted freedom and the duty of those in power to restrict the freedom of those below in order to maintain the society's integrity. The permissiveness of our age is ruining us, it is breaking up our families and has already destroyed our most precious values. Allowing every individual to set his own standards and make his own choices, without even the slightest hint of positive leadership from above, must lead to disillusion, cynicism and social breakdown. The ruling elites of ages gone by were right to lay down strict rules to be adhered to by the common people. They knew that it was their duty not to give the people what they would like, as this would seriously undermine the country's foundations, but to keep them in awe of power and authority. Since only in this way would the people cherish simple things and respect their leaders.

Even members of the nobility were expected to maintain certain standards in accordance with their rank. For example, in ancient Rome, as we have seen, the office of censor was established and had the specific task of removing from the Senate those members of it whose conduct was unbecoming of their rank. And this was not an uncommon occurrence; one remembers how the misconceived lust of the elderly patrician Appius Claudius for a young virgin led not only to him being removed from the Senate, but also thrown into prison. The ancient Romans took these matters very seriously. As for the middle ages, we all know about the importance that was attached to chivalry and decorum. Though no such office as censor existed at the court of the king, virtuous conduct was encouraged by the award of special titles (e.g., Knight of the Garter), and offices in the gift of the king, some of which were purely honorable, others of which involved great responsibility. Although members of the ruling class which will arise in the new age will be free to act as they please, and each noble will have his own idiosyncracies, those practices which are found to be the most congenial to the circumstances of this age will rapidly be enshrined in its customs and traditions, thereby remaining almost unchanged from one generation to the next. It is these customs, and not the idiosyncracies of individual rulers, which will be the most significant factor in the politics and social relations of the new age.

The supremacy of noble qualities is one of the foundations on which civilization is built. In fact, civilization could not have existed if a small minority had not possessed more than their fair share of all that is noble. This small minority has accomplished great deeds, a greatness which has been built upon the backs of the majority — it can be no other way. The contribution that the common people make to civilization is in their numbers, they provide an almost inexhaustible pool of undistinguished individuals. The majority know only one thing, the need to survive; this is how it was in the beginning, and this is the way it has remained. The noble ones not only have the desire to survive, but also the desire to rule. This difference produces the grandeur of civilization, its pathos and its vigor. Without it, mankind would have never passed beyond the stone age. For in those societies in which noble qualities are absent, man vegetates, he lives in hovels, he has no heroic tradition, his material culture is rudimentary and his literary culture non-existent, he has no ambition to achieve either for himself or for his society. Such a society's existence is also precarious as well as barren; it is highly vulnerable to environmental emergencies, since its members are not psychologically able to cope with major reverses in their fortunes, but instead accept the resulting disruption of their way of life as final. Not surprisingly, these simple equalitarian societies are fatalistic, and will move from one location to another if they feel that they will have better luck by moving on. Such a rootless way of life would be impossible for an aristocratic civilization which, by definition, must have a high degree of permanency. Another failing of these simple equalitarian societies is their susceptibility to incursion from outside, for such societies are generally peace-loving and not well versed in the art of war; hence, they are easy prey to more aggressive societies which are invariably hierarchical in organization.

Inevitably, we come down to the question of "what is noble?" Courage and generosity are obviously noble qualities, as is the love of good living and military adventure. But there is one quality which sums up better than any other what it means to be noble: this is the desire to dominate; the degree to which this desire is developed separates he who is noble from he who is common. The desire to dominate means the desire to take orders from no man; it means the desire to act as one feels, to live as a member of society and yet be a law unto oneself; it means the desire to stand above all other men in all that one does, to raise oneself and one's family to the greatest possible height, to achieve glory regardless of the cost, to be the source of all law and to take the law into one's own hands when one has a mind to do so, to involve oneself in great enterprises as the moving spirit, to stamp one's own personal tastes on such things as architecture, dress, art, music, drama and literature, in other words, the desire to control all that moves save the blind forces of nature. From this desire emerges all that is civilization, all that distinguishes aristocracy from other types of societies. We may add in passing that, conversely, one of the most consistent traits of the common people is the acceptance of the dominance of the nobility as part of the natural order of things. This makes for a stable, well-integrated society, something which Western man has lacked for a very long time. Admittedly, the desire to dominate has been greatly diminished corresponding to the degeneration of Western society, but the regeneration of mankind is at hand, and with it the desire to dominate, which will be greater than ever before.

So great will it be that it will prevent the reconstitution of the nation state. Instead, each society will be a contiguous cultural entity composed of numerous autonomous territories each with its own ruling elite. Because these territories will be united by the fact that they share a similar cultural heritage, the idea of nationality will not entirely disappear, but the idea of the centralized state will. For the autonomy of each territory composing the society will be jealously guarded. Should, on the other hand, the society ever be threatened by military incursion from outside, then national identity can be expected to come into play; warring factions would sink their differences and make war on the common enemy in defense of the homeland -- a duty which they would undertake in the name of their forefathers and the preservation of their culture. But assuming they are not threatened from outside, the nobles will make war upon one another almost unceasingly. No man could possibly set himself up as monarch of such a society. When not fighting domestic foes, the nobility will take their arms abroad in search of conquest and adventure. They will never for long remain at peace, but will always be anxious to display their nobility. The new age will be characterized by these perpetual power struggles. One man may be on his way to uniting an entire society under the leadership of his family, but well before this goal has been achieved, his power or that of his successor will succumb to the foremost obstacle in the way of national unity — a powerful, treacherous and fickle nobility. Some nations will undoubtedly have monarchs in the new age, but the leading societies of the age certainly will not.

With the return to dominance of aristocratic values will come a reordered system of social relationships. The class nature of the society will be present in every aspect of life. Thus, if a commoner should happen to meet with a member of the nobility, he will automatically defer to the noble, paying him the respect due to his exalted rank. If a noble sets aside land for hunting, it will be for his use only, and no commoner will be permitted to harm any of the larger animals inhabiting this land. But they could enter it for collecting firewood and hunting smaller animals, if they have received permission to do so from the ruling noble. There could be no possibility of an ordinary commoner eating at the same table with a noble or traveling beside a noble (unless specifically instructed to do so), or being treated as an intimate friend by a noble. Those persons of noble birth who are officials of a noble's household and members of his personal entourage will naturally rank well above both his domestic servants and all the other commoners within his domain. They will share his confidences, accompany him on distant journeys and act in his name whenever he instructs them to do so. As for justice, since the nobility alone will determine what is just and what is unjust, it will be based on rank rather than universal rules applicable to all. Ordinary commoners who anger their lord can expect to be severely punished and those commoners in his service who abuse his trust by going beyond his instructions or in some other way committing a serious indiscretion, can also expect to be firmly dealt with. But in deciding upon what is just in the case of the latter, the ruling noble will undoubtedly take into consideration past services rendered by the disgraced individual.

Because of the rebirth of aristocracy, the new age will recapture all that was best in the most heroic societies of ages gone by. The human spirit will once again soar to great heights. One remembers the noble Spartans at the pass of Thermopylae, three hundred of whom held off the attacks of a Persian army whose strength has been estimated at between one and a half and two and a half million men. And when these noble Spartans were betrayed to their enemy by a renegade Greek, and encircled, they fought to the last man led by their illustrious leader Leonitas. They were prepared either to conquer or to die; the easy option of surrendering as prisoners of war was not for them. We also have many examples of feudal chivalry at its most adventurous, for example, the Teutonic Knights, who considered it their destiny to being civilization to European Russia. The arrival of these knights and their settlement in the vast expanse of the Russian wilderness provided Russia with a new source of energy and vigor. This in a country which although great in size was never noted for the vitality of its nobility, but always for the backwardness of its people and the power wielded by its Tsar.

One thinks back to the Crusaders who were not only adventurers in search of battle and plunder, but had a mission from which they were not to be deflected. The fact that the Holy Land was no longer Christian and ruled by oriental potentates did not bother in the slightest these hardy warriors. All they knew was that Christian pilgrims could not travel freely through the Holy Land without harassment, nor worship in safety in such places as Jerusalem and Bethlehem, and something had to be done about this. And something was indeed done to put the matters right by the very first Crusaders who conquered the holy places and brought them under the control of Christian nobles. It is hard for us in this day and age to appreciate the sheer grandeur of such an enterprise and the courage it involved. The transportation of several hundred thousand fighting men from

Europe to the middle east was no easy undertaking in those days. The campaign involved a land whose territory was unfamiliar, whose climate was inhospitable to the European. Leprosy, malaria and other diseases abounded, sufficient supplies were never easy to come by, and the possibility of success very uncertain. But still they came, time and time again, to conquer or to die.

THE RETURN OF COMMUNITY

Contemporary sociologists have often compared the small intimate rural communities of bygone ages with the large impersonal, bustling communities which characterize the present day. Some of these sociologists maintain that the elimination of the intimate rural community, and its replacement by urban conglomerations, has led to many of the social problems which we are facing in most of the world's developed nations. This feeling is well summed up by Lewis Herber when he states that, "An incalculable percentage of urbanized Americans live on the brink of sheer hysteria. Economically insecure in their jobs, degraded by the herd-like congestion of public transit and large retail stores, packed into overcrowded dwellings, assailed by the interminable uproar of vehicles and machines, frozen in statuesque immobility by sedentary jobs throughout most of their working days — these urban dwellers often pass over the brink, or claw at its edge before spiraling into outright psychosis."[1] Although we must be careful in applying a cause and effect relationship to the movement of history, it is quite clear that there is substance to the belief in a link between increasing urbanization and the tendency towards social breakdown now evident in all industrialized societies.

The loss of community means that the individual and his family no longer has any input into his community more than paying his local taxes and sometimes shopping at the local supermarket. The decadent lifestyle of our contemporary industrial culture means that, depending on the hour of the day, an individual's mental life is centered on events at work, those on the television, or the happenings on a cinema screen. Alternatively, he is patronizing a nightclub, discotheque, or one of those numerous other places of entertainment set up to relieve us of boredom and surplus cash, i.e., his mind is anywhere but on the affairs of the neighborhood within which he lives. True, we have more opportunity than ever before for personal contact, but our social existence has become more spread out and hence more isolated than ever before. We work in one area, live in another, and satisfy our need for recreation in a third. So that those with whom we work often do not live in the same district as we do, and those with whom we fraternize in our leisure hours are not our next door neighbors (whom we hardly know), but acquaintances who may live many miles away, but who share the desire to lose their identity in an amorphous gathering at a downtown bar or discotheque. We are beginning to pay for this rootless way of life through hypertension, increasing incidence of neurosis and insecurity, which no amount of reliance on drugs, alcohol or tobacco will lessen.

What is so depressing about all this is that the problems of urban society and the fact that they are getting worse are common knowledge, but all solutions so far proposed are way off the mark. For instance, Thomas Blair, in his book *The International Urban Crisis*, prefaces his account of this situation with the following sage remarks:

> The major ills of our time are brutally apparent in the giant centers of population, finance, trade and culture — the multi-million cities like New York, London, Tokyo, Paris and Moscow. Everywhere that pattern is depressingly similar: unplanned growth, inner city decay and suburban sprawl, twice daily traffic jams on roads and underground transit systems, misused public funds, unrelieved poverty, slums still uncleared and growing larger, power and water shortages, and polluted environments. The richer the

resources, the worse the mess. What has gone wrong? Why does homelessness and squalor grow on a gigantic scale? Why are traffic and transport facilities strained to breaking point and no longer able to meet the travelling needs of urban dwellers? What are the forces of metropolitan growth that push whole communities into oblivion and kill the last vestiges of small neighborhood living? Why are urban planners, politicians, and administrators so insensitive to the needs of people and more frighteningly, unable to cope with the mounting crisis in cities?[2]

This is a powerful indictment of modern urbanization, but even a mind as incisive as Blair's fails to draw the obvious conclusion from these observations, which is that modern industrial society is rapidly on the way to becoming inviable. Instead, he talks about the need for radical reforms to achieve a more humane and socially just urban future. He, like all other modern writers who see the problem but not the solution, fails to realize that we have gone well beyond the point at which radical reforms can have any meaningful long-term effect. Something stronger is required, something far stronger. That this something will come, I have no doubt. The question is what sort of lifestyle will it bring for the majority. Needless to say, it will be nothing like the cramped and clock-regulated lifestyle of modern man. Gone will be the stresses and strains of modern city life, and the insatiable desire for material acquisition. It will be an age in which the common man is once again in touch with his inner nature. The common man of the new age, and his family, will live a simple life in a predominantly rural setting, a lifestyle that will always involve hardship and difficulties. It will be a life in which the common man will often be at the mercy of the elements at their most furious, with very little protection compared with contemporary man. But it will be a fully human age, unlike its predecessor; no longer will the tempo of life be dominated by the relentless urge to increase the national stock of wealth. The impersonal, isolated life of the large city will be replaced by the open and intimate life of the countryside. The wants of the common people will be simple; all their basic necessities they will be able to produce for themselves. Thus, the common people of the new age will build their own homes, make their own furniture and most of their tools, grow their own food and bake their own bread. The women, with the help of their younger children, will be spinners and weavers. All families will make their own soap and candles as well as shoes and clothes. Even those members of the community who perform important specialized tasks for the benefit of the community as a whole, such as the blacksmith or miller, will cultivate the soil as a secondary occupation. The common people will hardly have time to be bored or to brood about the rigors of their simple lives. Members of the same community will help each other in a direct and relevant way, not by the payment of local taxes to finance the provision of specialized services, but by personal participation in helping to do what needs to be done.

Neighbors will work all day in the fields side by side, help repair one another's homes after damage by bad weather or other causes. Each individual will contribute to the community according to his strength, talent and experience. Thus, the younger members will be expected to work for longer hours than the older members, and generally do a far greater amount of the physical work. On the other hand, the elderly will be responsible for the instruction of the young, for the leadership of the community, and for the mediation of disputes. Those who show well above average skill in the performance of a particular task (other than agricultural labor which will be obligatory for everyone), would be expected to devote more of their spare time to this activity than to any other. Working in the fields will be hard, back-breaking labor. For the most part, the soil will be of poor quality, and will require constant attention once seeds have been sown, if a good crop is to be produced. Make no mistake about it; the men, women and children of the new age will be a hardy breed. There will be no room for weaklings, or the physically and mentally infirm, unless they are able to make a worthwhile contribution to their community. No more will a society be able to lay back and expect a plentiful supply of food and other goods to be available day after day, season after season. In the new age, the individual will no longer be able to take life for granted. He will have to work hard for what little he is able to obtain from the land and will never be sure that a day will not come when he will not even be able to obtain the little that he has been accustomed to receive through the fruits of his labor.

There will of course be many other ways in which community life in the new age will differ from the present age. Differences which will give to life in the communities of the new age greater depth and dignity than could be achieved by any modern community, with their artificial communal solidarity, and their superficial understanding of what community life is all about. The extended family will be central to communities of the new age. For the extended family to make a reappearance, it will not be necessary for several generations to live under the same roof. Rather, the important point to note is that a wife and husband will live very close to their respective parents, and will be in frequent contact with them, as will be their children, unlike today, when the typical nuclear family may live many miles away from either set of parents, and therefore unable to look to them for immediate help in an emergency. The physical distance between the two generations also tends to create barriers to the development of a close personal relationship. This in turn creates divisions within society which are most painful to the elderly who are so often neglected by their wayward offspring. The organization of the family will be strictly patriarchal with the father remaining the head of the household for as long as he lives. Marriage would be entered into by mutual agreement among the parents involved, provided of course that neither the prospective bridegroom nor the prospective bride was adamantly opposed to the match. Once marriage ceremonies were completed, the union would be for life. Divorce among the common peoples (as among the nobility) will be unheard of, though the pressures for a man to repudiate his wife (as a last resort) if she should prove to be barren may sometimes be too great to resist. But other than this situation, there will be no other reason for the breakup of a marriage except the death of one of the partners. Promiscuity among the unmarried young people would be strongly discouraged by their parents, in favor of a close friendship leading eventually to marriage.

Children will be brought up to show the greatest respect to their parents and grandparents. Not that they will be cruelly abused, for to have many children will be the greatest blessing that can befall a man and wife; even the nobility will honor a women whose fertility sets her apart from most of her contemporaries. Thus, children will be brought up strictly, but with kindness and affection. Any child who becomes orphaned will be taken in by another family in the community. If more than one family should want to take in the same child, then the elders will decide the issue. The main factor they would consider would be how closely related by blood is each of the families to the child, and how large is each of the families. The closer one's blood tie to the child, the better would be the family's chance of being allowed to take him or her in, while the family with fewer children would have a better chance than the family with the greater number of children. The community will spare no effort to ensure that young children receive sufficient food, so that they may grow into vigorous and healthy members of the community, and that pregnant women and nursing mothers receive enough nourishment so as not to jeopardize the health of their offspring.

Formal education for the children of commoners will be non-existent, since as far as they will be concerned this would serve no useful purpose. All the same, it would be possible for a literate member of the community to teach a young relative or any other child the rudiments of reading, writing and arithmetic, if the child appears to be especially keen to learn. But as a rule, instead of receiving formal education, girls will be taught the practical skills to be expected of them, by their mother, grandmother or other female relative. These skills would include among others, washing clothes, cooking, baking and sewing, while boys will be similarly instructed in skills and knowledge appropriate to their age and sex, by their father, grandfather or elder brother. This instruction will include what is expected of them by their noble lord, as well as recounting the legends and stories about the origins of the community and about the race of noble heroes who brought order and security to the land. They will also receive instructions on more practical matters. Thus, every male child will be trained to defend himself from brigands by his father, and will be expected to develop proficiency in the use of the quarterstaff, so that if ever called into the military service of their noble lord, they can be quickly trained to become effective infantry men. Young children will probably begin to make themselves useful around the home at a very early age, probably five or six, and gradually do more as they grow older. The attitude to the education of children in the new age is best summed up by Plato as part of his quest to discover the ideal society.

Thus, Socrates, in the *Republic,* explains to Glaucon:

> "We shall," I said, "address our citizens as follows: 'You are, all of you in this land, brothers. But when God fashioned you, he added gold in the composition of those of you who are qualified to be Rulers (which is why their prestige is greatest); he put silver in the Auxiliaries, and iron and bronze in the farmers and the rest. Now since you are all of the same stock, though children will commonly resemble their parents, occasionally a silver child will be born of golden parents, or a golden child of silver parents and so on. Therefore the first and most important of God's commandments to the Rulers is that they must exercise their function as Guardians with particular care in watching the mixture of metals in the characters of the children. If one of their own children has bronze or iron in its make-up, they must harden their hearts, and degrade it to the

> ranks of the industrial and agricultural class where it properly belongs: Similarly, if a child of this class is born with gold or silver in its nature, they will promote it appropriately to be a Guardian or Auxiliary. For they know that there is a prophecy that the state will be ruined when it has Guardians of silver or bronze.'"[3]

I hardly need say that in the new age, the legitimate sons and daughters of the aristocracy will be the children of gold. We can go a step further, for Plato tells us clearly that in the ideal state each child should be educated according to his or her class background and expectations; any system of upbringing which deviates from this is bound to lead to the ruin of society. I feel sure that this sound advice will be taken to heart in the new age, especially so as the chances of the child of common parents proving himself to be of a higher quality are for all practical purposes nil. But neither must we forget Plato's other injunction; this is, if a child of noble parentage proves unworthy to succeed his father, he must be passed over in favor of a son who is.

The common people will have an outlook that is fraternal and parochial. They will know little about distant places with an entirely different culture, for they will rarely, if ever, meet with persons who have traveled in foreign lands or with those of different cultural background. In fact, the average commoner (and his family) will throughout his life never stray very far from the community in which he was born. For a man, the only exception to this would be military service in the army of his noble lord. The community into which one was born would be the central focus of one's existence throughout one's entire life. But there would be nothing to stop a family moving to another community within the same territory, something which they could do for a number of reasons, e.g., overpopulation, lack of security, or decreasing agricultural viability. News about what is going on in other parts of the territory or in territories other than one's own would come to the ordinary commoner by way of hearsay. The common people of the new age will be unsophisticated and not in the slightest bit bothered by their deficiencies in this respect, and neither will they be very much perturbed by their ignorance about matters of high policy.

The common people will have few reasons to travel to other territories, since all their close relatives and friends will live in the territory of their birth. Moreover, the idea of a vacation will be alien to common people of the new age. They will probably work five or six days a week, depending on the season of the year, and will cease working on the day of certain festivals which will be held on the same day in all communities throughout the territory. No fugitive could be removed from the territory in which he hopes to find sanctuary without the permission of the appropriate ruling noble. By agreement among the entire nobility, couriers would have unrestricted freedom of travel in all component territories of the society, provided that the noble through whose domain the courier was passing was not at war with the noble from whose domain he had been sent, or with the noble to whose domain he was on his way. The common people would keep a sharp eye open for strangers passing through the territory and report their presence to officials of their ruler. But in general, any noble could travel freely through the territory of any other noble with whom he was not at war, provided that he and his retinue conducted themselves in a manner that did not give offense to the noble through whose territory they were traveling. All strangers, i.e., those of noble birth who do not live permanently in the territory, will be welcome and free to visit the home of the ruling noble, assuming they bear him no ill will. No one will be allowed to recruit mercenaries to fight for their master in the territory of another ruling noble, though a noble will no doubt send gratuitous military assistance to one of his allies if this is requested.

The people of the new age will be naturally healthy and robust and those who are not will not survive. Herbal medicine will return to prominence. This weak age of ours pays far too much attention to matters of health. Most people could survive surprisingly well without the help of physicians and surgeons.

The existence of modern medicine does not stop people from getting ill, and neither does it always help them to get better. It is true that the application of modern medical science may at times produce wonderful results. But eventually man must die, and the really important point about human life is not when or how one dies, but how one lives, i.e., what use a man makes of his life, and this has nothing to do with the standard of medical care that is available. Great men will exist and live long lives regardless of the availability of modern medicine, and some of them will achieve greatness at a comparatively young age. The great medical problems of our age, cancer, heart disease, congenital deformities and mental illness, belong to this age, and this age alone. They have never been a significant matter in all previous ages, and will not be in the new age. Infants born with serious deformities are unlikely to survive through childhood the rigors of rural life, while adults regardless of age or medical condition will remain active members of their family and community almost to the day of their death; such will be the nature of the people of the new age.

We moderns have greatly overestimated the importance of health care, and in the process have turned into a society of hypochondriacs. Perhaps this was to be expected from such a weak, self-centered age such as our own, in which we have nothing to do but to pamper ourselves with material delights, stuff ourselves with food and worry ourselves sick about our health. The drug industry and the medical professional feed on this worry to provide us with futile services and useless or dangerous remedies for ailments which are sometimes real, but often imaginary or quite minor. Of course, some people must become ill — seriously ill — but the vast majority of those who visit their family doctor and obtain prescriptions are not in desperate need of medical care, and could well do without medical advice. Modern medical research for its part has not succeeded in making us immune to flu viruses or to the common cold. As a matter of fact, not only are antibiotics eventually rendered useless by new strains of the organism against which they are supposed to be effective, but new diseases are appearing all the time which seem to have been totally outside the cognizance of modern medicine up to the time. Moreover, medical research is itself threatening to become a source of these new diseases; witness the controversial experiments involving the manipulation of the genetic material of normally harmless bacteria.

In the new age, babies will be delivered by one or more close female relations who have had previous experience in performing this task. The sick would be nursed back to health by members of their family. Any person who has fully recovered from an illness whose symptoms are described to him by a friend or relative of a sick person, would give advice on the duration of the illness, the treatment he took to overcome it, and any other piece of information which may be helpful. It will probably also be true that the people of the new age will develop a high degree of tolerance to all sorts of infectious and non-infectious diseases, and will either recover from them fairly quickly, or not even be aware that they have a disease and live a normal life. Hence, the most important defense against illness in the new age will be a strong constitution and a buoyant spirit. These things the common people will have in abundance, for without them life would be impossible. Thus, if a person reaches his or her early teens, there will be a very good chance that he or she will live to a ripe old age. After all, modern medicine has not succeeded in increasing the life-span of the average man much beyond the biblical age of three score years and ten, and this figure was given to us some three thousand years ago. Since the absence of vaccination, anesthetic, the stethoscope and wonder drugs, was never a serious handicap to our ancestors, it is not at all absurd to ask whether or not we really need the benefits of modern medicine to survive. For I strongly suspect that we can get along quite well without them once we have put this age behind us. Individuals may suffer as a result of illness of one sort or another, something which happens just as much today as it ever did, but the society as a whole will survive and reproduce itself whatever the state of medical science.

Another of the features which will help to make the new age so very different from our own is the fact that the common people will have very little contact with money. Gone will be the economic individualism of this age. Things that the common people cannot produce for themselves, they will not need. There will be no way in which the common people could spend money within their community, and any money which might be received in payment for goods from the community would belong to the community as a whole, rather than to one particular person. The thought of becoming wealthy will not even enter the minds of the common people, for they will know that wealth and power are the prerogatives of the aristocracy and no other group. The communities of the new age will be much better off for the lack of money and the lack of desire to obtain it, for money is a destroyer of traditional values, and a disrupter of traditional community life. Karl Marx had the right idea when he told us, "Money, then, appears as a disruptive power for the individual and for the social bonds, which claim to be self-subsistent entities. It changes fidelity into infidelity, love into hate, hate into love, virtue into vice, vice into virtue, servants into master, stupidity into intelligence, and intelligence into stupidity."[4] It goes without saying, therefore, that an economy in which the cash nexus is highly developed, is incompatible with aristocratic leadership. The almost total absence of money will also mean that non-essential goods and services will not exist to enfeeble societies in the new age as their existence has enfeebled contemporary advanced industrialized societies.

The primary basis of economic organization in the new age will be commodity exchange, by which everyone from the ruling noble all the way down to the poorest commoner will exchange something he has in excess for something he wants. If he has nothing in excess, he will not be able to trade. But if he has many commodities in excess, as most members of the nobility will, then numerous exchanges will be able to take place. For as long as a noble controls his lands, he will have little need for silver and gold. All the same, a small amount of money may be minted by a ruling noble if he so desires, in the knowledge that this money would eventually represent a claim on the resources of his domain, a claim which he must honor on all occasions if his money is to be any use to him. The main purpose of this money would be to facilitate travel and to a lesser extent trade. Thus, a noble or any member of his family could use the coins of his domain within the territory of another noble to purchase say food or other items from the storehouse of the noble through whose domain he is traveling or from the common people if they have the required commodities in excess. The latter would be obliged to give these coins to their lord in return for whatever they had sold to the noble traveler or its equivalent. This money could in turn be used by its new owner for travel in the territory of the noble who minted it or in the territory of another noble. All coins would be a standard value, say, equivalent to a certain quantity of wheat which the noble who minted them would have to hand over on presentation, provided this was by another noble or his servant. A noble may change the value of any new coins he mints (though this would not affect the value of his old coins already in circulation), depending upon the availability of commodities.

Thus, in years of bad harvest their value would tend to be lower than in years of good harvest. A noble need not accept payment for wheat, or any other commodity for that matter, in the coins minted by another noble, but may instead demand trade by commodity exchange. Although the issuing noble would have to honor the face value (in wheat or other commodity) of every coin he mints, whenever it is presented to him, he can melt down returned coins and change their value to reflect changes in his economic situation. If a noble did decide to enter into monetary trade with a second noble who presents him with coins minted by one or more other nobles, he (the first noble) must accept them all at face value. By this system, money would be restricted to the use of the aristocracy alone, and its value (over a period of several years) would be determined by the availability of basic commodities, especially agricultural commodities. Some nobles may not even bother to mint their own money, seeing its existence rather as a liability than as an advantage. It will be a matter for each noble to decide. The standard of living among commoners in the new age will not vary greatly, since all will be eligible to share in the produce of the land according to need, i.e., the size of their family. But since some families will have members who show a high degree of talent in a particular activity, such as making clothes and shoes, this would obviously set them apart from other members of the community who are not so well endowed in this respect. Thus, if they were able to produce a surplus of shoes, this would obviously enhance their economic standing relative to other families, as they would be able to exchange these shoes for other things.

The carefully restricted use of money in the new age will greatly strengthen the position of the nobility. For one thing, this fact will eliminate the possibility of the rise of an unproductive commercial class. Such a class would certainly pose a long term threat to the political ascendancy of the nobility. Neither would it be a good thing for the common people to bear witness to the existence of a significant group of people who are, to even a limited degree, economically independent of the aristocracy. The absence of a commercial class will also ensure that the vast majority focus their energies on the production of food and on other important activities. Whereas the existence of a recognized aristocracy is essential for the revival of western civilization, the existence of a commercial class is not and could only serve to drain away manpower from the performance of far more useful tasks. Naturally, the possibility that industrial production would be re-instituted sometime in the future would also be negligible in a society which made only a very limited use of money, and spurned all those things necessary for the development of an industrial culture. Moreover, the circumstances of the new age would not be conducive to the involvement of a large number of people in non-agricultural pursuits on a full-time basis.

The simplicity of the lifestyle of the common people and their frugal habits will be ideally suited to the needs of a cashless society. Likewise, the aristocracy will not be able to go into debt to cunning moneylenders, and as a result forced to sell off their most treasured possessions and even their land. This is how money can come to distort traditional values to the point at which they become meaningless, turning true aristocrats into paupers, and upstart bankers into a so-called business aristocracy. This will not happen in the new age, for there will be no moneylenders, no bankers, very few merchants, and no industrialists. Just as the absence of money will negate the possibility of the re-institution of modern industry, so it will also negate the possibility of the re-institution of capitalist farming. All those who work on the land will automatically be working on land owned by a noble lord and therefore they will be under obligation to turn over part of their produce to him and also to whomever else he nominates. He would give nothing in return, except to acknowledge them as his loving and obedient subjects, and would of course provide military protection when this becomes necessary.

The nobility would have far more control over the productive powers of their subjects than they could ever have in a money economy. There are several reasons for this. For one thing, people would work without pay, so finding money to finance the construction of, say, bridges or irrigation projects, or to build homes for the nobility, would be no problem. But the people so employed would have to be fed, and they would be unable to engage in agricultural labor while they are working on the construction project. Then again, the number of people involved exclusively in providing services and in the production of high quality goods would depend not on the price mechanism, but on the size and demands of the territory's nobility and its resources in people and fertile land. The reason for the last proviso is quite simple, for the larger the number of commoners and the greater the fertility of the land, the greater will be the ability of the ruling class to remove people from the production of food and turn them to the provision of goods and services, either temporarily or permanently. The same considerations apply to large-scale construction projects, that is, the more people that can be removed from the performance of agricultural labor for a given period of time, the grander will be the scale of the projects that can be accomplished. Thus, the nobility will be able to exercise almost total control over all goods produced that will not be used by those producing them, since they will be the primary recipients of these goods, though it bears repeating one more time, that those commoners whose devotion to the needs of the nobility prevent them from producing sufficient food for themselves and their family, would have to be fed, and if necessary clothed, by the largess of the ruling class. Thus, the nobility will direct the economy of the new age simply by way of their exalted lifestyle, without need for any special attention being paid to economic matters.

With the restricted use of money and its subordination to custom and tradition, the idolization of Mammon will come to an end. No longer will gold and silver be what Marx aptly termed the fetish of the marketplace. These metals and other precious minerals will be considered primarily from the point of view of their aesthetic worth and turned into objects of beauty, just as the Incas and Aztecs used precious metals, not primarily to facilitate buying and selling, but mainly for the purpose of creating exquisite statues and other objects of beauty and veneration. On the other hand, the attitude of the Spanish Conquistadores to the precious metals is aptly summed up by Hernando Cortes, conqueror of Mexico: "We Spaniards are troubled with a disease of the heart for which gold is the specific remedy."[5] The disease was insatiable greed and the remedy was never there in sufficient quantity to cure it. But the stage had been set well before Cortes and his associates came to the New World, for in his famous letter from Jamaica, Columbus tells us, "Gold is a wonderful thing! Whoever possesses it is lord of all he wants. By means of gold one can get souls into Paradise."[6] When the Spaniards destroyed these civilizations, they also signaled the beginning of a new era which meant doing away with things of lasting value in favor of transient luxuries. All gold and silver objects the Spaniards could lay their hands on were melted down, cast into ingots, and shipped back to Europe, where the sudden arrival of such enormous wealth created a mighty inflation, and a short-lived economic boom for the merchants of Flanders, but did little else.

With the absence of money from general circulation, the parvenu will cease to exist; no longer will a penniless pauper have the chance to rise to the level of a prince almost overnight. For real wealth will no longer be there to be garnered by industry and commerce or by the plunder of gold and silver, but will be inherited from those who rule the land and these alone. There will be no way in which nobility could be purchased. Either a person will be born noble, or he will not. Neither distinguished service nor acts of great valor could confer nobility upon a person of common birth. Under these circumstances, noble qualities will shine through as they have never done before. For since the earliest days of capitalism right down to the present time, the average man has considered the bourgeoisie and aristocracy to be the same, when in fact they should be considered as two distinct types. The first is concerned solely with money and the gaining of power (if he even bothers to think in terms of power) through money; whilst the second is concerned exclusively with power, since he is already at the top of the social pyramid and intends to do whatever is necessary to remain there. Thus, the limited use of money in a stratified agricultural society would in no way affect the principle of aristocracy. But as for the bourgeois ethos, this is quite another matter; it won't even make an appearance, let alone flourish and grow.

Another important side effect of the restricted use of money in an age in which military engagements will be commonplace, is that it would make the hiring of mercenaries a rather difficult, if not impossible, undertaking. As a result, soldiers would be fighting out of loyalty to their lord, and not for pay. This fact will be highly beneficial; for one thing, it will mean that troops will always have to be obtained from one's own domain rather than paying outsiders to fight one's battles. The fact that the Roman empire was able to recruit sufficient manpower from the provinces for its armies, by attracting recruits with the prospect of regular pay, was one of the factors which led to a decrease in the number of Italians in the army and eventually to barbarian leadership of the military and control of the empire. Also, a mercenary army can present serious problems of discipline, since they are professional soldiers with no particular sympathy for the cause for which they fight. One is reminded of the plight of Carthage after the first Punic War, which was in danger of being turned upon by its own mercenaries after it had come to terms with the Romans. Then there is the matter of being too dependent on soldiers who will fight for the highest bidder rather than the most worthy cause. Thus, on one occasion they may be fighting for you, and on the next against you, as was the case with the condottiere of Renaissance Italy. Further, they may simply decide to stop fighting and return to their homes, or the nation from whence they came may ban its citizens from fighting for other nations, as the Swiss Confederation eventually did. All these points were masterfully dealt with by Machiavelli in his classic little book, *The Prince*, in which he concluded that whenever possible, the prince should train his own subjects to be soldiers rather than employ mercenaries. We may take the words of such an acute observer as putting the matter beyond all doubt.

The negligible presence of money among the common people will also have a positive effect on the quality of life in the new age. It will also greatly reduce mobility and the corrupting influence which is generated by people in search of quick financial gain. With the cash nexus all but eliminated, the individual will have to do far more for himself, his family and his community than he has had to do in the previous era. This fact cannot help but build a sturdy character confident in his ability to cope with his environment and independent of the need for any special help except that given on a gratuitous basis by other members of his community. The absence of a money economy among commoners would also help to keep old people active, vigorous and alert to the very last days of their lives, since having no savings to fall back on they would want to make themselves useful as contributing members of the community for as long as possible. The inability of the more talented members of the community to turn their talents to pecuniary advantage, would also do a great deal to maintain harmony. It will remove a major source of envy which seems to afflict those of lowly status more than those of higher status, namely resentment of the better lifestyle of those who are nevertheless on roughly the same social level as oneself. Then again, the almost total absence of money (among the common people) will do a great deal to reduce theft, in conjunction with the natural honesty of the people. In this connection, it is of interest to note that a number of Europeans who travelled through Africa in the eighteenth century (e.g., James Newton) noticed that they could leave their personal belongings in the open and unattended at any village they came to, and these would remain untouched. A similar degree of honesty will characterize the common people of the new age. Farewell then to the money economy; hail to the cashless society of the new age!

There will be no towns in the new age, only rural settlements. This will mean that there will be no gap between town and country, no large centers of trade, culture and entertainment to divert the common people from their simple life and corrupt their moral fibre. Life will be totally rural with almost everyone, save the aristocracy and the members of their household, engaged in the production of food at some time in their life, either on a regular basis or part-time. The nearest thing to city life will be the homes of the nobility. Although international trade will probably continue in the new age, its volume will not be very great, and it will involve for the most part agricultural commodities and very little in the way of manufactured goods. The fact that there will be almost no towns in the new age will differentiate it from all other civilized eras and will give to it special qualities unique unto itself. One of these will be the self-confidence of the nobility, whose homes will be bastions of civilization as well as centers of authority. Another will be the limited horizons of the common people, who will remain for the most part contented with their harsh and simple lifestyle, for wherever they travel within the territory of their birth, or within other territories, the situation will be the same. There will be no towns to which they can escape to live a life of sloth and indolence. The population density of these rural settlements will not be great. Furthermore, because there will be no towns, the people will be more evenly spread across the land than is now the case. Thus, instead of living in choking cities and over-crowded tenement blocks, they will be surrounded by plenty of open space.

The members of a community will also be emotionally much closer than they are today. What I am saying is that there will be a greater feeling of empathy for each other than could possibly be found in the highly mobile societies of today. Because of the very low level of mobility among the common people, the same families will live in the same community for many, many generations. The sadness of death, the joys of marriage and childbirth will be felt not only by those families most closely involved, but also by the community as a whole, since for all practical purposes, it will think and act as one family. Furthermore, when a son or daughter of the ruling noble has a child, every community within the domain will be expected to mark the occasion in an appropriate manner and send two or three of its most esteemed members to the festivities that will inevitably follow. Similarly, when a son succeeds his father as ruling noble, all communities within the territory will be required to send representatives to the ceremonies marking the transition of power, in order to pledge allegiance to their new lord. There will undoubtedly be other special occasions on which the ruling noble will desire to have the presence of representatives of all communities in attendance at his court. Once his wishes are made known to those communities, they will be expected to comply exactly as instructed. Each community will be expected to deal will local problems using its own resources, unless they involve matters which threaten to undermine the authority of the ruling noble, such as the persistent incursions of retainers of a neighboring noble. On the other hand, emergencies which affect the entire territory or most of it would gain the full attention of the ruling noble. He would do what he could to ensure that sufficient food supplies reach places where they are needed in times of shortages or to see that labor power is directed to help those communities which need to quickly complete a project requiring a large number of workers.

Do not think that the communities of the new age will be picturesque, tranquil associations of men and women that the romantic philosophers and social theorists have always written about, but never managed to get into operation. True, there will be a high degree of cooperation and harmony in these communities, and they certainly will not have a crime problem. But still there will be the occasional individual who must be subjected to communal discipline at its most severe, in order to preserve the community's integrity. Moreover, the physical circumstances of the new age are unlikely to be conducive to the languid, contented lifestyle pictured by the devotees of nature and the ideal of man in his natural state as a noble savage. The winters will, for the most part, be long and very cold, the summers will be relatively short, but very hot and will bring all those miseries and inconveniences with which we are so familiar, such as troublesome insects and stomach disorders. Furthermore, in certain places rain will not always be frequent, leading to severe drought conditions which may persist for several years at a time. It will not be easy to keep large herds of cows, sheep or goats, since the search for good grazing will be long and arduous day after day. The control of fresh water from a source of supply which lies on the boundaries of two domains, will be fought over constantly as the neighboring nobles battle for power. Foods such as eggs, milk, cheese, fresh meat, fish and fruits may not always be in plentiful supply. Thus, the common people will on occasions have to make do with what little they can get. The mortality rate among young children and babies will be so high as to become accepted as a normal fact of life. The fact that one's family name will live on will be the most important thing to any man of the new age (be he noble or common) who is close to death. Thus, although the new age will be a very human age, it will not be an age for the fainthearted. An important trait of communities in the new age then, will be their dedication to survival, a dedication which will on occasion help them to triumph over almost impossible odds.

Communities within the same domain will be natural allies, whilst those in different territories will tend to be natural antagonists, especially in regards to matters such as common pasture and the use of fresh water, though much will depend on the relationship between the appropriate nobles, for if this is good then the common people of the two domains will not have much difficulty in getting on when they come into contact. But if the relationship should be bad, then there will always be a strong possibility of hostilities breaking out over the most trivial disputes. There will be no man-made boundaries erected to divide one territory from another. Instead, the boundary of a noble's domain will be set as far as that point which he wishes his authority to extend. This will mean that in times when he is stronger than his neighbor, his boundary will tend either to remain firm or to expand a little in that direction, while in times when he is weaker, the reverse will happen, i.e., his boundary will tend to be shaky and may even contract under pressure from the increased power of his neighbor.

There will always be one or more areas of no man's land between neighboring domains, which will be a source of endless disputes as to grazing rights, fishing rights, timber rights and so on. Again, it will depend on relative strengths as to who gets the better of these disputes. And relative strengths will tend to change according primarily to the abilities of the opposing nobles, i.e., a son may not be as effective as his father was in maintaining the upper hand over a very aggressive, but so far unsuccessful neighbor. Another factor of importance would be the assistance given by allies of either party in terms of men and military supplies, should full-scale hostilities break out. This may depend on new alliances being struck up and old ones being dissolved. In fact, there are a host of possibilities which will keep the power struggles between competing nobles constantly in flux. But one thing we can say for certain is that whereas a community will be under obligation to assist another community in the same territory by virtue of their loyalty to the same noble, communities in different territories will be under no such obligation.

The availability of fertile land and fresh water will be two of the most important factors determining the location of communities in the new age. But over and above this fact, we may say that the largest concentration of people will be in those communities located nearest to the primary residence of the ruling noble. More distant communities will probably tend to be less populated and more widely separated from each other. But there would be incentives for people to form communities in the more distant parts of the territory. For instance, they could be allowed to give to their ruling noble a smaller proportion of their produce than those communities located closer to him. They would probably be also eligible for a higher level of exemption in regards to the supply of levies for military service than the nearer communities. When the common people need to transport a large load over a long distance, a donkey or donkey and cart would be the usual method of travel, whereas a team of horses hitched up to a large wagon will be used to transport the property of the nobles. There will be no paved highways in the new age, since road building would not be a strong point of the people. Instead, rough thoroughfares would be cleared out of the wilderness when necessary, and ground into regular highways mainly as a result of the constant to and fro travelling by caravans of the nobility.

There will be very few coastal communities, as sea-faring will not be much in favor in the new age. The main economic activities will be agriculture and the rearing of livestock. In addition timber will be taken from the forest as well as minerals from the various parts of the territory. These minerals will be used in such activities as the production of building materials, in the production of metals for the making of military equipment, and in the making of certain luxury items for the use of the nobility. Valuable (i.e., very rare) minerals and the goods that can be produced from them, will be used in commodity exchange with other territories. All timber and minerals within the territory will be the property of the ruling noble. Therefore, apart from what has the sanction of custom, they could not be appropriated by the common people of the territory, or those of another territory, for the purpose of personal use or commodity exchange without permission from the ruling noble. The same restrictions would apply to nobles -- they could not instruct any of their subjects or officials to take timber, water or minerals from the territory or another noble without obtaining his prior agreement. On the other hand, there would be no such control in regards to the timber, water and minerals of common land which occupies the area between two domains. To help ensure the security of his lands, a ruling noble would build fortresses at strategic points on the periphery of his domain and garrison them mainly with troops of his own class.

Wheat and other cereals will continue to be important food sources in the new age, just as they are at the present time. But we can reasonably expect new strains to emerge which will be better adapted to the climate and soil conditions that will characterize the new age. Storage of grain against bad harvests will also be a feature of the new age, and most of this stored grain will be kept in the granaries of the nobility. Communities in different territories which are located close enough to one another to do so, will be able to enter into the exchange of commodities (natural and man-made) provided prior permission has been given by both ruling nobles, and neither one rescinds his permission. Nearby communities located in the same territory would regularly enter into commodity exchange without the need to obtain permission from their ruling noble. The main items of exchange would be agricultural commodities and livestock, regardless of whether the exchanges were made within the same territory or between different territories. Most man-made commodities will involve a high degree of skill, i.e., a large input of specialized labor power, and moreover, surplus of this type of commodity will never be great. Therefore, they will tend to be not so freely available as agricultural products, and will be worth much more when they are, except in times of extreme drought. All commodity exchanges involving members of the nobility will be handled by functionaries of the nobles involved.

Communities of the new age will be models of the traditional societies, i.e., static, uninnovative, and cooperative, guided more by custom than by reason. The highest wants of the common people in the new age will be to see their children and grandchildren grow up to do the same things they did, face the same hardships, and experience the same pleasures and joys that they did. A great deal of attention will be given to the preservation and upbringing of children in the new age. The division of labor between men and women will be strict and unalterable with women doing most of the domestic work, such as looking after young children, cooking, keeping the home tidy, washing clothes, looking after the family vegetable plot, milking the cows or goats, weaving baskets, spinning wool, making clothes for themselves and the younger children, among other things. The men will do the heavier work, such as plowing the fields and harvesting the crop, taking cows to pasture, digging ditches and wells, building homes, cutting logs, making tools and furniture. They will also go hunting and fishing and participate in commodity exchange. In many of their tasks, women will be assisted by their younger children (both boys and girls). These tasks would include removing weeds from the soil, feeding the chickens and pigs, collecting firewood, picking fruits, and carrying water from the well or stream. Motherhood will be the source of greatest pride to all women. Fertility rites and festivals will be common in all communities. Sex before marriage will be taboo in societies of the new age, as will be abortion and the employment of any form of contraception. Instead of trying to compete with one another, men and women will once again complement one another, as they have always done up until very recently. Thus, women will be noted for their shyness in company, their tenderness and sympathy, and all those other qualities associated with the mother instinct. Men, on the other hand, will once again be the chief providers for the family; they will generally be far more assertive than women, able to bear hardship better and less prone to sentimentality in their judgments. Women will not be called upon to participate in warfare under any circumstances. Furthermore, as a general rule, they will not participate in discussions involving the affairs of the community as a whole. In the new age, a woman's place will firmly be in the home; involvement in the affairs of men will be left to the men.

The homes of the common people will be built of material that is nearest at hand. They will not be elaborate, but they will provide effective shelter and be easy to keep clean and in a good state of repair. They will be furnished in a very rough and ready manner, unless a member of the family happens to be adept at making furniture or is able to obtain the services of a member of the community who is. Wood and other abundant forms of carboniferous materials would be the main fuels, the open fireplace would provide warmth in the winter, and stone ovens would be used for baking. Although the homes of the common people will have few frills, they will nevertheless be very proud of them (since they built them with their own hands), and will do all they can to make them pleasant and attractive places in which to live. Each home will probably be a short distance from the nearest home to it. They will be constructed in such a way that there will be no serious difficulty in increasing the size of the house (i.e., by adding another room) as the family increases in size. Lighting will be provided in the main by the sun, although some commoners may have candles made by a family member or obtained in trade. Should this be the case, the candles would be placed in specially made holders so as to greatly reduce the risk of fire. There will be a number of dietary changes in the new age: foreign beverages will no longer be drunk, honey will replace sugar as a sweetener (used only by the nobility), and hard spirits will no longer be made, although wine and certain local alcoholic beverages will be produced. Certain fruits will become virtually unobtainable in most territories, including many that were formerly grown in very warm or tropical climates.

Because of the absence of money and their lack of contact with a decadent and enervating lifestyle, the common people will remain uncorrupted. Moreover, they will not seek to question as to why their life should be so hard, but will get on with the business of living and raising a family. Although the furnishing of the homes of the common people may be Spartan, each will nevertheless have distinctive features which will distinguish it from all other homes in the community, and the people will take pride in the upkeep of their homes. In this age, there is much talk about concern for the poor, but nothing which has been done in the last hundred years has completely eliminated poverty, and nothing that will be conceivably done in the foreseeable future is likely to achieve this objective. Is it not time we admitted that we are looking at the problem in the wrong way? Those who are poor now represent all who, no matter what is done for them, are unable to compete effectively in a market-oriented economy. The only possible way they will be able to become self-dependent and gain self-respect, is in a society in which the vast majority must also rely, not on special talent, connections, or on good fortune to be able to cope with the performance demands of industrial society, but on simple, hard physical work to derive their basic wants. Then there would be no subculture of poverty, but only communities whose members will have more than sufficient for their needs in good years, and perhaps a little less in bad years. Collin Ward explained succinctly how our treatment of the poor tends to degrade rather than elevate them, despite the fact that we sincerely believe that we have their best interests at heart: "One of the characteristics of the affluent world is that it denies its poor the opportunity to feed, clothe, or house themselves, or to meet their own and their families' needs, except from grudgingly doled out welfare payments."[7]

Time will be appreciated differently by communities of the new age than it is now. The common people will not have clocks, and will not know how to read the time. Instead, their appreciation of the passage of time will be determined by such things as the changing of the seasons, and with it the corresponding changes in their daily routine, the death of a ruling noble whose rule was especially remembered for various reasons, battles that were fought near their homes or in which a large number of men from the community took part. The common man of the new age will be up at dawn and fast asleep by late evening — at least on work days. He would have very few social commitments in the evening, and so would spend most of his evenings home with his family. Needless to say, the new age will not be a great one for bringing art, literature and entertainment to the masses. But it will be a great one for experiencing the basic pleasures of life, unadulterated by squalid commercialism or artificiality of manner. For the common people, these pleasures will include baking their own bread, and brewing their own beer, or other beverages. In the summer time, they will be surrounded by the scents and sounds of nature in full bloom. They will be able to fish, hunt rabbits and wild fowl, sit outside their homes and tell stories, or talk about old times and exchange news, tend their vegetable plots and make repairs to their houses, participate in communal labor such as the digging of ditches, cutting of logs, and of course harvesting the summer crop, and tending their livestock and poultry. In the winter, they will plough the fields, sow the seeds, collect firewood, find grazing for the cattle and sheep, obtain food for the pigs, goats and chickens. At home they will be making shoes and clothing. Thus, whether summer or winter, the life of the common people will be filled with things to do. The more delightful tasks will be looked upon almost as recreation, while the harder, more demanding tasks will be done in a spirit of cheerful acceptance.

There is one aspect of community life about which we have so far said very little, namely religious belief. When considering the future of religion, several points must be given their due weight. The first is that the existence of some sort of religious belief is essential for the existence of a healthy and well-constituted society, whether it be the simple animism of the primitive tribe or the complex theology of the Roman Catholic Church. Social anthropologists have attempted to define religion in a way that would be applicable to all societies, regardless of their level of complexity. Referring to their studies of backward societies in various parts of the world, they have come up with the definition that religion is any form of belief in spiritual entities. Whilst the apparent universal nature of this definition may recommend it to those who like simple answers to complex questions, it is also to be considered most inadequate on several counts. Most importantly, it suffers from the bias of the "rational man" who, like Sir James Frazer, author of *The Golden Bough*, would consider witchcraft and similar ritual practices as mankind's earliest attempt at groping for scientific certainty. From this point of view, all religions are just so much superstitious nonsense, which man will one day outgrow, just as the rational science of experiment, observation and deduction replaced the irrational metaphysics of the alchemists. This viewpoint fails utterly to understand religion as an interaction between a society and its natural environment. Admittedly, most modern social anthropologists are at great pains to point this out and refer to Frazer's beliefs as misguided and a product of cultural bias. Hence, the general tendency among contemporary social anthropologists to use such terms as simple societies, small scale societies, and non-literate societies, rather than the phrase "primitive societies," which conjures up all sorts of misleading connotations, especially in the mind of the untutored layman. Be this as it may, there still lingers the attitude that a society — especially a technologically advanced society — can get along quite well without widespread and sincere religious convictions in any shape or form, and not suffer accordingly.

Here again, our basic definition fails to perceive the essence of religious belief, which is in truth, not something that can be outlined in a simple sentence, but is rather something that has to be experienced and expressed. Nor should it primarily be a means of seeking compassion for the weak and defenseless, against the strong and omnipotent. Rather it is the only way in which man can reach out beyond himself and give tangible expression to his joy in being alive, to his transcendental feelings for the earth, its beauties, its awesome powers and not least of all for the great unending universe of which it is part and which is also within him. For the common man, as well as for the artist and the ruler, no purely rational system of thought will be able to do this, no matter how intellectually satisfying it may be. After all, the universe as we now know is quite beyond rational understanding, and man is best brought into sympathy with it by way of the senses and emotions rather than by way of the intellect. Be this as it may, we should not be surprised to find that attitudes towards all aspects of religious belief must become modified under the impact of far-reaching social and technological changes. This has been the lot especially of western man, who has transferred his restless search for "truth" to the realms of theology. In so doing, he has totally lost sight of the meaning of religious belief in a cloud of skepticism and cliche-ridden evangelistic piety.

"What has all this to do with the future of religious belief?," one may ask. Not very much until one realizes that it is possible to place all types of religious beliefs that we have had so far (and by implication, that we will have in the future), into two categories, namely Indigenous and Revelatory. Although the differences between these two types of religion are not always watertight, I believe they are significant enough to form the basis of a reliable system of classification. Indigenous religion is the most basic type of religious expression it is possible to have. It is generally confined to a particular region of a continent or empire, a particular country, society or a particular tribal group. Although on occasions, it may take root elsewhere among people of different culture and ethnic stock, it never achieves the same degree of ascendancy as it had in the land of its birth. Such religions are more often than not polytheistic; they rarely if ever have an explicit doctrine of morality, they make no offer of salvation to the unconverted, and do not profess to have as their objective the betterment of mankind. In harmony with their autochthonous quality, their origin is rarely associated with the teachings of an historic personage. Rather, they seem to have emerged fully fledged from the primeval darkness of the society's prehistoric past. We should also note that indigenous religions have little to say about the future of the society in which they are found, since, as a rule, they are considered as an integral part of the society's daily life, and not as a way of attaining perfection in this world or the next. Mainly as a result of this, vaticination is not a common feature of the writings produced by their priesthood. Examples of indigenous religions would be the religious cults of ancient Greece and Rome, the religions of ancient Egypt and Babylonia, Shinto and Hinduism.

Revelatory religions may be distinguished from indigenous ones by their ability to spread rapidly and take hold on a more or less permanent basis, despite political vicissitudes or resistance by followers of the indigenous religion. It is true that revelatory religions are proselytizing religions and actively seek converts, whereas indigenous religions do not, and also that the spread of such religions has more often than not been aided by military conquest. But these truths cannot detract from the fact that revelatory religions have spread far and wide to countries which share neither a common border, nor a common cultural heritage, let alone a common ethnic heritage. Typically, revelatory religions have originated from the teachings of one man, a fact whose importance was clearly appreciated by Machiavelli when he stated that the founders of religions deserve to be honored just as much as the founders of nations. They tend to be monotheistic and closely concerned with the relationship between man's life on earth and his life after death. Thus, they are for the most part strongly moralistic and their preachers tend to stress concern for the improvement of the individual and his society. With regards to Christianity, this was true from the earliest days of its ascendancy, i.e., after it had conquered ancient Rome. One recalls the famous saying of St. Augustine to the effect that if it were not the king's duty to ensure justice for all his subjects, then kingdoms were little more than highway robbery. Furthermore, such religions show a penchant for indulging in chiliastic prophecy and other visions of the better life, rather than accepting the present as the best possible way of life which can be either imagined or experienced. Examples of major revelatory religions include Christianity, Islam, and Buddhism.

Before proceeding, a few words must be said about the apparently anomalous position of Judaism. Although it may not be apparent at first sight, Judaism unmistakably belongs among the Revelatory religions. Some may dispute this assertion by pointing to the fact that until the great diaspora, it was always restricted to a tiny strip of Western Asia and to a specific tribal group. Furthermore, although widely dispersed throughout the world, its followers have made no attempt to seek converts from outside their own group, as is generally the case with revelatory religions. Granted also that its origin cannot easily be attributed to the teachings of one man, but is the product of the efforts of a long line of men. But regardless of all this, logic still demands that it be classified in the same category as Christianity, for it is the foundation upon which the latter religion is based. Why else do we so often speak of the Judaeo-Christian ethic as if we were talking about one and the same religion? It is the direct precursor of Christianity, a fact of which we are reminded by Disraeli, who once described Christianity as Judaism made acceptable to the masses. Without Judaism there could have been no Christianity, and without Christianity, there will be no Judaism.

The pre-eminent importance of the above dichotomy lies in the fact that the new age will witness the permanent eclipse of revelatory religions and the return of indigenous ones. People all over the world will once again want to express their emotions and feelings towards each other, for nature and for the universe in a way which is unique to them and not an import from another part of the world. Religion will once more be a celebration of man's feeling for the soil, sun and sky, for the trees and mountains, for the valleys and meadows, for the rivers and lakes, winds and rain. The wild beasts of the forests will once again be depicted in their true majesty as creatures to be feared as well as admired. Uncontrollable joy in the beauty of the human form will once again return and be given free reign. The religions of the new age, no matter where found or how practiced, will be an ode to joy — pure unadulterated joy. What is strong and powerful will be revered as blessed, what is weak and sickly will be despised.

THE FUTURE CONSCIOUSNESS

The new age will be an age of faith, as this age is not. If it were, western society would not be so deeply troubled as it is now. Faith has been transferred to science and technology, and the idea of progress. We are now paying the price for this loss of faith. We ask questions that cannot be answered, we support freedoms which can only lead to the destruction of the fabric of western society; in short, the present state of the western mind is a mass of contradictions. To understand what I mean by loss of faith, we can take the middle ages as an era in which men lived their lives steeped in faith. They were not concerned with social or scientific progress; they were not bothered about the impact their way of life was having on the environment; they did not expect the world to be a much better place in their time or that of their children's lifetime. They did not seek to find the reasons and causes for just about everything they were witness to, nor did they bother to embark upon futile discussions which left the basic facts unchanged. Neither did they need advice on how to run their lives, since they simply followed the time-honored customs of their forefathers. Their highest material desire was for a simple shelter to protect them from the severity of the elements, and sufficient food and water to give them the health and strength required to do a full day's work. They also accepted without too much difficulty their vulnerability as the lowest social strata. Crane Brinton tells us that "violence was to the medieval mind a part of God's plan, part of the expected regularities that govern the world."[1] It is not religion by itself that is important, although it has always been in the past a central aspect of an age of faith, but rather an attitude of mind which is neither interested in looking back to the past nor forward to the future, but accepts the realities of life as they are, and neither wants them to change nor expects them to change, being content to survive and reproduce. It is such an age of faith that will be heralded by the arrival of the new age. Societies will once again no longer be concerned about their future, for this is something that will take care of itself. One day will be very much like the next, year after year, decade after decade, century after century. Some years may be harder than others with poor harvests, while some years may be far better than others with very good harvests. But the structure of society will remain unchanged; attitudes, the technology and the way of doing things will all stay the same, and the power struggles among the nobility will go on and on.

It will be an age in which there will be no time for introspection; conscience will be replaced by faith; sin will be unknown. An individual's behavior and his opinions of right and wrong will be determined by his status and not by rules of conduct applicable to all. The average commoner will live among equals whose cooperation he will depend on for his very survival. The relationship among commoners then must involve a very high degree of reciprocity, i.e., an individual must treat others as he would like others to treat him. In this way, the community can work harmoniously as an association of people who are more or less equal. Any member of the community who could not accept his obligations would either be ejected from it into the wilderness, or dealt with in some other manner which would clearly display the community's determination to keep all its members on an equal footing, and not to tolerate behavior that would endanger its harmony.

The situation will be quite different in regards to the relationship between a noble and the communities within his domain. Since he is lord of the land, he will have the right to take whatever action he pleases. The communities would expect this, and for the most part accept it as the natural way of life. Since he and he alone laid down the law of the land, anything that he did would be right. His behavior would not be restrained so much by fear of communal reprisal as by the fact that he dare not depress the morale of communities in his domain too much for fear this would weaken his military position in subsequent conflicts with one or more of his neighbors. Only in relation to other nobles of equal status would an aristocrat's freedom of action be checked. The deep faith that will characterize the new age, does not mean that the people will do what is "good," but rather that they will act according to their feelings and inclinations; these will be determined not by their ethnic background, physical strength or temperament, but by status. The nobility, regardless of their ethnic attributes, will think one way, and all commoners will think another way. This difference is the key towards understanding the nature of authority in the new age.

Although life will be hard, the common people will be at peace with themselves. They will work with nature to survive, rather than trying to conquer it. They will not be envious of the aristocracy or jealous of other commoners whose greater talents cause them to stand out as exceptional members of the community. They will have no desire to continuously increase their standard of living. They will not be under pressure to produce more this year than they did last year. They will have no interest in bettering themselves, as this would be impossible. They will have very low expectations, but a high sense of morality. They will never question the permanency of their subordinate position, but will accept it as fixed and unchangeable. They will be unselfish, willing to share what little they have with their neighbor or a stranger who is hungry and lost. They will know nothing about the art of dissembling, but probably would not be above falsehood if they feel this could aid their survival or assist their cause. Their manners will be rough and ready, their attitudes unsophisticated. But this will not cause them any concern, for the nobility and their favored commoners will make up for the lack of refinement among the mass of the people.

The joys of the common people will be of the most basic kind, such as the birth of a child, the marriage of a son or daughter, and military success of their lord, particularly so when it involves the efforts of members of one's own community, and of course a good harvest. The fact that the simple pleasures are taken for granted or even scoffed at by modern man, shows how far we have gone in denying our unity with nature. Even though life will be far harder than it is now, there will be no such thing as a disturbed psyche in the new age. Neurosis and the far more serious condition of psychosis will be almost unknown. If someone is mentally ill, then he will be suffering from a physiological condition and not a psychological one, for all men in the new age, whether noble or common, will have healthy psyches (i.e., according to their status); those who do not will not survive. As far as ideals are concerned, the chief consideration of the common people will be the carrying out of their obligations to their ruling noble, and doing their full share of the work to ensure the wellbeing of their family and community. They will have no ambition and no enmity; greed and other strong desires will be quite alien to their nature.

But when we turn to discuss the consciousness and lifestyle of the nobility, things are quite different, for their beliefs, actions and way of life will together produce what we moderns call the spirit of the age. The first thing we must appreciate is one's emotions; all one's senses and bodily health will have a far greater role in the new age than they have had in any previous age. What we will have in fact is an emancipation of the senses quite unlike any that has ever taken place before, though such an emancipation is characteristic of all periods of disruptive change which link an age with the age succeeding it. The difference here is that the coming emancipation will be complete and sustained. It will not appear for a brief moment only to fade as people settle down to the new age, but will be the very life and breath of the new age. As Marx tells us, "Emancipation of the senses implies that the senses become practical in the reconstruction of society, that they generate new relationships between man and man, man and things, man and nature."[2] And the senses will indeed become practical in the reconstruction of society. If a noble feels angry, he will vent his anger rather than suppressing it; if he feels amorous he will satisfy his lust rather than restrain his appetite. If a noble feels generous, he will give without reserve. If he feels happy, or sad, disturbed or elated, his feelings will be there for all the world to see. Not for the nobleman of the new age will there be the toothy smile and equanimous temperament, regardless of one's true feelings and circumstances, a style which seems to be favored by us moderns as a mark of virtuous character. The nobleman of the new age will have no fear of showing his true feelings; not for him the double standards of modern mass society — a smiling cheerful outside and a bitter resentful inner self. This is the corruption that contractual society has brought to social relationships.

The aristocracy will be fully conscious of the power they wield over the lives of the common people. They will constantly strive to increase their power, prestige and influence at the expense of their weaker noble brethren. Unlike commoners, they will not hesitate to relieve their anger with acts of ferocious cruelty against those who have incurred their displeasure. They will enjoy good food and plenty of it. They will be excessively fond of riding and hunting. They will enjoy being entertained by those accomplished in any branch of the performing arts, whether the performance be given by a member of the family or by commoners. They will also be very fond of choral music and dancing. They will enjoy great spectacles, such as military reviews, pageants and contests of strength and skill. They may even participate in the latter with others of their own rank. Aesthetically, they will have a love for beauty and decorum which will surpass the nobility of any other age.

This phenomenal aesthetic sensitivity will be shown in the construction of their palatial homes, in their taste in dress, in the furnishing of their homes, and in their adoration of nature at its most glorious and awe-inspiring. With this love of beauty will go a level of indulgence of the passions never before met with a human history. They will revel in warfare, believing peace and tranquility to be for women and old men. They will regularly consume wine to the point of stupefaction without any ill-effects. If they set their mind on a particular objective, no sacrifice will be too great in order to obtain it. They will be merciless in dealing with those who challenge their authority. They will be unrelenting in pursuit of their enemies, and those who have betrayed their trust, but generous to their friends and kind to their servants. Their word will be the law of the land, and officials of their household will assist them to administer their land. In an age such as the one in which we are now living, where the spontaneous expression of one's health and vigor are impossible, even the possession of great wealth cannot give total contentment. This is an age which effectively represses those who are the most emotionally developed, those whose feelings and instincts are the highest possible embodiment of the essence of human life and history. The new age will be very different, instead of smothering these life-giving instincts and passions, it will allow their fulfillment to a far greater extent than has ever before been the case.

Too much intellectual contemplation will not be to the taste of the nobles of the new age. They will read and write as little as possible, leaving most of this type of activity to their trusted officials. At times, they may need to dictate a letter to another noble or familiarize themselves with the records of past events, records whose storage will be supervised by a trusted official who will be expected to make himself familiar with their content, so that the appropriate document can be brought to his master at a moment's notice. But on the whole, the nobility will not care too much for the written word. As for literature that existed prior to the new age, most of this will be lost or destroyed, and that which survives will be totally ignored by the nobility as well as by those of their officials who are the most learned. The ruling class of the new age will have no interest in the age that went before. Written laws will not be made in the new age; instead, when the need arises, the people will be given instruction by word of mouth. Neither will land deeds be drawn up or formal treaties made, for in the new age the sword will once again prove itself to be far mightier than the pen.

I should not need to point out to those familiar with western history that anti-intellectualism is the hallmark of a sturdy and vigorous nobility. It is an important aspect of the ideals of Lycurgus, the great lawgiver of Sparta. Mainly because of this, the Spartans had no time for literary pursuits, leaving these to the Athenians. One of Sparta's proudest boasts was that it did not need walls to protect it from the enemy, since the courage and bravery of Spartan manhood was sufficient protection, the truth of which was demonstrated over and over again. In this respect, the new age will be far closer to Spartan society than to classical Athenian society. The nobility of medieval society also cared little for the virtues of academic knowledge. Many knights could neither read nor write, while some kings (e.g., Charlemagne) could barely read, and found writing impossible. But the widespread illiteracy among those of noble birth did not detract one bit from the supremacy that these nobles enjoyed over both ignorant serfs and educated commoners. On the contrary, it was the spread of advanced education among the nobility which actually helped to further weaken their position, taking place as it did about the same time that the centralization of the state was gaining increased momentum. For with regards to higher education and aristocracy, there is one thing we can say for certain — universities produce thinkers, not warriors. Once a person of noble blood begins to defend his actions according to reason instead of according to birthright, then nobility becomes defenseless against the encroachment of the law, and is eventually toppled by the ideal of equal justice before the law. The less contact the nobility have with the evils of knowledge, the better off they will be. But there will be one area in which the nobility would put forth all their best efforts, including their intellectual abilities; this will be in regards to the gaining and holding of power and influence which will be the driving force of the new age. Reading and writing, detailed consultations and careful consideration will be undertaken if necessary to gain one's ends. When not involved in scheming for power, the last thing the nobility will want to indulge in is pastimes which require excessive mental concentration and provide so little sensual reward in return. The things that amuse them, that help them sleep soundly, that stimulate their senses in a pleasurable manner, that take their mind off the power struggle of the moment, that require the least mental effort in return for maximum satisfaction. These are the activities that the nobility will find most congenial to their nature when at home.

The personality and tastes of a ruling noble will dominate the territory which he controls. He will see to it that fortifications are constructed where he wants them, and to the specification that he demands. He will likewise take a keen interest in the construction of homes built for himself and his family, and in any other large construction project which he has sanctioned. In regards to furniture, personal possessions, clothing and the like, he will often give precise instructions as to the design and materials he wants to be used; if the finished product did not meet with his approval, he would reject it. But once it has met with his approval, it will become a treasured possession to be kept within the family for generation after generation. Every article he uses will be handmade, produced by craftsmen on his orders, or sent to him as a gift by another of equal rank. His home will be the grandest within the territory. No other noble will be able to pass through his lands without paying him a visit or at least sending him a messenger to inform him of the fact. For a ruling noble who was totally ignored by another of greater or equal rank passing through his land would treat such an oversight as a personal affront which could easily embitter future relations.

A ruling noble will want to know about everything that is happening in his territory that is out of the ordinary, so that he can deal personally with the matter if necessary. But he will not employ spies; instead he will rely on information supplied to him by the commanders of his more distant outposts, by those sent to him by the communities within his domain, and on reports given to him by officials of his household who sometimes might be required to make an on the spot investigation. The wisdom of the noble ruler will not come from books, but from his exalted status and the knowledge that he is the living representative of his forefathers who have ruled the land and protected the common people since the age began. No matter will be too great for him to cope with or too small to merit his attention. He will probably know almost as much about the communities within his territory as he does about his family ancestry. If subjects of one noble are caught committing misdeeds in the territory of another noble, they will have to answer to the ruling noble in whose territory they were caught. A ruling noble will regularly visit communities in the territory under his control. These visits will be made without fanfare, and the noble will never have more than a few companions with him — since he will always be sure of the loyalty of his subjects, and therefore will not need protection when he is visiting them. The ruling noble may be away from his home for several weeks at a time with his exact whereabouts unknown to all members of his household, except those who are with him. It is during these absences that he will make extensive tours of the territory under his control. During them he will personally sit in judgment on disputes brought before him; he will also carefully observe how his subjects are coping, and if necessary, decide whether or not he needs to substitute new customs to help them cope with a changing situation.

The home life of the nobility will be a model of order and good sense. Everything will have its place, stewards will be in charge of the servants and they will receive their instructions directly from the lady of the household. All members of the household will act towards one another in accordance with their respective status. Thus, everybody will defer to a lord and his lady, while the wife of a noble would defer to her husband. All officials of noble birth will occupy a higher position than all commoners in the noble's service, while indoor servants would rank above outdoor servants. Hierarchy among officials of noble birth will depend on their closeness to their lord. If they are among his most intimate advisers, they will rank above all other nobles of the household who are not so favored and who do not participate in the highest councils. The daughters of these high officials will be the companions of the daughters of the ruling noble, and their sons will be the companions of his sons. The style of the nobility at home will be leisurely and unhurried; they will have time to consume sumptuous meals of several courses. If they feel tired at any time during the day, they will lie down and rest. If they do not feel like attending to a particular matter they will instruct one of their officials to do so, or leave it for another time. Similarly, if they do not feel like giving an audience to a commoner, whether he be an emissary from another ruling noble, or a subject, they will put off the meeting until they feel they are ready for it, which may be a few hours later or a few days later, depending on the pleasure of the noble. The nobleman will have total discretion as to how he uses his time and whether to be active or indolent. The nobility will spare no effort to make their homes not only attractive to look at, but also beautiful places to inhabit; noble women will dress according to their rank, and under no circumstances would they be allowed to dress as men do.

As for the children of the aristocracy, no effort will be spared to bring them up in a manner befitting the high status of their parents. In early life, they will have nursemaids as well as receiving a great deal of attention from their mother and father. As they grow older, they will be given tutors and taught the rudiments of reading, writing and arithmetic. From their early teens onwards, girls will learn about such things as dressmaking, needlework, knitting and the management of domestic affairs, while boys will learn about the martial arts and military strategy. Both girls and boys will become expert horse riders, beginning with their own pony at a very early age. Just as the case with children of common birth, girls of noble birth will obtain most of their education from their mother, whereas boys will obtain most of their education from their father. The education I am talking about here is not academic, but practical instruction, for children of noble birth can only learn about "what is noble" from those who are best qualified to tell them, i.e., their parents. This (i.e., the learning of what is noble) will be the most important part of a noble child's education; academic knowledge will play only a relatively minor part. Needless to say, boys would receive a far more energetic education than girls. They would go regularly on hunting expeditions with their father, during which they would learn how to survive in the wilderness. In some cases (especially so the eldest son), they may be sent away to enter the service of a friend of their father for two or three years, as part of their preparation for their future responsibilities. On returning to their father, after completion of their service, they would automatically receive a high military command and would be allowed to stand in for their father in the leadership of some military campaigns and the administration of the land under his control. From their earliest days, the children of the nobility will be taught to be obedient to their parents at all times. In their relationship to commoners, they will be taught what is expected of them, and will practice it daily.

All aristocracies treat matters of heritage and ancestry with great seriousness, and the aristocracy of the new age will be no exception to this rule. All noble families will keep elaborate written records of marriages, legitimate births, and deaths; these records will be the family tree, and of great importance in matters of succession. Only members of the nobility will be able to lead an army on the battlefield. The legitimate son of a noble father would be expected to marry a woman of noble birth. Only under the most exceptional circumstances, could the child of a noble father and common mother succeed to the position of his aristocratic father. If a noble is taken alive in battle, he would be treated by his captors with the respect due to his rank, and eventually allowed to return home after terms of accommodation have been worked out between himself and his successful adversary. If a noble should be killed in battle, his body should be returned to his family if this is at all possible. If not, it would be taken care of according to the custom of the age, and kept separate from the bodies of all those of lesser rank. A noble will generally be identified by the richness of his attire, and by the family crest and motto imprinted on his clothing and personal possessions. Anyone who, not being a member of the nobility, attempts to impersonate one, would be dealt with in a most rigorous manner, so as to set an example to others, as would anyone who steals from a member of the nobility.

Members of the nobility will always know exactly what they want. Remorse will be unknown to them, they will rarely regret any action they take, whether in a fit of temper or after cold calculation. Sons of the nobility will under no circumstances engage in any type of manual work, since it will be beneath their dignity to do so. This applies especially to agriculture. In the main, those members of the nobility which did not inherit land from their father would leave home and enter the service of a ruling noble who will be able to give them the opportunity to use their abilities to the fullest extent. A ruling noble will have the power to order the execution of any other individual resident in his territory. Although they will enjoy the good life when at home, when away from home the nobility will be inured to the harshest conditions, e.g., deprivation of food, persistent foul weather, and fatiguing travel, and will be able to stand up to these and other hardships as well as the most hardy commoner. Nobles will not be worried about their personal safety, whether on the battlefield, on the hunt, or when travelling about their domain, for they will believe that they have nothing to fear as long as they have no fear of dying. In battle, they will throw themselves into the thick of things; during the chase they will take the lead in attacking the quarry. Although they will not be immortal, the principle of aristocracy will survive their demise so long as they have legitimate children to continue their line. Therefore, they will be totally unworried about their fate.

Members of the aristocracy of the new age will not be men of reason, but men of action. Their deeds, far more than their words, will express their thoughts and feelings. Members of the nobility would never involve themselves in a brawl. If they are insulted by someone of equal rank, they could obtain satisfaction by offering a challenge to armed combat. If their sensibilities have been offended by a commoner, they would either strike him down on the spot, or order that he be punished in an appropriate manner. But on no account will those of noble blood engage in fist-fights. The favorite pastimes of the nobility will include hunting deer, wild boars, bears, wolves and so forth, as well as hawking and combat practice. Any noble who strays into the territory of another noble during a hunting expedition would not expect to meet with a hostile reception, unless he and his companions acted in such a way as to provoke such a reception. In the summer time, the noble families will visit friends in other territories or travel further afield to a society other than their own. In the winter time, horse-drawn sleigh rides through the countryside will be very popular among the nobility, military campaigns would cease, armies would be disbanded, and troops would return home.

One of the great tragedies of our age is that modern man is unable to appreciate the difference between "life" and "being alive," which are not the same, but two entirely different things. The first propels man to create history; the richer and more diverse a society's history, the greater its abundance of "life." Thus, in one age, life may mean the creation of beautiful mythology and legends, original philosophy, great advances in mathematics and astronomy, or it may also mean the building of great armies, the conquest of many lands leading to the formation of one great empire. In another period, it may mean the spread of a new and vibrant religious belief and the overthrow of the old religions. In a different age it may mean rejection of the pursuit of knowledge and its replacement by the pursuit of power. Or in yet another age, "life" may mean the greatest possible freedom given to the pursuit of wealth and knowledge. What we are talking about is life-giving action, for since man must die, it matters not how long he lives or how he dies, but what he does with his life. Thus "life" means great enterprises which could lead to the death of tens of thousands and involve the efforts of hundreds of thousands. It means great ambitions, unquenchable desire, towering rage, blind fury, high pride and burning passion; it is the very stuff of history as merely being alive could never be.

The essence of being alive is to do only what is necessary to survive and not much else. It means barely existing, making one's living in a humble way, living a peaceful life, attacking only when one's need to stay alive becomes desperate enough to prompt such action. The survival customs of the society may be surrounded by elaborate rituals, but they can hardly be said to be the stuff of which history is made. Where are the great individual leaders, the generals and religious teachers, the great poets and philosophers? What are the beliefs and principles for which the society would be prepared to die, or which compels them to keep themselves separate from a race they have subjugated? Where is the great heroine whose smile has launched a thousand ships in whose name great armies have marched and great men have died? Where are the great conflicts between contrasting ideologies, between one's devotion to duty and one's personal feelings? Where is the man who is ready to stand forth and boldly oppose the direction in which his society is moving? All these things are almost unknown to the simple equalitarian and generally peaceful societies studied by social anthropologists, and which have been the building blocks of the less dynamic nations throughout the world. It is in this sense that many of these simple societies such as the Trobriand Islanders and Australian aborigines can be said to have no history. It is in this sense also that history will continue to be made and recorded in the new age, though not in the same self-conscious way that it is now made and recorded.

Those who look forward to the resurrection of aristocracy must ignore the outcry of the weak and insecure, and place their faith in the future. The opinions of those who oppose its coming will not count because the people will not be asked to vote on the new age; it is coming whether they want it to or not. It will be a great age that truly knows itself like none before it has ever done. For too long now, we have been stumbling in the dark without light and without hope. Man now has both; there should no longer be any reason for him to be afraid.

REFERENCES

THE CRISIS OF A LOST SOCIETY

1. M. Mesarovic & E. Pestel: *Mankind At The Turning Point,* p. 152. Hutchinson & Co., 1975, London.
2. Robert L. Heilbroner: *Between Capitalism and Socialism,* p. 100. Random House, New York, 1970.
3. E. F. Schumacher: *Small Is Beautiful,* p. 135. Blond & Briggs, London, 1973.
4. M. Mesarovic & E. Pestel: *Op. Cit.,* p. 135.

THE STAGNATION OF CONTEMPORARY POLITICS

1. Max Horkheimer & Theodor Adorno: *Dialectic of Enlightenment,* p. 169. 1972.
2. H. Marcuse: *Counterrevolution and Revolt.* Beacon Press, Boston, 1972.
3. Z. Bauman: *Socialism: The Active Utopia.* London, 1972.
4. Chris Harman: *Bureaucracy and Revolution in Eastern Europe.* Pluto Press, p. 26, London, 1974.
5. R. Wolff: *The Poverty of Liberalism,* p. 160. Beacon Press, 1968, Boston.
6. Anthony de Crespigny (ed.): *Contemporary Political Theory.* Thomas Nelson & Sons, London.
7. J. S. Mill: *Considerations On Representative Government,* p. 246. J. M. Dent & Sons, London, 1972.
8. Alexis de Tocqueville: *Democracy In America.* Eds. J. Mayer & Max Lerner. Harper & Row, Vol. II, p. 666.

THE BANKRUPTCY OF MODERN ECONOMICS

1. R. L. Heilbroner: *Between Capitalism and Socialism,* p. 120. Random House, New York, 1970.
2. R. L. Heilbroner: *Between Capitalism and Socialism,* p. 120. Random House, New York, 1970.
3. E. Schumacher: *Small Is Beautiful,* p. 135. Blond & Briggs, London, 1973.
4. R. L. Heilbroner: *Op. Cit.,* p. 281.
5. R. L. Heilbroner: *Op. Cit.,* p. 281.

6. K. Marx: *Communist Manifesto.* Trans. S. Avineri. Cambridge University Press, 1968.
7. J. Schumpeter: *Capitalism, Socialism and Democracy,* p. 82. George Allen & Unwin, London, 1943.
8. D. Riesman: *Abundance For What? And Other Essays,* p. 304. Doubleday & Co., New York, 1964.
9. Karl Marx: *Early Writings* (Trans. & Ed. T. Bottomore). 1963, C. A. Watts & Co., London.
10. S. Avineri: *The Social And Political Thought of Karl Marx,* p. 251. Cambridge University Press, 1968.
11. G. Sorel: *Reflections on Violence.* The Free Press, 1950 (Glencoe).
12. C. Wright Mills: *The White Collar Worker.* 1956.
13. D. Bell: *The Coming Of Post Industrial Society,* p. 44. Heineman, London, 1974.
14. *The Ecologist* (editorial): "Blue Print for Survival." January 1972, London.
15. T. L. Blair: *The Poverty of Planning* (the introduction). MacDonald, London, 1973.

THE COMING AGE OF REACTION

1. Alexis de Tocqueville: *Democracy in America,* Vol. II, p. 667.
2. H. Kahn & A. Wiener: *The Year 2000,* p. 412. Hudson Institute, 1967.
3. R. L. Heilbroner: *Between Capitalism and Socialism,* p. 260.
4. Paul & Anne Erhlich: *Population Resources and Environment,* p. 141. 1970, W. H. Freeman & Co.
5. *Journal Of The History Of Ideas 1960.* Gwyn Williams: "The Concept of Egemonia in the Thought of Antonio Gramsci," Vol. 21, p. 594. 1960.

THE RETURN OF CLASS RULE

1. R. L. Heilbroner: *Between Capitalism and Socialism,* p. 81.
2. R. L. Heilbroner: *Op. Cit.,* p. 101.

LEGALITY IN PERSPECTIVE

1. George Sabine: *A History Of Political Theory.* Cornell University Press, 1933 edn.

THE END OF MODERN IDEALISM

1. Paul Thompson: *The Work of William Morris,* p. 245. Heineman, London, 1967.
2. J. Schumpeter: *Capitalism, Socialism and Democracy,* p. 10. George Allen & Unwin, 1943.
3. *Marx & Engels Selected Works,* Vol. I. Moscow, 1969.
4. Beatrice Webb: *My Apprenticeship,* p. 112. Longman, 1926, London.
5. E. Mandel: *Marxist Economic Theory,* Vol. II, p. 614. Merlin Press, 1968.

6. Vernon Bourke: *History of Ethics,* Vol. I. Image Books (Division of Doubleday), New York, 1970.
7. D. Kagan: *The Great Dialogue,* p. 166. The Free Press, 1965.
8. Erich Fromm: *Fear of Freedom.* 1942.

BEYOND POLITICAL MAN

1. J. S. Mill: *Considerations On Representative Government,* p. 245. Everyman's University Library, 1972.
2. Sigmund Freud: *The Future Of An Illusion.*
3. Jacob Burckhardt: *The Civilization Of The Renaissance In Italy,* p. 122. The New American Library, A Mentor Book, 1960, New York.

THE RETURN OF COMMUNITY

1. Lewis Herber: *Crisis In Our Cities,* p. 135. Prentice Hall Inc., 1965.
2. Thomas Blair: *The International Urban Crisis.* (Preface) Hart-Davis, MacGibon, London, 1974.
3. Plato: *The Republic.* Trans. H. D. Lee. Penguin, 1955, London.
4. T. Bottomore (ed.): *Karl Marx Early Writings.* C. A. Watts & Sons.
5. Andre Gundar Frank: *Capitalism and Underdevelopment in Latin America,* p. 151. Penguin Books, 1967.
6. E. Galeano: *The Bleeding Veins of Latin America,* p. 24. Monthly Review Press, New York, 1973.
7. Collin Ward: *Anarchy In Action.* George Allen & Unwin, 1973, London.

THE FUTURE CONSCIOUSNESS

1. Crane Brinton: *A History Of Western Morals.* Weidenfeld & Nicolson, London, 1959.
2. Karl Marx: *Economic & Philosophical Manuscripts,* p. 139. Lawrence & Wishart, London, 1970.

YOU WILL ALSO WANT TO READ:

☐ **94041 THE WORLD POWER FOUNDATION: ITS GOALS AND PLATFORM, *edited by Harold Thomas.*** The purpose of the World Power Foundation is to prepare an intelligent warlike religion for the future — a power philosophy that lets bold men take advantage of the opportunities that history may present them, and translates their desire for slaves and control into a workable systematic social policy. ***1980, 5 ½ x 8½, 90 pp, soft cover. $7.95.***

☐ **34035 CURIOUS PUNISHMENTS OF BYGONE DAYS, *by Alice Morse Earle.*** This interesting book, first published in 1896, about torture inflicted by the Church and State, will be of interest to anyone interested in crime and punishment, in guilt and justice, and in the never-ending saga of man's inhumanity to man. ***1896, 5½ x 8½, 149 pp, illustrated, soft cover. $7.95.***

☐**17028 HOW TO START YOUR OWN COUNTRY, *by Erwin S. Strauss.*** This book tells you the story of dozens of new country projects, most of them since the 1960s. It also explains *how* you can start your own country. Covers the 5 approaches for starting a new country most likely to succeed, and more. Includes over 100 pages of fascinating case histories illustrated with dozens of rare photographs. ***1984, Second Edition, 5½ x 8½, 174 pp, illustrated,indexed, soft cover. $7.95.***

★ *RA*

Loompanics Unlimited/PO Box 1197/Port Townsend, WA 98368

Please send me the books I have checked above. I have enclosed $....................(including $3.00 for shipping and handling).

Name ....

Address ....

City/State/Zip ....

"Yes, there are books about the skills of apocalypse -- spying, surveillance, fraud, wire-tapping, smuggling, self-defense, lockpicking, gunmanship, eavesdropping, car chasing, civil warfare, surviving jail, and dropping out of sight. Apparently writing books is the way mercenaries bring in spare cash between wars. The books are useful, and it's good the information is freely available (and they definitely inspire interesting dreams), but their advice should be taken with a salt shaker or two and all your wits. A few of these volumes are truly scary. Loompanics is the best of the Libertarian suppliers who carry them. Though full of 'you'll-wish-you'd-read-these-when-it's-too-late' rhetoric, their catalog is genuinely informative."

-THE NEXT WHOLE EARTH CATALOG

Now available:
THE BEST BOOK CATALOG IN THE WORLD!!!

- *Large 8½ x 11 size!*
- *More than 500 of the most controversial and unusual books ever printed!!!*
- *YOU can order EVERY book listed!!!*
- *Periodic Supplements to keep you posted on the LATEST titles available!!!*

We offer hard-to-find books on the world's most unusual subjects. Here are a few of the topics covered IN DEPTH in our exciting new catalog:

- *Hiding/concealment of physical objects! A complete section of the best books ever written on hiding things!*
- *Fake ID/Alternate Identities! The most comprehensive selection of books on this little-known subject ever offered for sale! You have to see it to believe it!*
- *Investigative/Undercover methods and techniques! Professional secrets known only to a few, now revealed for YOU to use! Actual police manuals on shadowing and surveillance!*
- *And much, much more, including Locks and Locksmithing, Self Defense, Intelligence Increase, Life Extension, Money-Making Opportunities, and much, much more!*

Our book catalog is truly THE BEST BOOK CATALOG IN THE WORLD! Order yours today -- you will be very pleased, we know.

(Our catalog is free with the order of any book on the previous page -- or is $2.00 if ordered by itself.)

Loompanics Unlimited
PO Box 1197
Pt Townsend, WA 98368
USA